The Genius of Valhalla
The Life of Reginald Goodall

JOHN LUCAS

The Genius of Valhalla
The Life of Reginald Goodall

THE BOYDELL PRESS

Originally published as *Reggie: The Life of
Reginald Goodall* by Julia MacRae Books, 1993

This edition first published 2009
The Boydell Press, Woodbridge

ISBN 978-1-84383-517-2

The Boydell Press is an imprint of Boydell & Brewer Ltd
PO Box 9, Woodbridge, Suffolk IP12 3DF, UK
and of Boydell & Brewer Inc.
668 Mt Hope Avenue, Rochester, NY 14620, USA
website: www.boydellandbrewer.com

A CIP record for this book is available
from the British Library

This publication is printed on acid-free paper

The drawing on the facing page is by Milein Cosman

Produced by Toynbee Editorial Services Ltd

Printed in Great Britain by
CPI Antony Rowe, Chippenham and Eastbourne

FOR ANNIE

Contents

List of Illustrations

The author and publishers are grateful to all the institutions and individuals listed for permission to reproduce the materials in which they hold copyright. Every effort has been made to trace the copyright holders; apologies are offered for any omission, and the publishers will be pleased to add any necessary acknowledgement in subsequent editions.

Dedication page Drawing of Reginald Goodall by Milein Cosman (© 1985 Milein Cosman)

(*Between* pp. 176 and 177)

Foreword

In July 2008 a live broadcast of Reggie Goodall conducting *The Mastersingers of Nuremberg* at Sadler's Wells Theatre in 1968 was made available on CD for the first time, released on Chandos Records' "Opera in English" label. The impact of hearing Goodall's legendary performance, forty years on, was a knock-out, not only among those who, like me, were lucky enough to have witnessed the original production, but also among younger generations. No wonder that after his magisterial account of *The Mastersingers* Goodall was invited to conduct an "English" *Ring* at the London Coliseum in the 1970s. This in turn had inspired *me* to go knocking on doors to ensure that his *Ring* performances were preserved on record. So, the fortieth anniversary year of the seminal *Mastersingers* seemed to me the right moment to hold a public event that would celebrate Goodall's musical legacy, something that would reflect why his influence continues to reverberate through generations of British musicians.

This event, *The Genius of Valhalla*, took place at the London Coliseum on 23 November 2008, bringing together his biographer John Lucas, a panel of artists and administrators closely associated with Goodall – Dame Anne Evans, Norman Bailey, Margaret Curphey, Sir Brian McMaster, Anthony Negus and Nicholas Payne – and a large audience of Goodall fans. The discussion was chaired by Humphrey Burton, whose 1984 BBC-TV profile, *The Quest for Reginald Goodall*, completed a moving and memorable testament to an extraordinary figure in British musical life. But such events are ephemeral and what had become very evident, from both the reception of *The Mastersingers* recording and the enthusiastic response to *The Genius of Valhalla*, was that a new edition of John Lucas's biography of Goodall would not only feed renewed interest in this remarkable musician, but also restore an important strand in the history of operatic development in Britain during the latter half of the twentieth century.

Sir Peter Moores, CBE, DL

Introduction and Acknowledgments

"When you conduct other things – things other than by Wagner – you find there's something lacking. You miss the richness and the depth and the potency of his music" – Reginald Goodall, talking to the author, 1987.

I FIRST HEARD Goodall conduct in the 1950s. He was on the staff of Covent Garden, though his appearances in the pit there were sporadic. He gave performances of *Manon*, *Turandot* and *Bohème* that were cogent and illuminating, and he breathed life into Britten's *Gloriana* after its unfortunate premiere under John Pritchard. His *Meistersinger* – "Not my *Meistersinger*," I can hear him saying crossly, "Wagner's" – won him glowing notices in the press, as did the performances of *Die Walküre* he conducted on tour. Yet by the end of the decade he had all but disappeared from view. It was puzzling, but I knew nothing then of operatic politics.

At a party at the 1961 Edinburgh Festival I was introduced to a Covent Garden stalwart, the baritone Geraint Evans, who regaled his fellow guests with tales of the Opera House. What, I asked him, had happened to Goodall? He adopted a solemn expression. "Ah, Reginald," he said, rolling the initial R theatrically. "Poor Reginald." He then changed the subject. Clearly, as far as Covent Garden was concerned, Goodall was a spent force. Yet seven years later, at the age of sixty-six, he made an extraordinary comeback, with a production of *The Mastersingers* for Sadler's Wells Opera that demonstrated beyond dispute that here was a great Wagner conductor in a tradition stretching back through Hans Knappertsbusch and Karl Muck to Hans Richter, conductor of the first *Ring* cycle at Bayreuth in 1876.

Goodall had watched Knappertsbusch at work during his visits to Bayreuth throughout the 1950s, and from him had learned how to build the acts in great, seamless arches, how to relate one tempo to another, how to balance the sound so that each individual strand in the orchestral fabric could be heard, how to ensure, through close attention to the dynamic markings in the orchestral parts, that singers were never drowned. Goodall complained that most conductors failed to observe Wagner's dynamics; as a result, he said, singers were encouraged to sing stridently in order to compete with the orchestral flood. Big steely voices were not for him – he liked voices that were even in quality and sonority from top to bottom of their range. "Too much metal, dear," he grumbled at even his favourite sopranos when they sang high notes – and he would stick his fingers in his ears to underline the point. In low-lying passages he demanded the rich characteristic of the violin's bottom string – "More G string, dear" was a constant plea.

Not all singers could cope with Goodall and the demands he made of them. But those who could revered him. A Goodall regular, the bass Gwynne Howell, has written, "He could be infuriating and cuttingly critical with, at peak moments, a quick stamping of the feet. With luck the next singer would arrive – preferably female, he liked female company – and calm would be restored. I would return home on some exhausted high, but just as I felt I wanted to give up it would all fall into place. All those shaky gestures of his conducting style would become clear and meaningful."[1]

Goodall attached the greatest importance to Wagner's final injunction to his singers before the 1876 *Ring* at Bayreuth: "Die grossen Noten kommen von selbst; die kleinen Noten und ihr Text sind die Hauptsache" – "The big notes look after themselves; the little notes and their text are the main thing." All the semi-quavers, said Goodall, were to be given their proper sonority; they were not to be "snatched at". Words had to be sung with the utmost clarity and attention to meaning. Notes had to be "coloured", either to mirror the harmonies in the orchestra or to reflect the emotional mood of the scene or phrase. "Angel of death," he would say to his Brünnhildes in the *Todesverkündigung* in Act 2 of *Die Walküre,* urging them to adopt a dark, grave sound; during King Marke's long solo in Act 2 of *Tristan*, he would ask the singer to match the timbre of the accompanying bass clarinet. Goodall was responsible for a remarkable flowering of Wagner singing that led to a generation of British and Commonwealth Wagner singers he had coached taking leading roles at Bayreuth, stretching from Jon Vickers in the late 1950s to John Tomlinson and Anne Evans thirty years later.

Goodall was sometimes mocked for his painstaking rehearsal methods, yet he worked in a way that would have been considered natural by Wagner's earliest interpreters. He was shocked by the fact that international conductors in the latter part of the twentieth century rarely took the trouble to coach the singers for their own productions: "Imagine Klemperer behaving like that! That's one of the things I like about Barenboim – he works with his singers. He's one of the few who does, and it shows. Most of the others are flitting here and there, conducting this and that. It makes me tired."

Goodall worked equally hard to achieve the correct balance in the orchestra. He set great store by sectional rehearsals: strings only, Wagner tubas, the harps. Often he worked with individual players: the timpanist, perhaps, or the bass trumpet. He regarded orchestral musicians not as his servants, but as his peers, though the respect he showed them was not always reciprocated. His detractors accused him of being incompetent in his conducting technique; he was criticised, too, for slow tempi.

"At the sectionals," said Goodall, "we would discuss balance, and how notes, phrases, should be played. In this way the players could see how they fitted into the picture, how each one of them contributed to the whole. Wagner should be like playing chamber music on a big scale. If all the parts are brought out, it gives the music movement and makes it much richer. The whole meaning and movement of the music must come out of the harmonies. Boulez has said that in Wagner the movement is often in the inner parts, between the top line and the bass, and he's quite right.[2] Listen to an average performance of *The Ring* and you'll find that half of these inner parts are lost. I always say that in Wagner no note is superfluous. Everything must be heard."

He practised what he preached. Reviewing the CD version of Goodall's complete recording of *The Ring,* Nigel Simeone picked out the the last seven bars of *Götterdäm-merung* as an example "of just how potent Goodall's handling of Wagner's orchestral sound-world can be: not only is there more audible detail than is often the case, but the sense of spaciousness and flow is extraordinary. The very last chord is a typical instance, with the harps beginning their arpeggios before the rest of the orchestra arrive at D flat major. This is no accident of live performance: Goodall achieved this effect every time I heard him conduct the work and the resulting sense of expansive serenity is one I have never heard matched. Almost every page of music has some similar example of the deepest imaginable knowledge, understanding and love of the score."[3]

Goodall continued to study the scores of *The Ring* and *Tristan* and *Parsifal* until the end of his life. "Even if you lived to be 150 years old," he said, "you would still not discover all the secrets of *The Ring.*"

I did not get to know Goodall until the early 1980s. He was already an old man, but he still had three new productions ahead of him: *The Valkyrie* for the Welsh National Opera, *Tristan* and *Parsifal* for the English National Opera. None of those who knew him, myself included, ever thought he would agree to having a biography written about him, but we were all wrong. As I wrote in *Opera* at the time of his death, he seemed to think that by its very existence the book might stand as proof to the world (as if proof were needed) that he had achieved something of note; it would cock a snook at all the bogeymen and bully-boys, both real and imagined, who had dogged his long career. It irked him that his gifts had never been properly acknowledged by Covent Garden, the house that had employed him for most of his career, but he was not a bitter man.

I have used many quotations from Goodall's conversations in the book. In public he tended to be monosyllabic, but in private his talk was full of musical insights, jokes and piquant observations on the "poseurs" and "routineers" (two favourite words) of his profession. Goodall did not try to cover up his Mosleyite past – and nor does this book. His unwillingness in the immediate aftermath of the second world war to believe the full extent of the atrocities committed by Nazi Germany seems inexplicable and unnerving. In the end he faced up to the terrible truth, but always found it hard to accept that a country that had spawned creative artists as great as Beethoven, Goethe and above all Wagner could also have been capable of such barbarity. "It's what I thought at the time," he said. "I can't change that." The political views he expressed in later years could be catagorised as "left-wing"; the very mention of Margaret Thatcher sent his blood-pressure rocketing skywards. Goodall's memory for dates, names and places was poor, and it was a red-letter day when, quite unexpectedly, he handed me a bundle of his diaries, some of them dating back to the early 1930s. They were hard to read, incomplete and concerned almost exclusively with appointments, but they provided vital clues to the course of his career.

Scores of people helped me to fill in the gaps. They were headed by the late Maisie Aldridge, who knew Goodall for more than fifty years, and Goodall's nephew, the late Colonel David Tetley, who not only encouraged me at every turn, but gave me permission to quote from Goodall's letters and diaries. Others with long memories of Goodall included Philip Blake, a fellow conducting student in the 1930s, Wilfred Stiff, who as a boy sang in Goodall's church choir in Holborn, and Felix Aprahamian, who allowed me to use extracts from his pre-war diaries. He and Nicholas Kenyon both read parts of the typescript and made valuable comments on it, as did Peter Heyworth and Terence Kilmartin, who, alas, both died before the book was completed. The Peter Moores Foundation provided generous financial help that enabled me to carry out research in Canada and other places.

Others who provided information and assistance include Elizabeth Abercrombie, Richard Adeney, Joyce Aldous, Ande Anderson, Eric Anderson, Sir Richard Armstrong, Richard Austin, Norman Bailey, John Barker, Geoffrey Bennett, John Blatchley, Christopher Bornet (Royal College of Music), Robert Bossert, Bruce Boyce, John Burrows, Moran Caplat, Jeremy Caulton, Clare Colvin (English National Opera archives), Hilda Connell, Patrick Connell, John Copley, Canon Robert Cowan, Joan Cross, Eric Crozier, John Cruft, Jeremy Cullum, Sir Colin Davis, John Denison, Patrick Dingle, John Doe, Lord Donaldson, Denis Dowling, Sir Edward Downes, Leslie Duff, Brian Duffie, Ruth Dyson, Ruth Edge (EMI archives), Sir Mark Elder, Lionel Elton (South Place Concerts), Laurence Elvin, Kenneth Essex, Dame Anne Evans, John Evans, Nancy Evans, Sir Keith Falkner, Norman Feasey, Richard Fisher, Francesca Franchi (Covent Garden archives), Lionel Friend, John Gardner, Fr John Gaskell (St Alban the Martyr, Holborn), James Gibson, Reginald Giddy, Alexander Goehr, Sir William Glock, Livia Gollancz, Elise Goodall, Linda Esther Gray, John Greenstone, Romayne Grigorova, Sir Charles Groves, George Hallam, Suvi Raj Grubb, Arthur Hammond, Derek Hammond-Stroud, Leonard Hancock, the Earl of Harewood, Michael Heyland (Royal Choral Society), Douglas Hopkins, Gwynne Howell, Joan Ingpen, Robert Irving, Roderick Jones, Fr Frank de Jonge, Iris Kells, Michael Kennedy, Leo Kersley, Janet Kersley, Lotte Klemperer, Jean Korn, Adele Leigh-Enderl, Iris Lemare, Marion Littleboy, David Lloyd-Jones, Jonathan Lofft (Royal St George's College, Toronto), John Ludlow, Sir Donald McIntyre, David McKenna, Sir Brian McMaster, Victorine Martineau (British Council archives), Alan G. Melville, John Mitchinson, Sir Peter Moores, Gareth Morris, Victor Morris, Nancy Morse, Anthony Negus, Ralph Nicholson, Richard Nunn, Nicholas Payne, Anna Pollak, Andrew Porter, Dr Alan T. Prince, Henry Prouse, Philip Reed (Britten-Pears Library), Alberto Remedios, Betty Richards, Cressida Ridley, Malcolm Riley (Percy Whitlock Trust), Charles Robinson, Rosy Runciman (Glyndebourne archives), Richard Temple Savage, Robert Slotover, Irene Speir, Canon D. Ralph Spence (St Luke's Church, Burlington, Ontario), Nellie Stannie, Sir John Stephenson, Renee Stewart (Leith Hill Festival), Rosamund Strode, Dame Joan Sutherland, David Syrus, Kendall Taylor, Wilfred Thomas, Marion Thorpe, Sir John Tooley, Edmund Tracey, Jon Vickers, Robert Virgo, Paul Ward, Susan Ward, Derek Williams (Cambridge University Library music department), Douglas Wise, Anne Wood, Reg Woodward, and Emanuel Young. To this list must be added the staff of the Bishopsgate Institute Library; the Deutsche Oper, Berlin, archives; the Diocese of Toronto archives; the Finsbury and the Holborn local history libraries; the archives of the Hallé, Royal Liverpool Philharmonic and Philharmonia orchestras; the Imperial War Museum; the John Lewis Partnership archives; the Lansdowne Library, Bournemouth; the Lincolnshire Archives; the Mills

Memorial Library, McMaster University, Hamilton, Ontario; the Theatre Museum; and *Opera* magazine.

The quotations from the unpublished correspondence and diaries of Benjamin Britten are © the Trustees of the Britten-Pears Foundation and are not to be further reproduced without written permission.

Finally I must thank the book's original publisher, Julia MacRae, for her boundless wisdom and patience, as well as Boydell and Brewer for publishing this slightly revised edition, which has been made possible by a further generous contribution from the Peter Moores Foundation. The ever-vigilant Bruce Phillips has given me invaluable help with the text.

JOHN LUCAS
November 1992; July 2009

CHAPTER I

Lincoln

A S WITH so much in Reginald Goodall's life an air of mystery surrounds
the date of his birth. According to his passport he was born in 1902, but
the correct date is 13 July 1901. Goodall himself was to blame for the confusion. In the earlier part of his career he would adjust his age to suit the circumstances. When applying for conducting jobs, he might add a few years, to
suggest greater maturity and experience than he possessed. Sometimes he took
a few years off. Sometimes, it seems, he so confused himself that he could not
remember how old he actually was. According to his marriage certificate he
was 28 when he married in 1932. In fact he was 31 – just a few months younger
than his wife, who was astonished to discover his real age when in 1940 she
registered his application for deferment of military service.

Goodall's birthplace was a modest terraced house in Monks Road, Lincoln,
a street of red-brick homes and shops that had grown eastwards from the
centre of the city in the latter half of the nineteenth century. Then, as now,
78 Monks Road had a small garden at the front and a paved yard at the back.
A brass plate on the gate announced that it was the home of A. E. Goodall,
music teacher. Albert Edward Goodall, Reginald's father, taught the piano,
and was organist and choirmaster at St Peter-at-Arches, a galleried church of
1724 by William Smith that stood on the north-east corner of the High Street
and Silver Street.[1] Music, however, was not Albert's main occupation. He was
confidential clerk to E. E. Tweed, a leading Lincoln solicitor. Tweed was Clerk
to both the city and county magistrates.

Albert's father, Thomas Goodall, was a leather-dresser by trade, though by the
time he died his business activities had expanded in other directions. The Lincoln directory for 1894 describes him as a glue manufacturer, with premises at
Bracebridge, then a separate parish to the south of Lincoln, but now part of the
city itself. His entry for the following year reads, "Glue powder and size works
and firewood merchant, asphalter and miller." Thomas and his family were strict
Nonconformists. They attended St Catherine's Wesleyan Methodist Church,
which urged temperance on its members, a reason perhaps why his son Albert,
a convivial and gregarious man, switched his allegiance to the Church of England. One of the few women at St Catherine's who declined to join the temperance league was Reginald's Aunt Ada, who had no objection to the occasional

drink. It was her private joke to lace the trifles she made for church socials with sherry. They were much in demand.

Reginald's mother, Adelaide, was the daughter of a Leicester draper, James Jones. Albert Goodall was 37 and a widower when he married her in June 1900 and brought her to Lincoln to live in Monks Road. They were not rich – Albert's salary as a solicitor's clerk was £160 a year, though he had a small additional income from his musical activities – but they could afford a maid-of-all-work, who slept in a room on the top floor, next to the nursery. A second son, William, was born on 20 July 1902, exactly a year and a week after his brother. Both boys were given only one Christian name, soon shortened to Reggie and Billie. Their father did not care for long strings of names; he found it irritating having to write them out in full at the solicitor's office or in court.

Monks Road is down at heel now, but in the first decade of the century it was considered well-to-do. Next to the Goodalls' terrace was the Arboretum, a pleasant park on the side of a hill, with pavilions, a fountain and a brightly painted cast-iron bandstand, where bands from the barracks and the local engineering works played in the summer. Sometimes the concerts were followed by firework displays. Reggie and Billie were pushed round the Arboretum in their prams, and later played there with their hoops. When they were old enough, they went to Miss Wileman's private school in Nettleham Road.

The boys' parents were very different in temperament. Adelaide Goodall, the least musical member of the family, thought pubs were vulgar and disapproved of her husband's habit of staying out late with his drinking companions. His life revolved round three establishments, all within a short distance of each other: St Peter-at-Arches church, the solicitor's office in Silver Street where he worked, and the Spread Eagle Hotel in the High Street.[2] Adelaide was well aware that the Spread Eagle's waitresses held a special attraction for her husband, and was wracked with jealousy and unhappiness as a result. Curiously for a man of sybaritic tastes (though the fact that he had once been a keen sportsman may have accounted for it), Albert favoured a strict regimen for his sons. There were cold baths every morning. In 1988, almost eighty years after she joined the Goodalls as the family skivvy in 1910 at the age of 19, Mrs Nellie Stanney remembered:

> When I got there, I saw these two little boys, Billie and Reggie. Billie was just as plump as his father, and Reggie was as thin as his mother. Reggie – poor little mite. I always felt sorry for him. They were all for Billie. I don't know why. Reggie always looked so cold and miserable. He always had to have cod liver oil, every morning. When I put the cod liver oil in the spoon he looked at me so miserably. He didn't like it a bit. He was sort of put on. He was ignored too much.[3]

Reggie was four when he was given his first piano lessons by his father, though Albert was convinced that it was the extrovert Billie who had the greater potential. While Billie continued to be taught the piano at home, the shy and retiring Reggie was sent to have lessons with his half-sister, Agnes, eighteen years his senior and the child of Albert's first marriage. At the time she was living behind the station in Tentercroft Street, where she taught music for a living. Not long afterwards she married Captain Eric Tetley of the Yorkshire brewing family and moved up the hill to live in Greestone Terrace, a cul-de-sac of late-Georgian houses situated just below the cathedral. Unlike Albert Goodall, Agnes had no doubts about her young half-brother's musical abilities. She lavished a good deal of love on him and built up his confidence. In 1910 she persuaded her father that Reggie should attend the Lincoln Cathedral choir school. Albert approached the organist and choirmaster, Dr G. J. Bennett, who agreed to hear the boy.

Bennett was comfortably off, for his wife, Marion, was the daughter of Joseph Ruston, founder of Ruston, Proctor, a Lincoln engineering firm with a world-wide reputation. They lived at North Place, a Queen Anne-style mansion they had built for themselves in Nettleham Road. Reggie was taken there by his father for an audition. Bennett sat at a piano fitted with a pedal-board that corresponded exactly to that of the cathedral's organ. Presumably he liked what he heard, for shortly afterwards Reggie became a fee-paying boarder at the old choir school at 1 Northgate, a terrace of little houses that still stands at the junction with Nettleham Road.

For an English cathedral organist of his time, Bennett had unusually wide sympathies in both religious and secular music, and Goodall always considered himself exceedingly fortunate to have come under his influence. Bennett, said Goodall, laid the foundations of his own musical interests. In his youth Bennett had spent a year at the Hochschule für Musik in Berlin, followed by two years in Munich, where his masters had included the celebrated organist and composer, Joseph Rheinberger. Back in London, he had been appointed a professor of harmony and composition at the Royal Academy of Music at the age of 25. His own works, strongly influenced by German Romanticism, included an overture, *Jugendtraum,* which August Manns conducted at the Crystal Palace concerts in 1887. Eight years later he went to Lincoln, where he remained until his death in 1930.

Bennett was a thick-set, fierce-looking man with a reddish face and a large ginger moustache. On Sunday mornings he wore a top hat, morning coat and spats, and carried a rolled umbrella, which he was once seen brandishing at a precentor who had been unwise enough to say he did not wish to hear a certain anthem by Gounod in the cathedral again.[4] Goodall found Bennett an impressive, if somewhat frightening, figure. Another Lincoln chorister, Reg Woodward, has described some of Bennett's more alarming practices:

In the Song School he would haul a boy by the collar over the music benches at which we stood and administer a beating with a hard and heavy hand. On one occasion this was administered in error to the wrong boy. A shocked silence followed. [On learning of his mistake,] he roared with laughter and said, "Well, it will do for next time." Once he irrupted into the choir during a service and led out a malefactor by the ear.[5]

A dedicated cigarette-smoker (at home he enjoyed a hookah), Bennett was given to sticking his nicotine-stained fingers into the choristers' mouths to make sure they were kept wide open. The boys preferred it when he used the end of his baton for the job; it tasted better. Sometimes the whole choir was the subject of his wrath. The Lincoln historian Laurence Elvin remembered an Evensong at the end of which Bennett played the shortest of voluntaries, rushed to the vestry before the choir could leave the building, admonished the boys and men for their mistakes and took them through the anthem until it was sung to his satisfaction.[6] But Bennett was not all gruffness and bad temper. He gave sumptuous Christmas parties for the choristers at his home. There were summer parties, too, when he joined in cricket matches on the lawn and whammed tennis balls over the roof of the house to boys waiting on the other side. Anyone who caught a ball got a sixpence. If there were those who disapproved of Bennett's methods as a choir-trainer, few disputed the excellence of the results he achieved: the choir was held to be one of the best of its kind.

Not surprisingly for a pupil of Rheinberger, Bennett had an outstanding technique as an organist. Goodall said it was Bennett's playing of Bach's organ prelude in B minor that first made him aware of the power of great music. Goodall was also introduced to Wagner's music through Bennett, who often played excerpts from the operas at his organ recitals, notably the prelude and Good Friday Music from *Parsifal*. (When "Father" Henry Willis, who had designed and built the cathedral organ, died in 1901, Bennett played in his memory, not some pious piece of Victoriana, but the funeral march from *Götterdämmerung*.) Bennett introduced new compositions by Reger and Karg-Elert, and performed a good deal of French music by Guilmant, Widor and Franck. English organ music rarely featured in his programmes.

The Lincoln choral foundation consisted of nine lay clerks – three altos, three tenors and three basses – and sixteen choristers. A lay clerk could live on his salary then, though some earned extra money by giving singing lessons. In Goodall's time, and for some years afterwards, the basses were Messrs Endersby, Lofthouse and Woodward, whose son Reg Woodward has described them lovingly:

Their idiosyncracies afforded us endless entertainment, their sheer professionalism a standard we envied ... Mr Endersby, a very distinguished looking man, had a vast voice, like the Lord thundering out of heaven. Mr Lofthouse was a Yorkshireman and very proud of it. "Eh, lad, 'ast tha never bin to Leeds? Tha doesn't know tha's born." He had trouble with his aspirates and we listened eagerly for the verse in the psalm which he rendered as "Why 'op ye so, ye 'igh 'ills. This is God's 'ill." Occasionally he had an argument with his wife, which always ended, "Who's maister in this 'ouse then?" "You are, but I'm nek."[7]

Although a Lincoln chorister's round was arduous, Goodall thrived, for music was now central to his life: in addition to singing in the cathedral, he was having regular lessons in piano and theory from Bennett's assistant, Harry Trevitt. On weekdays the timetable at the choir school included PT before breakfast, morning and afternoon choir practice, and Matins and Evensong in the cathedral; ordinary school lessons had to be fitted into the few gaps that remained in the day. Games were played on Thursday afternoons, when Evensong was sung by the men alone. Services in winter could be a miserable experience, for St Hugh's Choir was unheated; the fantastical canopies of its stalls might be masterpieces of the medieval woodcarver's art, but they went unappreciated by small boys suffering from chilblains brought on by the extreme cold. The rewards were pitiful. The choristers had two 12-day breaks – one after Easter, the other after Christmas – and a fortnight's holiday in August, which even by the standards of the day was very little.

By the time Goodall joined the choir, Bennett had leavened the cathedral's typically English repertoire – canticles by Croft, Smart, Stanford and Harwood – with anthems by Mendelssohn, Bach, Mozart and Spohr. In addition he had reintroduced several works by his most distinguished predecessor at Lincoln, William Byrd, including the Short Service, known then as Byrd in D minor. At the time Byrd's music was rarely heard in Anglican cathedrals, though, simultaneously with Bennett's efforts at Lincoln, Sir Richard Terry was reviving the composer's music for the Roman liturgy at Westminster Cathedral.

In October 1912 there came a change in the services at Lincoln that was to have a dramatic effect on the music performed in the cathedral. The new High Church precentor, the Rev. John Wakeford,[8] abolished the Litany, which had traditionally followed Matins on Sunday mornings, and replaced it with a Choral Eucharist. Bennett introduced settings of the Mass by Schubert and Silas, Dvořák, Gounod and Guilmant – all of them adapted to the words of the English prayer book. Bennett's own favourites included Schubert's Mass in G, Dvořák's in D (sung on both Easter and Christmas days in 1913), and Gounod's *Messe solennelle de Ste Cécile,* all of which were to become staples of Goodall's own repertory when he too became an organist and choirmaster some years later. Not everyone in Lincoln liked the unfamiliar works. Frank Woolley, Bennett's one-time assistant, detected a dangerous whiff of the Continent about them: "The music of these Masses was florid and chromatic, and of great length, and almost inclined to produce an atmosphere of the secular; that

which is so alien to the great tradition of English cathedral music."⁹ Goodall
loved them.

In addition to providing music for the liturgy, Bennett conducted choral
concerts in the cathedral. The choir was boosted by an amateur chorus from the
city and there was also an amateur orchestra. Thus Goodall sang in performances
of *Messiah,* the *St Matthew Passion* and Haydn's *Creation.* Even more important
from the point of view of Goodall's musical development were the annual
choral and orchestral concerts Bennett conducted for the Lincoln Musical
Society, which he had founded in 1896. Planned on an extravagant scale, they
gave Lincoln the chance to hear works that in some cases were rarely, if ever,
heard outside the main cities. Thanks to Bennett, Lincoln probably heard more
of Wagner's music than any other comparably-sized town in England.

The concerts took place in the Corn Exchange, which was normally used as
a cinema. The acoustics were not perfect, but the building was large enough
to take a choir of 200 and an orchestra drawn mainly from the London Symphony Orchestra. There were distinguished soloists. Goodall and his colleagues
from the choir school had specially reserved seats. In November 1911 Bennett
conducted Act 3 of Wagner's *Tannhäuser* and Sullivan's oratorio, *The Martyr of
Antioch.* It is a measure of Bennett's influence on the musical taste of Lincoln
that the Sullivan turned out to be a relative failure with the audience, while the
Wagner was judged a triumph.¹⁰

The following year Bennett conducted Act 3 of Wagner's *Die Meistersinger
von Nürnberg.* But it was the concert which took place on 28 November 1913
that Goodall remembered more clearly than any of the others, for he took
part in it. It marked the 100th anniversary of Wagner's birth and was devoted
entirely to his works. There were 250 performers in all. Bennett's programme
was typically generous:

Lohengrin
Act 1, omitting Sc.1; prelude and bridal chorus from Act 3

Parsifal
Grail scene from Act 1

Der fliegende Holländer
Senta's ballad

Die Walküre
Ride of the Valkyries and Wotan's Farewell

Siegfried
Forging songs

Tannhäuser
March and chorus from Act 2

The soloists in the *Parsifal* extract included the leading British Wagner tenor of the day, Frank Mullings, in the title-role, Frederic Austin as Amfortas, and Charles Woodward, the cathedral lay clerk, as Titurel. The Montsalvat bells "did not produce the deep solemn tones the composer intended," said the *Lincolnshire Chronicle,* but Goodall and the other Lincoln choristers, who provided the boys' choir at the end of the scene, came in for particular praise, "their well-trained voices adding much to the charm of the music."[11]

In the meantime the Goodall family had been struck by a catastrophe from which it never fully recovered. On 2 April 1911, Albert Goodall was dismissed from his job, and rumours quickly spread through the city that he was connected with irregularities discovered at the solicitor's office. The following evening he was arrested at home on a charge of "forging the name of Dr Winter to a document at Mr Tweed's office on February 16th." After being warned that further charges would be made, he was driven in a cab to the Lindsey police station in the High Street, where he spent the night in the cells. His distraught wife sent a message to her step-daughter Agnes, who rushed round to Monks Road to offer comfort. The following morning Albert appeared before the city magistrates at the Session House, where Mr Tweed, his old employer, "betrayed signs of emotion" as he read out the charge.[12] The *Chronicle's* headlines were dramatic:

SENSATIONAL ARREST AT LINCOLN

WELL-KNOWN OFFICIAL IN CUSTODY

ON A CHARGE OF FORGERY

A PATHETIC FIGURE

Mr Scorer, the prosecuting solicitor, put his case. Witnesses at magistrate's courts, he explained, were entitled to certain allowances, but before they could receive the money, the magistrate had to sign an order which could then be presented at a Lincoln bank for payment. To save time, it had become the custom for magistrates to sign blank certificates, leaving Goodall to fill in the details. Dr Winter had been allowed a sum of 10s 6d for attending a case heard by the county justices on 16 February. Goodall had made out the order, not for 10s 6d, but for £2 2s. He had then forged Dr Winter's signature on the document, collected the money from the bank, sent 10s 6d to Winter by post, and kept the rest for himself. Further examples were cited.

Goodall was remanded for six days and refused bail on the grounds that he might leave the city, though he protested vehemently that he would do no such thing: "I'll turn up like a man and stand my trial." When he reappeared in court the following week, a number of charges were read out. He admitted his guilt and was committed for trial at the June Assizes, where once more he pleaded guilty.[13] In his summing-up, the judge, Mr Justice Pickford, said he thought it most irregular that the accused should have been allowed to fill in the certificates in the first place, but he should not have fallen to temptation. Goodall was sentenced to eight months' imprisonment. By the time he was released, his marriage had collapsed and he emigrated to Canada to start a new life. It was never fully explained in court why he had resorted to forging the certificates, but it was widely assumed in Lincoln that his frequent visits to the Spread Eagle had contributed to an unbridgeable gap between income and expenditure.

It is not hard to imagine the effect that the trial had on the family. Adelaide became deeply embittered. Beset with financial difficulties, she was forced to take in foreign apprentices from the Ruston engineering works as lodgers. The faithful Agnes helped to pay off the debts and made sure that Reggie could stay at the choir school, but Billie was taken away from his private school and sent instead to the Rosemary Lane Wesleyan elementary school, a few streets away from home.

The letters Reggie wrote to his mother from the choir school betray his feelings of loneliness at this time (the spelling and punctuation have not been altered):

June 1st 1913

My Dear Mother,

Thankyou very much for the letter you sent yesterday morning and also for the 1/- postal order you sent you needn't of bothered of sending me it at all I would a lot rather you had come I was very disappointed you did not come up. I expect you will be very lonely without Billie to keep you company especially today (Sunday) I wish I could have come to keep you company. My garden is getting on alright the radishes which Billie brought me up are coming up ripping.

A school report that has survived from the summer term of 1913 shows Goodall top of his class in the history exam and second in scripture, English and Latin. The headmaster thought this a big improvement on past results, but wrote, "His progress is still slow, as he is very lacking in application." In arithmetic and algebra he still worked "without much intelligence & will not tackle difficulties." Goodall's general conduct was considered "good," though Wakeford, the cathedral precentor, found him "inattentive to orders: he must learn obedience."

Early in 1914, Adelaide Goodall, exhausted by her efforts to struggle on in Lincoln, accepted an invitation to go and live with her married sister, Florence, in Springfield, Massachusetts. Agnes Tetley pleaded with her to allow Reggie to stay on at the choir school, offering to pay all his fees and expenses, but, to Reggie's dismay, her entreaties fell on deaf ears. Mrs Goodall and the two boys sailed for America. Reggie was not to return to England for another eleven years.

CHAPTER 2

Exile

S PRINGFIELD lies in the south-western corner of Massachusetts, about
ninety miles from Boston. Its most notable feature is the Springfield
Armory. Founded during the American Revolution, it produced America's first
military musket and laid the foundations of the city's industrial and commercial
prosperity.

Reggie, homesick for Lincoln, found Springfield strange and alien. He and
Billie were laughed at by their schoolfellows for their shorts and long socks.
Once again it was the outgoing Billie who, musically, fared better than his
brother. He was taken up by a group of admiring women, who arranged for him
to have piano lessons in Boston; later they sent him to study at the Damrosch
and Mannes music schools in New York. Reggie, beside himself with jealousy,
reckoned that if music were to play any part in his own life, he would have to join
his father in Canada. Albert had settled in Burlington, a small town surrounded
by market gardens and apple orchards at the western end of Lake Ontario. Mrs
Goodall was sympathetic to the idea, for money was short, and within months
of the family's arrival in Massachusetts Reggie, to his great delight, was packed
off to Canada. Billie remained in Springfield.

Although Burlington's population has grown from 5,000 to 164,000 since
the first world war, and most of its market gardens have fallen prey to property
developers, the area round St Luke's Anglican church, with its bosky avenues
and stone-and-clapboard summer homes, has changed little since the day the
13-year-old Reggie arrived there. Albert Goodall had fallen on his feet and was
making a living as a piano teacher. He was also organist and choirmaster at St
Luke's, where he had been rewarded with a $50 increase in salary for raising the
standard of its music.[1] He lodged near the church at 432 Burlington Avenue,
home of a Mrs Oliver. Albert's name was linked romantically with that of her
daughter, but there was no question of marriage. Albert and Adelaide Goodall
never divorced.

Reggie, who stayed with his father at Mrs Oliver's, went to school in Burlington, sang in the church choir, and was taught piano, organ and theory by William Hewlett, co-director and later principal of the conservatory of music at the
nearby steel town of Hamilton. Hewlett was no provincial. English by birth, he
had studied in Berlin with the composer Hans Pfitzner and the Russian pianist
Ernst Jedliczka. A noted organist, he gave regular recitals on the big Casavant

instrument at Hamilton's Centenary Methodist Church, and conducted the city's Elgar Choir in performances of Mendelssohn's *Elijah* and the Verdi Requiem. Hamilton's musical life may not have been extensive, but it was supplemented with visits by leading recitalists and travelling opera companies.

Reggie enjoyed his time in Burlington, but it was not to last. In 1916 his father, to whom he had grown close, volunteered for the army. At first sight it was a surprising move. Conscription was not introduced in Canada until the following year, and it is unlikely that Albert would have been called up even then, for he was already in his early fifties. Goodall believed that his father enlisted firstly out of financial necessity – demand for music lessons had dropped dramatically with the war – and secondly for reasons not unconnected with his continuing fondness for drink. After Ontario introduced prohibition in 1916, many men found that the army offered them better opportunities for obtaining alcohol than did civilian life, particularly if they were serving abroad. As things turned out, Albert remained in Canada for the rest of the war.

Reggie was forced to return to his mother in Massachusetts, where he took a job to help support the family. He was now 15 and had left school for good. At first he was a messenger for the local railway company, which he enjoyed, but the pay was poor and before long he joined an engineering works, "drilling holes in pieces of metal". There was one consolation about life in Springfield. Once a month Billie was taken on the train by his patrons to hear the Boston Symphony Orchestra; sometimes Reggie got the chance to go too. Occasionally the Boston or the Philadelphia Orchestra visited Springfield, the latter under Leopold Stokowski, who had been appointed its chief conductor in 1912. Goodall remembered Stokowski dashing on to the platform at Springfield and, without bothering to acknowledge the applause, plunging straight into the introduction to Act 3 of *Lohengrin*. Such showmanship appealed to Goodall's theatrical sense, though he never tried to emulate it.

Stokowski was to make a vital contribution to Goodall's growing musical awareness, for just as Bennett had opened his ears to the possibilities of the organ, so Stokowski revealed to him the infinite range of colours that could be coaxed from an orchestra. Throughout his years in North America, Goodall was fascinated by the "Philadelphia sound" and the immense care Stokowski took to achieve it. Goodall never lost his love of beautiful tone; it was a crucial element in his own performances. "I know there are other things in music that are more important," he said in his eighties, "but after all, sound is what we're selling. I hate nasty tone. Even the timpani should sing. I remember the cymbals in the Bruckner Seventh when Furtwängler did it with the Berlin Philharmonic – a shower of stars. Not a bang or a clap, which is what you seem to get these days. I don't care what they say about Stokowski. He was good. He could achieve a lovely sound. I learned something from that." When in May 1974 Stokowski gave his last concert in London, Goodall was there to hear it.

After several months of discontent in Springfield, Goodall wrote to Hewlett, asking if he could return to Canada to study with him at the Hamilton Conservatory. Hewlett replied that he could, but that he would have to support himself, since no scholarships were available. Thus, at the age of 16, Goodall went back to Burlington, where he stayed once more at Mrs Oliver's, though this time without his father, who was to remain in the army for at least another year. Hewlett found him a job as a clerk and general dogsbody in a bank, which more than paid for his fees. Goodall's studies at the conservatory progressed rapidly and at the end of his first year he won a gold medal from Toronto University for his showing in the junior examinations (the conservatory was affiliated to the university). Two years later he graduated with first-class honours and received another gold medal. On the strength of his success he got a job as church organist and choirmaster at Dundas, a small town just inland from Hamilton. The pay was not much, but with the additional money he earned by giving piano lessons, he could afford to resign from the bank. He was now 19 years old, and his life as a professional musician had begun.

Goodall remained in Dundas for little more than a year. One of the friends he made there was a young Cambridge graduate, Gordon Reid, the son of a local factory-owner. Reid, who was more interested in music than he was in the factory, thought Goodall was wasting his talents in the backwater of Dundas and commended him to Dr Albert Ham, a minor composer but a good teacher and choir-trainer whose opinions carried weight in Canadian musical circles. Ham was English, and the thought of meeting someone who had sung in the choir at Lincoln appealed to him. He was impressed by Goodall's piano-playing and in June 1922 secured for him the post of organist at the Anglican cathedral of St Alban the Martyr, Toronto, a curious, but imposing edifice in Howland Avenue, which at the time served as the seat of the bishop. Because of a chronic shortage of funds, the only part of the building that had been completed was the chancel, a splendid example of late nineteenth-century Gothic boasting the only double-hammerbeam roof in Canada. Lacking a nave, St Alban's had distinct limitations as a venue for synod services, episcopal enthronements and civic ceremonies, for the chancel could seat little more than 400 people. Goodall's choir took up a disproportionate amount of the available space.[2]

Reid also introduced Goodall to another important Toronto musician, Healey Willan, a larger-than-life figure who was to leave a strong mark on him. Willan, who had been born in Balham in 1880, was vice-principal of the Toronto conservatory and later professor of music at Toronto University. "Any fool can play notes," he said, quoting his old organ teacher, William Stevenson Hoyte.

"I want to hear the music." Willan liked to claim that he was "English by birth, Irish by extraction, Canadian by adoption, and Scotch by absorption." The Irish part was doubtful, but the rest was true. According to his biographer, Willan's enthusiasms included good food, good drink, good fun, good conversation, good music and attractive women. He wrote excellent limericks:

> There was a young lady from Wantage
> Of whom the Town Clerk took advantage.
> "Of course you must pay her,"
> Said the District Surveyor,
> "You've altered the line of her frontage."[3]

Willan was Rabelaisian by temperament and a devout Anglo-Catholic by conviction. He saw no inconsistency in this: there was, he said, a time and place for everything. For an impressionable young man from Burlington, it was heady stuff.

As a composer, Willan was an unrepentant conservative, though he rarely failed to encourage students working in advanced contemporary forms. He wrote orchestral works strongly influenced by Wagner and Brahms, brilliant organ music whose roots lay in Bach, Rheinberger and Reubke, a post-Wagnerian opera called *Deirdre* and finely crafted motets. He was an authority on Gregorian chant as well as Renaissance polyphony and passed on his love of both – as well as his passion for Wagner – to Goodall, who, whenever his own duties allowed it, attended services at the Anglican church of St Mary Magdalene in Manning Avenue, where Willan had recently been appointed organist and choir-master. The aim of the vicar, Father Henry Griffin Hiscocks, was to make his church the spearhead of the Anglo-Catholic movement in Canada, and with Willan's help he achieved it.[4]

Willan saw the Mass as sacred drama, and at first the ritual was regarded with suspicion by Toronto's Orange-influenced popular press. It took the *Montreal Standard* to notice the choir's "exquisite and expressive singing." Goodall was deeply affected by the combination of liturgy and music, and his visits to St Mary Magdalene's marked the beginning of his lifelong commitment to Catholicism, first the Anglican variety and later the Roman. The last vestiges of his forebears' rigid Methodism dropped away; he had come to think of it as cramped and lacking in joyousness.

Goodall's job at St Alban's Cathedral ended in farcical circumstances. The bishop, James Sweeny, had been invited to attend a special service at St Paul's Church in Bloor Street, Toronto. Since its organist was ill, Sweeny offered Goodall as replacement. The churchmanship at St Paul's was exceedingly Low, and Goodall wondered how he might inject some colour into the proceedings. The only solemn ceremonial allowed was a procession of sidesmen in morning coats who carried the collection plates to the chancel rail, where the Evangelical rector, Canon Henry Cody, a former education minister for Ontario, stood waiting. Goodall watched the prosperous-looking burghers line up at the west end of the church in military order. As they set off down the nave, he struck up with the jaunty "March of the Robbers" from *Chu Chin Chow* – "We are the robbers of the woods/And we rob ev'ryone we can." It caused a sensation.[5] Whether Goodall was pushed by the bishop into resigning from the cathedral, or whether he thought it prudent to leave of his own volition, is not known, but very shortly afterwards he became organist and choirmaster at the nearby church of St Mary the Virgin, Westmoreland Avenue. Like St Mary Magdalene's, it had been built in the 1880s to serve the new residential streets of west Toronto.

Healey Willan maintained that because there were no choir schools in the country, it was impossible to have a first-class boys' choir in Canada. He replaced the boys he had inherited at St Mary Magdalene's with women, who were made to sing without vibrato. Goodall, still only 23, was determined to prove Willan wrong. The artisan parish served by his new church seemed at first an unpromising source of choristers, but he found twenty boys and rehearsed them for up to seven hours a week with a fanatical attention to detail. Former choristers remember his hot temper. When the singing went adrift, he would sweep service books to the floor or let out "a howl of pain".[6] Sometimes boys were whacked over the head with a hymn-book if they sang out of tune.[7] News of the choir's excellence soon spread and parents from all over Toronto began to ask if their children could join it.

Goodall's zeal knew no bounds. Believing that a knowledge of Bach's works was fundamental to an understanding of all other music, he made the choristers write essays about the composer and took them to performances of the cantatas at the Timothy Eaton Memorial Methodist Church, where they followed the music with the scores he provided. For weeks he rehearsed the boys in a Bach cantata for a concert at Westmoreland Avenue, but to the disgruntlement of both choir and congregation cancelled it at the last minute because he thought the results were not good enough. When he was not working with the boys, he spent hours in the church practising Bach's preludes and fugues. The rector's wife, worried that he never seemed to eat, took to putting sandwiches on the organ console for him but, as often as not, when she returned for the tray, she found them untouched, though Goodall was still playing.

Meanwhile Goodall's brother Billie had gone to Paris as tutor-companion to the children of an American doctor, and while there had taken the opportunity to study with one of the most sought-after teachers of the day, Isidore Philipp, professor of piano at the Conservatoire. After six months, however, Billie abandoned all thoughts of a career as a pianist and returned to America to concentrate on something that interested him a good deal more – organising recreational facilities for young people. Goodall was incensed by his brother's decision and even in old age could not help but reflect on the benefits he might have had from all the money that had been spent to no purpose on Billie's musical education. The idea that anyone might consider running summer camps preferable to pursuing a musical career was beyond his comprehension.[8]

Goodall might well have stayed in Canada for the rest of his life, but for a chance meeting with Sir Hugh Allen, who was both director of the Royal College of Music in London and professor of music at Oxford University. During his time at St Mary's Church Goodall had also been appointed music master at Upper Canada College in Toronto, Canada's best-known independent boys' school. Healey Willan had recommended him for the job. In 1925 Allen visited the college in his capacity of examiner for the Associated Board of the Royal Schools of Music and was much impressed by what he heard. He urged Goodall to return to England and study at the Royal College, where, he promised, he would be given all the help he needed. Goodall jumped at the chance. There was no problem about money, for he had saved enough during his four years in Toronto to pay for a passage. He resigned his posts and sailed for England. His only regret was that he had left his father behind. He never saw him again.

After the first world war, Albert had returned to Burlington and in time had been reinstated as organist at St Luke's church. Prohibition was not repealed in Ontario until 1927, but the town had become the playground of Toronto's new rich and there was no shortage of bootleg liquor for anyone who wanted it. Many of the "social events" that took place in the basement of St Luke's church hall hardly complied with the law, but the rector of the day, George Tebbs, who was almost as free a spirit as Albert, turned a blind eye to them. When Albert died of a severe heart condition in July 1936 at the age of 73, the *Burlington Gazette* paid tribute to "a well known and esteemed resident of the town." The Burlington Sons of England Society and the local branch of the Canadian Legion attended his funeral at St Luke's in force. Unlike her husband, Goodall's mother did eventually return to Britain, where she died in 1950.

Goodall often railed against "English hypocrisy," which he felt had forced his father into unnecessary exile. Though he never expressed regret about the years he spent in Canada, he nevertheless wondered what turn his life might have taken had he been allowed to remain at the Lincoln choir school. He found it hard to forgive his mother for taking him away from it. In 1988, while being driven down Earls Court Road in London, he stared morosely at the multinational passers-by. "People should stay in their own countries," he observed. "And that goes for English people, too."

CHAPTER 3

Sacred and Profane

A GNES TETLEY, who had not seen her half-brother since he was 12, was waiting for him on the quayside when his ship docked at Liverpool in September 1925. He was lean and wiry in appearance, and, though timid in manner, full of enthusiasm. Agnes took him to London by train and found digs for him in Rowland Gardens, South Kensington, near to the Royal College of Music, where Sir Hugh Allen, as good as his word, enrolled him for the winter term. The college register shows that Goodall gave his year of birth as 1903, instead of 1901. He may have believed that at 24 he was rather old to be a student. He need not have worried. He looked so boyish that most of his fellow students thought he was much younger anyway.

Goodall's principal study was piano, his second one organ. To meet his rent and living expenses, as well as the college fees of 12 guineas a term, he took a job as a pianist at the King's Picture Playhouse (now the Cineworld), on the corner of King's Road and Old Church Street in Chelsea. For several nights a week he accompanied the silent films, playing jazz, popular music, excerpts from the classics, anything that fitted the pictures on the screen. Later he played the cinema organ.

Goodall also answered an advertisement for an assistant organist at the church of St Alban the Martyr, Holborn, an Anglo-Catholic stronghold that enjoyed a high reputation for the quality of its music. The resident organist, Owen Franklin, wanted one of his own pupils as assistant, but the vicar, Father Henry Ross, insisted on auditions being held. There were eight candidates in all. Goodall, who came towards the end in the playing order, noted that his predecessors were all cautious in their choice of test-pieces. Instinct told him that this was the wrong approach, and in contrast he gave a bravura performance of Marcel Dupré's F-minor prelude and fugue. "I rattled the windows," he said later. Ross was bowled over and gave him the job on the spot. For 2s 6d an hour, or about £50 a year, Goodall helped to train the choir, played the organ for the children's service at 9.30 a.m. on Sundays, and stood in at the main Sunday services – the High Mass at 11 a.m. and Evensong and Benediction at 6.30 p.m. – when Franklin was on holiday.

Ross, a tall, dignified man, was famous for his oratory; he packed the 900-seat church for his Lenten addresses, which he delivered with a pronounced

Cockney twang. At High Mass on Sundays, he would berate his listeners: "Last Thursday was Ascension Day. Where were you? And you? And you?" The congregation enjoyed a nervous frisson and returned in their hundreds for more the following week. Ross's ideas about music were unsophisticated. On St Alban's day, 22 June, he liked nothing better than to have a trumpeter from the Brigade of Guards to lead the congregation as it processed round the church singing "For All the Saints." But he was a man of perception, and he was not to regret Goodall's appointment. Goodall came to look on him as a father-figure.

Owen Franklin remained at St Alban's until September 1928, when he left to become assistant organist at York Minster. His successor, Bertram Orsman, said he did not want a full-time assistant. Goodall was given notice, though he was asked to hold the fort for the six weeks or so between Franklin's departure and Orsman's arrival in November. Thanks to his experiences in Toronto, he was able to carry out his duties with confidence. Ross wrote prophetically in the parish magazine: "In the short interregnum our assistant organist, Mr Goodall, has done remarkably well, and I venture to think that he will make his mark most successfully in due course. He has thrown himself into his opportunity with enthusiasm, and I am very grateful to him and the members of the choir who have responded so well to his efforts."[1]

By now Goodall had been back in England for three years. He had found the Royal College of Music a dispiriting place and had left it temporarily, mainly for financial reasons. Standards at the college were low. Allen struggled hard to raise the level of teaching, but many excellent musicians had been killed in the war and a new generation of teachers had yet to emerge.

In the circumstances Goodall was fortunate in his professors – the Australian pianist and composer Arthur Benjamin, and Henry Ley, organist of Christ Church Cathedral, Oxford, and later Eton College. Ley wanted him to apply for an organ scholarship at Oxford, but Benjamin thought Goodall was too old for university and urged him to join the rough and tumble of professional musical life before it was too late. Goodall took Benjamin's advice. He always regretted that he never attended a conservatory on the Continent, but scholarships for foreign study were rare and he had no private means. It is not difficult to understand the despairing cry Goodall uttered many years later when he looked back on his early days in London: "Think of people in Vienna or Berlin, sitting at the feet of Schoenberg or Richard Strauss. And what was I doing? Playing the piano in a cinema. I had no proper education."

Goodall was also disappointed by the low standards of orchestral playing he found in London. He had been used to the sound produced by Stokowski's superb Philadelphia Orchestra and Koussevitzky's Boston Symphony. When he went to hear the New Queen's Hall Orchestra under Sir Henry Wood, he was confronted by scratchy cello tone and ill-tuned woodwind: "I like cellos to sound like cellos. I was appalled by Henry Wood and the orchestra and the whole damned thing." It meant nothing to Goodall that Wood was some kind of national hero, who could achieve miracles on minimum rehearsal-time. Goodall had come face to face with the British musician's ability to muddle through. He thought it amateurish.

There is plenty of evidence to support Goodall's view of British orchestral standards at that time. The quality of the London Symphony Orchestra can be judged from a sarcastic comment made by the critic Ernest Newman on his return from a visit to America in 1925:

> I was afraid that after the splendid American orchestras our own would sound very poor, but I was agreeably disappointed. The LSO, I suppose, ranks as our premier orchestra; and I am glad to be able to record that at its concert last Monday it compared not unfavourably with the orchestras in some of the New York picture houses.[2]

It would be five years before London got its first contracted orchestra, the BBC Symphony, and seven before Sir Thomas Beecham's London Philharmonic burst upon an astonished audience at the Queen's Hall.

One of the first people to help Goodall with his career in London was a friend from Canada, a young baritone called Leslie Holmes, the son of the Bishop of Moosonee and a pupil of Albert Ham in Toronto. Goodall had invited him to share his digs. Though both of them were virtually penniless – visitors to Rowland Gardens got the impression that Goodall lived on a diet of porridge – they managed to spend several weekends in Paris, where Goodall marvelled at the playing of the great organists: Joseph Bonnet at St Eustache, André Marchal at St Germain-des-Prés, Charles Widor at St Sulpice, Charles Tournemire at Ste Clotilde, Marcel Dupré who with luck might be giving a recital at Nôtre Dame cathedral. Holmes had come to Europe to study with both the Irish bass-baritone Harry Plunket Greene and the German baritone and teacher, Reinhold von Warlich. Holmes introduced Goodall to both of them.

Goodall played the piano for Holmes at his lessons with Plunket Greene. As a singer, Plunket Greene was no longer in his prime, but he knew a vast amount about interpretation and Goodall listened carefully to what he taught. Plunket Greene held that words and music were inseparable. He stressed the importance of consonants. Used correctly, he said, they reinforced the rhythm: "There is not a jingle in the world ... which does not owe its rhythm to its consonants." Anyone who has been coached by Goodall, particularly in the Wagner repertoire, will recognise the ideas set out in this passage from Harry Plunket Greene's book, *Interpretation in Song*:

> The uses and abuses of consonants are hard to put in writing. To find the happy medium between incisiveness and demonstrativeness is the difficulty. The British singer, as a rule, is inclined to underdo his consonants, the German to overdo them. But the German is trained in a finer school. If Wagner had done nothing else, his achievements in musical elocution alone would have left his country for ever in his debt. Of all composers Wagner wrote the truest vocal music from the point of view of dramatic diction. The actual physical powers required to sing his operas are, no doubt, abnormal, but his works for purity and ease of declamation are never likely to be surpassed ... All that [the singer] has to remember is that the mumbled jargon of the ordinary English conversation is not speaking in its true sense, and that the speech which he has to exalt into song must be clear and clean-cut as the music it adorns.[3]

Articulation, Plunket Greene insisted, should be "done with the tip of the tongue, the teeth and the lips," a rule that Goodall was later to seize on and turn to his own purposes.[4]

Plunket Greene was an enthusiastic supporter of the South Place chamber concerts and performed at them every season – rather unwisely as time went on – until 1935; he died the following year at the age of 71. A generous man, Plunket Greene saw to it that his best pupils got a chance to appear there too. Leslie Holmes's turn came in the 1926–27 season, the last to take place at the concerts' original home, the South Place Institute off Moorgate. Holmes was invited back the following season and this time Goodall accompanied him. Their recital, on 19 February 1928, marks Goodall's first known appearance on a public concert platform in London. It was held at the City of London School on the Victoria Embankment, "accessible from all parts," said the society's leaflet, "by Trams, Buses, or the Underground Railways." But the audience was sparse. Many of the concerts' regular supporters had already discovered that the hall not only had poor acoustics, but, worse, was usually unheated.

Holmes and Goodall, who shared the bill with a string quartet and a solo pianist, gave a group of songs by Schubert, Schumann and Reger in the first half and a selection of folk song arrangements in the second. They went on to give five more South Place recitals, all at the Conway Hall in Red Lion Square, Holborn. They broadened their repertoire to include songs by composers as diverse as Pfitzner, Vaughan Williams, Rameau, Purcell, Mahler, Mozart and Healey Willan; their performance of Schumann's *Dichterliebe* was described in the society's annual report as "masterly". By the time of their last two recitals Holmes had adopted a new first name, Laurence, to avoid confusion with a radio singer who was also called Leslie Holmes. Holmes's voice was not large, but he was an intelligent and sensitive artist. In later years he taught at the Royal Academy of Music.

Goodall acknowledged that the influence exerted on him by Holmes's other mentor, Reinhold von Warlich, was "immeasurable". If Bennett in Lincoln had sown the seeds of Goodall's interest in German music, it was Warlich who brought it to flower. Warlich first met Goodall with Laurence Holmes in 1928. Impressed by Goodall's playing, he asked him to work for him. Goodall accepted the invitation and played for Warlich's master-classes until the mid-1930s, not only in London, but also in Munich, Vienna and Salzburg during the summer months.

Warlich was born in St Petersburg in 1879 of Baltic German parents. His father had been chief court musician, in charge of the Tsar's military bands and the court orchestra. The accompanist Gerald Moore, who claimed that much of what he knew about *Lieder* came from Warlich, thought that in many ways he was "typically Russian and might have been a character out of Dostoievski. He could be radiant, especially if he were the centre of an admiring circle of eager but silent listeners, but the morrow would find him in the depths of a black depression, his large blue eyes staring at you unseeing."[5] Warlich may have seemed typically Russian in his darker moments, but culturally he was German to the core. He revered Germany's poets as much as he did its composers.

Warlich urged Goodall to hear the Berlin Philharmonic Orchestra when it visited London in November 1928 under its chief conductor, Wilhelm Furt-wängler. Many British critics expressed strong reservations about the German conductor's tempi and choice of dynamics. He was even accused of eccentricity. But for Goodall there was a Dionysiac charge in Furtwängler's interpretations that he found intoxicating. The Berlin orchestra played with all the precision and beauty of tone he had missed since leaving North America. From then on Goodall attended all Furtwängler's rehearsals and concerts at Queen's Hall. In February 1932 he and Warlich sat behind the orchestra for Schubert's Great C-major Symphony. Goodall remembered the last movement as being "bacchanalian". "You will never hear another performance of it as good as that," said Warlich.

Although he continued to give *Lieder* recitals during the 1930s, Warlich was not a singer of the first rank: he had a suspect technique and in later years was inclined to sing under the note. His forte was interpretation. Like Plunket Greene, he attached the greatest importance to the marriage of words and music. For Warlich, a singer who could not get the meaning of every phrase across to the audience, no matter how beautiful the sound, was a failure.

Warlich was a courtly man and something of a snob, and in England was sought out by society. No doubt the fact that he had been brought up in the shadow of the Tsar was part of his attraction. Women admired his good looks and he kissed their hands assiduously. Sometimes he was invited to perform at country houses: "Now Goodall, we're going away for the weekend; take your black tie." They went to Ickworth, the Suffolk home of the Marquis of Bristol

(Lady Bristol was a leading member of the Warlich fan club), where they performed Schubert's *Winterreise* one night and *Die schöne Müllerin* the next.

Goodall played for Warlich in Austria and Germany almost every summer from 1929 to 1935. While he was in Munich he heard numerous operas conducted by Hans Knappertsbusch. In Vienna he watched Franz Schalk rehearsing *Fidelio,* and for the first time encountered Bruckner's symphonies. In Salzburg he heard Bruckner's church music. At the 1933 Salzburg Festival he attended *Figaro, Der Rosenkavalier* and *Die ägyptische Helena,* all conducted by Clemens Krauss, and *Tristan* and *Die Zauberflöte* under Bruno Walter. The Vienna Philharmonic Orchestra was in the pit. There were marvellous casts: Adele Kern as Susanna and Sophie, Alfred Jerger as Almaviva, Lotte Schöne as Pamina, Richard Mayr as King Marke and Sarastro, Helge Roswaenge as Da-Ud in *Die ägyptische Helena,* Tamino and, for good measure, the Italian singer in *Rosenkavalier* and the seaman in *Tristan.*

Goodall was always self-conscious about his lack of formal education and liked people to believe that he had studied with Furtwängler, Krauss and Knappertsbusch, even though he had never done so. His biographical notes claimed that he had been educated in Vienna and Munich. In a way it was true, for he learned more from his travels with Warlich than he would have done from whole terms at Oxford.

At the end of January 1929, only three months after he had left St Alban's, Holborn, Goodall received a letter from Father Ross, asking if he would go and see him. He called at the clergy house, where Ross explained that the new organist had not been a success and had departed, leaving the church without anyone to direct the music. Ross hoped that Goodall might agree to act as stand-in once more until a new organist could be appointed. There was one problem, however. The customary setting for the liturgy at St Alban's on Easter Day was Beethoven's Mass in C, which was always accompanied by a small ensemble of strings, trumpet and timpani drawn from the ranks of the London Symphony Orchestra. Ross confessed to Goodall that he had thought him too inexperienced for the task. However he had consulted the professional men of the choir on the matter and they had urged him to give Goodall a chance – "he knows how to conduct." Goodall, who had never conducted an orchestra of any sort before, accepted the challenge.

The Beethoven turned out to be something of a triumph, or as Goodall himself preferred to put it, "It went quite well. Father Ross called me into his study afterwards and said, 'Well, Reginald, would you like to be our regular organist?' And I said, 'Yes, if you think I can do it.'" The salary was £200 a year, which for Goodall was wealth. Five years later, J. A. Westrup, then editor of the *Monthly*

Musical Record and a critic for the *Daily Telegraph*, was to write of a concert of twentieth-century church music that Goodall gave with the St Alban's choir: "Incredulous readers may object that it is impossible for an ordinary church choir to sing complex modern music. We can only suggest that they go to St Alban's ... and judge for themselves. They will be astonished, as we were, at the perfection of the ensemble and the nuances of interpretation."[6]

CHAPTER 4

High Holborn

T HE CHURCH of St Alban the Martyr, Holborn, designed by William Butterfield and consecrated in 1863, was a masterpiece of Victorian architecture. It had a nave of extraordinary grandeur, 87 feet in length, which soared above its squalid surroundings, while the alabaster-lined chancel provided a further 40 feet. All those who worshipped at St Alban's regarded it as the pro-cathedral of Anglo-Catholicism, but the original church was destined to last for only 78 years. On the night of 16 April 1941 it was destroyed by German fire-bombs.

When the war ended, many hoped that it might be possible to rebuild St Alban's exactly as it had been before, but insufficient funds were available, and eventually Adrian Gilbert Scott, brother of Sir Giles Gilbert Scott, was asked to produce a new, more economical design. From the outside, his church looks similar to its predecessor, for he was able to incorporate several features of the old building that had survived the fire more or less intact, including the massive saddleback tower, the east wall and the memorial chapel by the south entrance dedicated to the church's first vicar, Father Alexander Mackonochie. But the interior is a different matter. Though dominated by a vast, gaudy mural of the Blessed Trinity by Hans Feibusch at the east end, it is otherwise coolly austere, with few of the elaborate architectural details and rich furnishings that made the Victorian St Alban's a place of wonderful mystery. Many old hands who attended the re-opening ceremony in 1961 could scarcely recognise where they were.

Until 1952, when it was united with the adjoining parish of the bombed St Peter's, Saffron Hill (and also acquired a chunk of St Andrew's, Holborn), the parish of St Alban the Martyr was tiny. Measuring roughly 500 by 200 yards, it was bounded by Clerkenwell Road to the north, Leather Lane to the east, Holborn to the south, and Gray's Inn Road to the west. At the time the church was built no fewer than 8,000 people were crammed into this space. There were cows, too, kept for milking in a shed in Brooke Street. It was a place of appalling destitution, a rookery of lodging houses, children's brothels, workshops and thieves' kitchens. Dickens drew on his knowledge of the area for *Oliver Twist,* where he describes it as "one of the lowest and worst that improvement has left in the midst of London."

Even in the 1920s and 1930s, when Goodall was there, the parish was considered one of the poorest in central London and its clergy spent much of their time grappling with social problems. The last of the cows had recently gone, but 5,000 human beings remained. Many of them relied on casual work in Leather Lane market, many others were out of work. The lucky ones, among them the families of postmen from the nearby Mount Pleasant sorting office, lived in the north of the parish on the Edwardian Bourne Estate. Most of the rest were cooped up in the crumbling tenement buildings round the church. Factories and warehouses took up what little space was left. The boys' playground was on the flat roof of the church school in Baldwin's Gardens; there was nowhere else for it.

To learn more about conducting, and thus protect his new job, Goodall applied to join one of the conducting classes at the Royal College of Music. Auditions were presided over by Malcolm Sargent, who was in charge of the senior class. "Good God," said Sargent, as Goodall struggled through his test-piece, "he can't even beat four in a bar." None the less Goodall was given a place in the junior class, run by W. H. Reed, leader of the London Symphony Orchestra. "Willie" Reed was not much of a conductor. Most of his practical experience came from conducting amateur groups, such as the Great Western Railway Choral Society, which rehearsed at Paddington station and gave concerts in Ealing Town Hall. A man of charm and something of a joker, Reed regaled his students with anecdotes about the celebrated musicians he knew. There was a lot of laughter, but not much conducting, and Goodall quickly came to regard the class as a waste of both time and money. On 13 December 1930 he left college for the second time.

Only two days earlier, at St Alban's church, Goodall had conducted his choir of sixteen boys and eight men in what came to be regarded as one of the most important concerts of his career, for it included the first performance in Britain of Bruckner's great Mass in F minor. The soprano Leslie Duff led a quartet of young professional soloists, and George Thalben-Ball of the Temple Church accompanied the work on the organ. There was no money for an orchestra. It had taken more than fifty years for the work to reach London. Had Goodall not happened to hear it sung liturgically in Salzburg cathedral the previous year, it would have taken even longer.

Goodall made clear his commitment to Bruckner in a short preview article he contributed to the St Alban's magazine:

> If one studies his church works – the Masses in D Minor and E Minor – the Te Deum – and the monumental Festival Mass in F Minor, we [*sic*] must recognise his greatness ... It is religious music, but at the same time free and daring in its individual outlook, and modern in its idiom.[1]

Goodall's admiration for the composer was not shared by London's music critics. When in the previous month Otto Klemperer had conducted Bruckner's Eighth

Symphony at Queen's Hall, only Ernest Newman of the *Sunday Times* had shown enthusiasm for the work. A. H. Fox Strangways wrote in *The Observer* that he had "never heard such a number of platitudes and mannerisms within an hour ... But the melodies are worst: they really have no meaning."[2] Klemperer thought the playing of the London Symphony Orchestra was "very bad."[3]

Goodall, however, was not deterred by the general apathy and just over a year later, on 21 January 1932, gave a second concert at St Alban's devoted to Bruckner's church music. This time the programme included the British premiere of the composer's setting of Psalm 150 – as well as performances of his *Te Deum* and the Kyrie, Sanctus and Benedictus from the Mass in E minor for eight-part choir and wind orchestra, which, though then unknown in London, had once been heard at the Jesuit church in Farm Street, Mayfair. Thalben-Ball, highly skilled at transcribing orchestral colours, again played the organ. Goodall left nothing to chance. He even wrote his conducting gestures into his vocal score of the Mass: "curved and round beat down – sweep of palm" for the beginning of the Sanctus; "draw back L.H. to closed fist" in the Benedictus.[4]

This time Goodall's enterprise paid off. At least two critics from the national press turned up, though their reviews continued to reflect the prevailing misapprehensions about Bruckner's music. For C.G. in the *Daily Telegraph*, the concert confirmed his opinion that the "first and last thing about Bruckner is that he is essentially a church composer."[5] The anonymous critic of *The Times*, who devoted a whole column to the event, shared this view and took the opportunity to contrast Bruckner unfavourably as a composer of symphonies with Brahms, Franck and Elgar, "with all of whom he has something in common and compared with whom he is undeniably weak." He ended his review:

> It is certainly strange that a choral country such as this is should have begun at the wrong end with Bruckner, should have heard the symphonies occasionally and, not being gripped by them, should have neglected to take what for us is the most obvious avenue of approach to him. But this modest attempt at St Alban's, Holborn, suggests that it is not too late to explore it. These examples of his most characteristic work were listened to with rapt attention by a very large congregation, not of musicians but apparently of the ordinary parishioners. We congratulate Mr Goodall on his enterprise.[6]

The concert was actually the third that Goodall had conducted at St Alban's (the first, in December 1929, was devoted to Mozart's Requiem and motets by Victoria, Rachmaninov and Tchaikovsky). The fourth one, on 24 January 1933, was remarkable for including the first London performance of Szymanowski's *Stabat Mater*, which had received its British premiere only four months earlier at the Three Choirs Festival. It shared the programme with Haydn's *Theresienmesse*, then a rarity in Britain, and a repeat of Bruckner's *Te Deum*.

For the first and only time at a St Alban's concert there was a small string orchestra of a dozen players from the LSO, led by George Stratton. Anthony Collins, who later took up conducting, was first viola and Adolf Lotter, the last surviving pupil of Dvořák, played the double bass. Thalben-Ball filled in the wind parts on the organ. Ralph Nicholson, a fellow-student of Goodall's at the Royal College, was the timpanist:

> The one orchestral rehearsal we had was most revealing, for Goodall rehearsed each desk separately and in great detail. Experienced orchestral players would normally have taken unkindly to a young conductor working in this way, but not on this occasion. They were only too glad to have a chance to get to know the music and practise the tricky parts as quickly as possible. Goodall was thorough and patient and very helpful. Everything was done with great concentration and not a moment was wasted. The concert left me in no doubt that here was a conductor of the future. He conducted the whole complex programme from memory.[7]

The soloists were Margaret Ritchie (then known as Mabel Ritchie), Anne Wood, Ian Glennie, a pupil of Reinhold von Warlich, and Goodall's recital partner, Laurence Holmes. Anne Wood noted that "Goodall treated the boys of the choir as though they were professionals. I was startled how tough he was with them."[8]

Most of the boys came from the parish itself. Few of them could sing even the simplest sequence of notes without prompting from the piano when they joined at the age of seven or eight. To make them look smarter on Sundays, Goodall put them in Eton collars, which, with their surplices, gave them a deceptive air of innocence. The men of the choir were a mixture of amateurs and professionals. The latter, mostly recruited from the choruses of West End musicals, were paid £25–30 a year, which compared well with the wages offered by other churches. Boys got between 10 shillings and £3 a quarter, depending on how long they had been there. The money came from collections, bazaars and special appeals.

Goodall's fifth concert at St Alban's, on 21 November 1934, was the last he gave there. The church could no longer absorb the deficits incurred. The programme was devoted to unaccompanied twentieth-century choral music – Stravinsky's *Pater Noster* (almost certainly its first British performance), two carols by Herbert Howells, two motets by Sibelius and one by Healey Willan, and a Mass for two soprano choirs and flute by a young Dutch composer, Jan Mul. Two of Bruckner's motets were added for good measure. The audience, which was not large (it was a muggy night, which may have kept people away), included the future music critic Felix Aprahamian, then a broker's clerk on the London Metal Exchange. He noted in his diary: "Goodall is a genius. The motets and other choral works were rendered to real perfection by a handful of choristers."

The concert was reviewed by both *The Times* and the *Daily Telegraph*. The former said that the setting of *Pater Noster* "showed Stravinsky perverse as usual," though "Mr Goodall conducted his excellent choir through all this difficult music with unfailing confidence and ability."⁹ J. A. Westrup in the *Telegraph* found the performances "extraordinarily good. Mr Goodall, who conducted everything without a score, has succeeded in training his singers to observe every nuance with surprising unanimity. The perfect acoustics of the church gave an added richness to the choral tone."¹⁰ Westrup had more to say in the *Monthly Musical Record*:

> We should like to know how many church choirs in London would have the enterprise to sing a programme of this kind, let alone sing it with the finish and subtlety which the St Alban's choir put into their performances. Mr Goodall has no exceptional material to draw upon. The excellence of the singing must be due to a combination of a patient perseverance and expert tuition on one side and loyal and devoted co-operation on the other.¹¹

Blood, sweat and tears came into it too. Leslie Duff, who often sang as a soloist at High Mass on Sundays, recalled:

> Every Sunday there was a different Mass, and at the main Friday rehearsal – the only one with the soloists – I would think, how on earth are these boys going to do it? How can they do it? You cannot imagine the labour and the struggle and strife that was necessary to achieve anything that could be called a perform-ance – and Reggie wouldn't have anything but a performance, because his per-fectionism made it hard for him to put up with any failures, though inevitably there were some. He was very temperamental and he had a tremendous temper. It wasn't funny at all, it was very hard work, but the results were staggeringly beautiful. I have never got over that feeling of absolute rightness about the per-formances.¹²

Like many others who knew Goodall at St Alban's, Leslie Duff was fascinated to find that when he was not working he was modest, humble, shy and courteous, but that as soon as he began to make music a demon seemed to leap out of him: "Obviously he was fiery and mad inside. He had terrific power."

At rehearsals in the old schoolroom in Baldwin's Gardens, the boys became adept at avoiding the missiles hurled at them by their fanatical choirmaster – rulers, ink-wells, hymn-books, hard-backed blackboard dusters flew through the air, usually accompanied by a stream of swearwords. It could be quite frighten-ing, with Goodall, brimful of nervous energy, stamping his feet, shouting at the top of his voice and banging the piano-lid up and down to instil an elusive rhythm into the choristers' heads.¹³

Once, to everyone's astonishment, an irate mother accompanied by a police-man and her small tearful son irrupted into the rehearsal to complain that Goodall had clouted the lad over the ear. Goodall tried to explain that he had only given him a light cuff for some musical misdemeanour. While the constable did his best to quieten things down, the mother stormed out, saying the boy would never return to the choir again. But he did return, and after he had been back a couple of times, the mother said to Goodall, "You know, it's an extraordinary thing, but I can't keep him away," The boy's friends were not at all surprised to see him back. There was a strong *esprit de corps* in the choir.

Several of Goodall's old choristers have testified that in later years they came to recognise that their whole outlook had been changed by their experience of singing in the St Alban's choir. Goodall had shown them that they were capable of achieving something of value in their lives. Some had difficulty in reading and writing English when they joined, yet Goodall taught them to sing, not only in Latin, but also, when they came to perform Bruckner's Psalm 150, in German. Rehearsals were held on Mondays, Wednesdays and Fridays, and, if things were going badly, on Saturday mornings as well; on such occasions Goodall rewarded the boys afterwards with tea and cakes at Lyons in Holborn. There were summer jaunts to Richmond Park for picnics and cricket matches, with Goodall umpiring in his shirtsleeves. For those who were interested, there were visits to Queen's Hall.

In spite of the reign of terror at rehearsal, the boys were fond of their choirmaster, for as often as not his rage quickly turned to laughter. Among themselves they called him "Bags," after the baggy "Oxford" trousers he wore. They were intrigued by his old trilby hat, worn right through at the point where he lifted it to the women he met; by his accent (they assumed he was Canadian by birth); and by his prowess as a runner (he always seemed to be in a tearing hurry). It is a measure of the boys' enthusiasm for their task that Goodall had no difficulty in persuading them to join him on Sunday-afternoon expeditions to the Temple Church to hear the monthly performances of major choral works given there by Thalben-Ball's choir, made famous by Ernest Lough, the boy wonder. Once they were late and raced down Chancery Lane at the double, with Goodall, coat-tails flying, well in the lead. Not even the parish school champion could catch him.

Goodall taught the boys their parts note by note, phrase by phrase. He passed on the lessons he had learned from Plunket Greene and Reinhold von Warlich. To improve articulation he made them repeat over and over phrases such as "The tip of the tongue, the teeth and the lips" and "Hot potatoes in the throat." (For variation, the latter was sometimes repeated in German: "Heisse Kartoffeln in der Kehle.") Before embarking on an unfamiliar work, Goodall would explain what it was about and then make sure that the boys understood every word of the text. He tried to impart to them the sense of overwhelming profundity he felt in much of the music they performed. "Imagine it," he would cry ecstatically, as the boys struggled with the Gloria of the Bruckner F-minor Mass.

"It's the whole cosmic universe!" It was a phrase he often used to describe his transcendent musical experiences. Once, tidying up after a rehearsal, he noticed that one of the choristers, a small boy with red hair, had drawn on his score a little circle with a dot in the middle of it. Underneath he had written, "The cosmic universe." Goodall loved the joke.

Those who heard the St Alban's choir marvelled not just at the beauty of the singing, but also at its expressiveness (a quality rarely encouraged in Anglican choirs at the time), whether in the unaccompanied Masses of Victoria, Palestrina and Byrd that were sung throughout Advent and Lent, the Masses of Schubert, Mozart and Gounod given during the rest of the year, or the motets by Liszt and Sibelius, Tchaikovsky and Rachmaninov, performed at Benediction on Sunday evenings (see Appendix II, page 214). By all accounts the plainsong, sung in the tradition of Solemnes and used for the Psalms, the antiphons, the canticles at Evensong and the responses, was like a great tidal river in its ebb and flow. For Goodall, plainsong evoked the same feeling of mystery as *Parsifal*.

The musical standards Goodall achieved at St Alban's helped to attract huge congregations. To ensure a seat at High Mass on Sunday mornings it was necessary to sit through the Matins that preceded it. People from the smarter areas of London, from Mayfair and Belgravia in particular, flocked up Brooke Street to the south entrance. The local people preferred the north door to the church in Baldwin's Gardens, which still bears its original Victorian superscription, "Free for ever to Christ's poor."

The organ at St Alban's, a powerful, four-manual instrument built by "Father" Willis in 1893, was famous for its brilliance and its colour. Felix Aprahamian "never ceased to deplore its loss, for its Great division was probably Willis's finest."[14] But it was not easy to play: the combination pedals had to be given a hard kick down before the stops came out; if the pedals were only halfway down, only half the air got to the pipes. Aprahamian, who was secretary of the Organ Music Society, showed Goodall his Opus 1, a set of variations on a ground bass, which Goodall played as the organ voluntary after Mass on 14 January 1934. The budding composer wrote in his diary: "The usual clattering and shuffling was going on, but what was audible was finely played ... I must write something really worthy of [Goodall's] great interpretive talent." But Aprahamian never got round to it. When he heard Goodall play the variations a second time, he started to have doubts about his future as a composer. The piece held together successfully, but it contained too many echoes of Dvořák and Franck, Vaughan Williams and Karg-Elert, for his liking.

Thanks to Aprahamian, some of the Organ Music Society's recitals took place at St Alban's, and Goodall, to his delight, found himself playing host to three of the French masters he had heard in Paris – Joseph Bonnet and André Marchal in 1935, Charles Tournemire in 1936. (Olivier Messiaen gave the first complete performance in London of his *Nativité du Seigneur* at St Alban's in June 1938, but by then Goodall had left). Tournemire's visit was not a success, for the elderly *maître* failed to cope with the combination pedals; Marchal's on the other hand was a triumph. Though blind, he had no difficulty in mastering the instrument, which he had never played before, and he finished his recital with a *tour de force* – an improvisation in the form of a four-movement symphony on themes which had been specially written for the occasion by a quartet of distinguished composers, Roussel, Sibelius, Jongen and Vaughan Williams, who submitted them in sealed envelopes.

Marchal opened the envelopes and handed the themes to an assistant, who read them out to him and then transcribed them into Braille. Having memorised them, Marchal launched into his long and complex improvisation, which in the end had five movements, for he built not only a fugue on Roussel's deliberately awkward theme, but a prelude as well. It was an astounding performance. For Goodall, it provided further proof of the technical superiority of the French organists, whose virtuosity and brilliant registration he admired so much. Although never a virtuoso in the class of Marchal or Dupré, Goodall was none the less a force to be reckoned with as an organist. "His playing," said Aprahamian, "was full of temperamental fire." Goodall played a good deal of organ music by Tournemire, Widor, Vierne and Dupré. "Dear God," he said, looking back, "we used to shake them up at St Alban's. I hated the staid Church of England sort of playing you used to get then – Yom, Pom, Pom, Pom – though Thalben-Ball was marvellous, of course; he could play. I took lessons from him. But Bonnet, Marchal … They were my models, real Catholic organists. They made the whole place rock."

Father Ross had retired as vicar in April 1931 and had been succeeded by Ralph Shakespeare Eves, who came from the parish of St Barnabas, Pimlico. Eves was short and roly-poly and known to his curates as "Rootles," because he was "always rushing and rootling around."[15] His preaching style was florid: "And our Lady will take me in her lilywhite hands and lead me to the high altar of God, and there I will play the harp." Fellow clergymen listened in disbelief; pious ladies from Belgravia swooned in their seats with admiration.

There was a comical streak of camp in Eves. He would call his curates "Doggy" or even "Darling," and was once overheard having a long telephone conversation with a mysterious person called George, who turned out to be the sister superior of the nuns attached to the parish. He was always ordering taxis to visit old friends in other parishes, where, without the sanction of the local incumbent, he would hear their confessions or give them the Sacrament. Goodall once found himself in one of these "sacrataxis," as they were dubbed by the St Alban's curates. He had gone to the clergy house to ask Eves to hear his Easter confession. "I'm off to Victoria," said the vicar, "but come along too." Goodall climbed into the waiting taxi. By the time he climbed out, at Charing Cross, he was "shaken, but absolved."

In spite of his boundless eccentricities, Eves was widely regarded as one of the most saintly slum parsons of his day, a humorous, affectionate man who worked hard on behalf of the young, the deprived and the unemployed. Although hopelessly unmusical, he recognised that he had a choirmaster of genius and was proud of Goodall's achievements. When the parochial church council complained that the choir fund was overspent, he made up the deficit himself. Six months after Goodall had given the concert performance of Bruckner's F-minor Mass, Eves agreed to let him perform it liturgically with orchestra at the 1931 patronal festival. "I hope, Goodall, it is not too long," he said. "Well, Father, it's done in the Catholic church in Austria, you know." "In that case it may be all right." As things turned out, Eves's fears were justified. It made for an immensely long service and the experiment was not repeated, though the E-minor Mass, more suited to liturgical use, was given regularly on Sunday mornings.

Eves and Goodall had great respect for each other, but their professional relationship was abrasive. There were tremendous rows. Goodall was inclined to treat the Sunday High Mass as a great sacred concert and resented anything that interfered with the music. The oaths he uttered when the Sanctus bell at the altar clashed in pitch with the choir's singing could be heard by the front rows of the congregation. There were oaths, too, when the choir went wrong, and on more than one occasion he was so upset by a mistake that he fled into the choir vestry and had to be lured out to complete the service. If the boys held their books incorrectly, he would walk over and slap their hands in mid-Mass; if the clergy sang the versicles out of tune, he would put his head in his hands and groan. He could not stand the sound of congregational singing and sometimes took the hymns at Evensong so fast that nobody could keep up. When, at the end of one Mass, Eves shut the chancel gate with a clatter during a pianissimo passage in the organ voluntary, Goodall stopped playing, glanced in the organ-mirror to identify the culprit, slammed the stops in, banged down the organ-lid, picked up his hat and coat, and rushed out of the church, leaving the bemused vicar standing on the chancel steps. Eves never grasped that, as far as Goodall was concerned, anything that destroyed the musical moment was unforgivable.

At times of crisis Goodall was fortunate in being able to count on the support of the senior curate, Colin Gill, who helped him plan the music at St Alban's. Whenever Eves threatened to fire Goodall for his cussedness, Gill, who had been a chorister at Christ Church Cathedral, Oxford, would point out the difficulty of finding anyone as dedicated to replace him. Eves and Goodall had their final dispute in early 1936. It had been a constant source of irritation for Goodall that when the boys of the parish left school at the age of 14, they always left the choir as well, which seemed to him a waste, considering the amount of time it took to train them. Generally speaking, boys in the 1930s took longer to mature physically than they do now, and their voices broke later – Ernest Lough was 16 when he made his famous recording of *Hear my Prayer*. As a result, choirboys could acquire greater musical experience than is possible now. Goodall pleaded with Eves to stop hiring an orchestra and use the money instead to encourage the senior boys to remain with the choir by paying them more. But the vicar would have none of it and Goodall resigned.

Eves was distraught. He may have been driven mad by Goodall's intractability, but he had a deep affection for him and wrote a generous encomium in the magazine:

> During the past five years [actually seven] he has, at great cost to himself, produced music which has raised S. Alban's to a height unsurpassed in London, and, although there may be some who have felt that our music has become a little too elaborate and too expensive, yet on all hands, both in London and all over the country, I have heard expressions of appreciation for the standard which has been attained. Mr Goodall will leave us at the height of his fame here.[16]

In the course of his search for a replacement, Eves tried to entice Boris Ord away from King's College, Cambridge, but without success, and eventually appointed Arnold Richardson at a salary of £150 a year, which was £30 less than Goodall received. Eves told the annual parochial church meeting that as a further economy measure he would in future pay for the orchestra himself. Goodall worked for the last time at St Alban's at the patronal festival in June 1936.

Sadly, no records were made of Goodall's choir. Benjamin Britten once owned a private recording, taken from a broadcast, of his first large-scale work, *A Boy was Born*, in which the BBC Chorus was joined by the St Alban's boys, but it is now lost. Altogether the St Alban's choir was involved in three collaborations with Britten. In the long term they were to prove highly significant for Goodall.

CHAPTER 5

Young Britten

A BOY WAS BORN, Britten's Opus 3, is a formidable achievement for a student of 19. Completed in 1933, it is based on texts ranging from fifteenth-century carols to Christina Rossetti's "In the Bleak Mid-winter," and is cast in the form of a theme and six variations for unaccompanied men's, women's and boys' voices. Most choirs found it so difficult that in 1955 the composer felt obliged to revise it and add an optional organ part. He never wrote another piece as challenging for voices.

The work's premiere was given by the BBC's Wireless Chorus on 23 February 1934 in the concert hall of Broadcasting House. Peter Pears was among the tenors. Britten wanted his old mentor, Frank Bridge, to conduct[1], but the BBC preferred Leslie Woodgate, the Chorus's newly appointed director. The important part for boys' voices was assigned to the choristers of a fashionable Mayfair church, St Mark's, North Audley Street. At rehearsals, Britten found their singing "occasionally somewhat on the lumbering side; but I think I have put most of that right."[2] He judged the performance itself a success, but must have had lingering doubts about the St Mark's choristers, for when plans were being laid for the work's first public performance, to be conducted by Iris Lemare the following December at the Mercury Theatre in Notting Hill Gate, he approached Goodall and asked him if there was any chance of the St Alban's boys taking part.[3]

Goodall agreed at once to the proposal. The composer, who was just 21, sat by the stove in the St Alban's schoolroom, while Goodall, twelve years his senior, hammered the notes into the heads of his six best choristers – the Mercury's small stage put a strict limit on the number of performers. "He was a very shy boy," Goodall remembered. "He treated me with respect; but it should have been the other way round." In fact they were both shy. They got on well – apart from anything else they shared a low opinion of the Royal College. Both suffered from inferiority complexes.

The performance, on 17 December 1934, was given under the auspices of the pioneering Macnaghten-Lemare concerts of contemporary music, which had been started three years earlier by a trio of women, all in their twenties: Iris Lemare, the composer Elisabeth Lutyens and the violinist Anne Macnaghten. The concerts' first purpose was to promote the work of young British composers, Britten, Tippett and Rawsthorne among them. Their second was to provide a shop-window for the talents of the three founders, who felt themselves cold-shouldered in a predominantly male musical world. They were among the first to recognise Britten's gifts and premiered several of his early works. When Lemare conducted the first performance of his Three Two-part Songs for female voices in 1932, it was the first time that any of his music had been heard in public. The Royal College, which Britten left in 1933, paid scant attention to it.

For *A Boy Was Born* Goodall's choristers were joined by the Carlyle Singers, an amateur group trained by Lemare and bolstered for the occasion by two professionals, Anne Wood and Jan Van der Gucht. It was a tough assignment for an amateur choir, even one as competent as Lemare's, and looking back she thought the performance was probably "hearty but not tight-knit."[4] Wilfred Stiff led the St Alban's contingent and sang the solo part in the third variation, "Jesu, as Thou art our Saviour."[5] Britten, who attended the performance with Frank Bridge and his wife, had mixed feelings about the evening. He wrote in his diary:

> Mostly very poor I'm afraid – Herod [Variation II] being esp. wobbly – I came out after it, not being able to stand the strain!

> Funnily enough so many people like the work. The boys (St Albans Holborn) were very, very good and beautiful.[6]

Whatever Britten's misgivings, the performance undoubtedly helped to consolidate his position as a new force in British music. The critics turned up in strength and most of them looked favourably on both work and performance. Fox Strangways devoted his whole column to the occasion in *The Observer*.[7] Westrup in the *Daily Telegraph* was almost alone in striking a discordant note. "The solving of technical problems," he wrote, "seems at times to have occupied the composer's mind to the exclusion of musical ideas."[8]

A Boy Was Born received its second broadcast a year later, on 29 December 1935, with Leslie Woodgate again conducting. This time, not surprisingly, Goodall's choristers were chosen to take part, in preference to their posher and better known rivals from North Audley Street. Unlike the St Mark's choir, which was employed quite frequently by the BBC and even made some gramophone records, the St Alban's boys had never sung on the wireless before. An official of the BBC's music department, caught unawares by the quality of their singing, told them that he found it hard to believe they were not the product of a choir school.

The rehearsals went smoothly, though for both Britten and Goodall a shadow was cast over them by the news of Alban Berg's premature death on Christmas Eve. Goodall was keenly interested in the music of the Second Viennese School; Britten had wanted to study with Berg in Vienna, but the college authorities had blocked the idea. Of the broadcast, Britten noted in his diary:

> ... to B.B.C. at 9.25 for show of my Boy Was Born by B.B.C. Chorus under L. Woodgate & St. Alban's boys (fine) [.] Apart from contretemps in Finale it goes well – beginning fine & some very exciting. I can't help but like this work, as I feel it is genuinely musical.[9]

In a comment in the *Musical Times*, which Goodall cut out and kept, W. R. Anderson wrote:

> B. Britten's "A Boy Was Born" grows in interest on a second hearing. The boy singers (St Alban the Martyr's, Holborn: congratulations to Mr R. Goodall) were extremely good ... I wish the men's top As didn't sound so snatched and savage. Oh, for some of the tenors I used to know![10]

To which Goodall added in ink: "Wait until they hear our Byrd 3 part."

Goodall's second collaboration with Britten involved the composer's *Te Deum* in C for treble solo, choir and organ, written in 1934 for the North Audley Street choir, which may have given its first performance in the course of a service, though this cannot be substantiated, since the choir records disappeared following the closure of St Mark's in the 1970s. The first known performance was given on 13 November 1935 by the St Michael's Singers under Harold Darke at the St Michael's, Cornhill, festival in the City of London. Darke's singers were also due to perform the *Te Deum* the following month in a new version with string orchestra and harp that had been specially commissioned by the BBC, but Darke found he was too busy to rehearse with the BBC Orchestra and the broadcast had to be postponed. Meanwhile Britten had asked Goodall to conduct this new version at a Lemare concert on 27 January 1936 with the St Alban's choir. It turned out to be its first performance.

Goodall started to rehearse the choir, men and boys, at the beginning of December 1935. By now Britten was working for £5 a week as resident composer and sound-track supervisor for John Grierson's GPO Film Unit, based at Blackheath. He confessed in his diary that his colleagues at the unit – who included W. H. Auden, the film-makers Grierson and Basil Wright, and the painter William Coldstream – made him feel ill at ease intellectually. A meeting with them on the morning of 6 December, he wrote, had left him, as usual, with "a pretty violent inferiority complex [...] but this is somewhat eased by my going to a rehearsal of Goodall's choir of St Alban, Holborn, where I take them through my *Te Deum* – & they are flattering to say the least."[11]

Wilfred Stiff was no longer at Holborn and his successor as head chorister had difficulty with the solo part. There were the usual explosions. "Goodall is rightly indignant," noted the composer.[12] He did not start to orchestrate the work until 14 January, a task he found dull, for he was absorbed at the time in recording the sound-track for one of the film unit's most famous documentaries, Harry Watt's *Night Mail,* for which he had composed the music and Auden had written the verse commentary.[13]

Britten finished orchestrating the *Te Deum* on 20 January. That night King George V died. Many concerts in London were cancelled or postponed, and the BBC started to broadcast solemn music, but it was decided that the Lemare concert should go ahead as planned. Britten wrote in his diary for 22 January:

> Fetch parts of Te Deum from copyists after breakfast & take them (thro' immense traffic blocks & diversions on account of Proclamation of New King at St. James's Palace) to R.C.M. for first rehearsal with Goodall. Considering we have only one string to each part they sound very well.

By the day of the concert the number of string players had grown to nine – two first violins, two seconds, two violas, two cellos and one double bass – which was all that the Mercury Theatre's stage could accommodate with the choir in place. Since there was no harp, the optional piano part was used instead. Britten himself played one of the violas.

Auden was in the audience and so was Goodall's conducting teacher at the time, Constant Lambert, who in a review in the *Sunday Referee* complained rather oddly that the *Te Deum* "displays that combination of a brilliant technique with ultimate greyness of effect that we have already come to expect from this young composer. Mr Britten is, I admit, a problem to me. One cannot but admire his extremely mature and economical methods, yet the rather drab and penitential content of his music leaves me quite unmoved.[14] Fox Strangways, on the other hand, thought the work "bespeaks attention at once and holds it to the end." Goodall and the choir, he said, "know their music and sing it like musicians."[15]

Goodall had opened the programme with the first performance in England of Bruckner's little Mass in C, an early work for alto soloist, two horns and organ (or in this case string quintet, for the Mercury had no organ). Appropriately it was the work he chose to perform at his very last service at St Alban's five months later. By now he was so closely associated with the composer that the *Musical Times* reviewer referred to him as "Mr Reginald Goodall (of St Alban's, Holborn, Bruckner expert)".[16] Expert he may have been, but twenty-five years were to pass before he was given another chance to conduct a work by Bruckner in London.

CHAPTER 6

Amateur Nights

G OODALL'S MUSICAL activities during the early 1930s were by no means confined to St Alban's and his collaboration with Reinhold von Warlich. For a week in April 1930 he accompanied the baritone Keith Falkner in a variety show at the London Coliseum. Falkner, a noted oratorio singer, had been asked to top the bill by Dennis Stoll, musician son of the theatre's impresario, Sir Oswald Stoll. Supporting acts included "silly dances," Albert Sandler's Trio, the British Movietone news, various comedians, a Mickey Mouse cartoon and songs of "Old Ireland" from Talbot O'Farrell.

There were three performances daily, at 2.15, 5.15 and 8.15. Falkner, who thirty years later became director of the Royal College of Music, had two spots. In the first he sang popular operatic arias with the theatre orchestra under its resident conductor. For the second, the curtain went up to reveal Goodall alone on stage, seated at a grand piano. Falkner sauntered on and sang selections from Keel's *Salt Water Ballads* and Vaughan Williams's *Songs of Travel*. His singing, said the *Daily Telegraph*, "was warmly appreciated." Only *The Stage* mentioned Goodall's role in the proceedings, but made no comment on it.[1] The most spectacular item on the bill was "Beauty and Dance," in which, said *The Stage*, "a company of around 70 young ladies go through various forms of dancing, including capital scenes representing Toy Town, a garden of orchids, a fan dance and a final parade ... The company are drawn from the Plaza Girls, the Paramount Girls, the Mangan Tillerettes and other show and ballet girls." Goodall enjoyed himself.

There were also more sober jobs that year, for example a pair of organ recitals Goodall gave for the BBC from the church of St Mary-le-Bow in the City. Works by Dupré, Vierne and Franck figured prominently, though the second programme also included a scherzo by G. J. Bennett, Goodall's old choirmaster at Lincoln, and a transcription of the berceuse and finale from Stravinsky's *Firebird*. Such engagements helped Goodall to make ends meet, but did nothing to satisfy his ambition to become a full-time conductor.

In May 1932, after a gap of more than two years, he rejoined the Royal College, this time as a member of the senior conducting class. It was not so much the class that attracted him back, as the fact that the college was an excellent place for hearing about freelance jobs. Between the wars many musicians treated the college like a club and remained there long after they had started their professional careers; nobody paid much attention, provided the fees were paid. In all, Goodall was a student at the college for 24 terms, or the equivalent of eight academic years.

The senior conducting class was still being run by the debonair Malcolm Sargent. Goodall had mixed feelings about him:

> Sargent was all right if all you wanted was four in a bar. Four here! Two there! Four, two, three, watch the beat! I once said in an interview that I had no technique and was rather proud of it, but it was quite wrong of me. You've no right to stand up in front of an orchestra if you have no technique at all. It wastes the players' time. It's just that from Sargent and others I got nothing but technique. There was no interpretive depth, and in the final analysis that's what makes one conductor different from another.

Some of the students copied Sargent's conducting style slavishly, but that was not Goodall's way. He modelled himself instead on two celebrated conductors who had effective, but highly unconventional techniques. The first was Beecham, the second Furtwängler. Goodall was particularly fascinated by Furtwängler's use of the *Luftpause,* the split-second pause he sometimes made at the top of an upbeat to add emphasis to the ensuing phrase. Goodall worked hard to achieve the effect himself, but at first had difficulty in judging the exact moment for the downbeat, for although the pause must be apparent to the listener, it must not cause a hiatus in the natural flow of the music (the trick is to make up the lost time in the following bar). The *Luftpause* – or "rock" as Goodall christened it, after the rocking movement of the body with which Furtwängler indicated the downbeat – became a trademark of his own conducting. It can be heard in the first bar of his recording of *Tristan und Isolde*, where the *Luftpause* before the celebrated "*Tristan* chord" helps to create an extraordinary sense of impending doom. Goodall first heard Furtwängler perform the prelude at Queen's Hall in 1937. "I can hear, even today, the way he conducted it," Goodall recalled fifty years later. "It changed my life."

Goodall divided musicians up into those who "had rock" and those who had not. Sargent "had no rock in him at all." Yet if Goodall had acquired more of Sargent's clarity, not to mention his savoir-faire, his career might have advanced further than it did in the 1930s. His fellow conducting students were sharply divided about his talent. Some thought his beat stiff and ungainly. Others, like the future conductor Charles Groves, were so impressed by his innate musicianship that they assumed he would be the next Beecham.[2] Another former student, Emanuel Young, maintained that "if Reggie had developed a technique, he would have been a worse conductor. Conducting for him was making music, not beating time, though that sort of approach does demand more rehearsal time than is often available."[3]

In 1933 Sargent contracted tuberculosis and the class was taken over by Goodall's old teacher from the junior class, W. H. Reed. Goodall felt Reed was ignoring him and wrote a letter of complaint to the college bursar:

> Dear Sir
>
> I am enclosing a cheque for 3 pounds to be applied to my arrears of fees.
>
> But I must say there is not much inducement to pay this money – I have been in the 1st and 2nd conducting classes five terms and have had exactly 8 min actual work with the orchestra, and have never been "allowed" to conduct at any concert, and the last half of last term was simply wasted.
>
> As I earn my living at music and pay my own fees I naturally object, in these hard times, if I don't receive any return for what I pay – it is of course a different matter for the scholarship people and wealthy amateurs some of whom receive far more attention than their ability warrants.
>
> Yours faithfully,
> Reginald Goodall[4]

The letter seems to have had some effect, for not only was Goodall "allowed" to conduct the rondo from Brahms's D-major Serenade at the second orchestra's summer concert, he was also awarded the annual Theodore Stier prize for conducting, worth £9, or a term's fees. In 1934 Sir Hugh Allen noted in Goodall's summer term report, "I wish we could find him a full rigged symphony orchestra. He'd make them play all right." The following term the senior class was taken over by the composer and conductor Constant Lambert. He was four years younger than Goodall, who considered him far a better conductor than Willie Reed, but too much of a dilettante in his musical tastes. Why, Goodall once asked him tactlessly, had he wasted his time editing the symphonies of Boyce, when he could have been preparing a new edition of *Boris Godunov* instead? Lambert laughed nervously.[5] Goodall liked to claim that Lambert had a low opinion of his work, but in fact Lambert's written reports on him were consistently enthusiastic.

Goodall reckoned he learned more from attending concerts and rehearsals at Queen's Hall than he did from the conducting classes. He had a pass for the BBC Symphony Orchestra's rehearsals and watched a whole gallery of celebrated conductors at work: Toscanini ("he had great clarity, but he was too Italian for me; I like my music to come up from the bowels of the earth"), Sir Adrian Boult ("rather overrated"), Ernest Ansermet, Beecham ("we were damn lucky to have him, when you think of the state of music in England at that time; he knew what was what"), Hermann Scherchen, Hamilton Harty ("a very fine conductor; his Brahms was wonderful"), Bruno Walter, and a conductor he had first admired in America, Serge Koussevitzky, whose insistence on thorough and detailed rehearsal made a lasting impression on Goodall.

Of all Goodall's fellow conducting students, only Muir Mathieson managed to establish himself as a full-time conductor before the start of the second world war – he was appointed musical director of Denham film studios. A despairing student asked Sargent for advice on how to succeed as a conductor. "Give good sherry parties," said Sargent. Goodall thought the reply was preposterous. Former students remember him as someone who kept to himself at the college: conversations with him were almost exclusively about music. To extend his knowledge of orchestral instruments, Goodall took lessons in the double bass with the BBC Symphony Orchestra's principal, Eugene Cruft, in the timpani with another BBC player, Frederick Wheelhouse, in the horn with the LSO's principal, Alan Hyde, and in the violin with W. H. Reed. "Finds the violin more difficult than he imagined," wrote Reed in Goodall's report for the 1935 Christmas term, "but he is forging ahead." Later Goodall studied the violin with one of the most distinguished teachers of the day, Carl Flesch, "not so much because I wanted to play well – though I did improve – but because I wanted to know more about bowing. I told Flesch that I was a conductor, that I had read two of his books and that I wanted to study with him from an orchestral standpoint. He was very helpful." Flesch must have been impressed by Goodall's enthusiasm, for he refused to accept payment for the lessons.

Sir Hugh Allen continued to support Goodall. One of the first jobs for which he recommended him was the conductorship of the Bishopsgate Institute Musical Society. Founded in the City of London in 1896, it was typical of myriad amateur choirs and orchestras in pre-war Britain that hired professional musicians to train them to a respectable standard. Such work was considered an important source of income, not just for tyros, but also for established conductors like Wood and Sargent. The Bishopsgate Society, which consisted of a chorus and a small string ensemble, met once a week to rehearse for the two concerts it gave annually in the Bishopsgate Hall. It favoured oratorios like *Messiah* and *Elijah,* though it sometimes branched out with Parry's *Blest Pair of Sirens* or Stanford's *Songs of the Fleet.*

Goodall saw opportunities for introducing more adventurous works, but first secured the Society's confidence with Bach's Christmas Oratorio, which he gave at his opening concert in December 1933. The following April he conducted two unaccompanied choral works by Sibelius – the hymn *Natus in curas* and *Hail to the Moon* – Vaughan Williams's Magnificat and what was only the third performance in London of Bruckner's F-minor Mass (Goodall had given the first two himself at St Alban's). Felix Aprahamian noted in his diary, "Orchestra disappointing, the choir lusty singers." A critic from *The Times* thought that the choir needed to look to the articulation of its words and that the "technical aspect" of Goodall's conducting left something to be desired, though in the

Bruckner there was no doubt "as to his ability to procure a vivid performance of this highly coloured music even when he had only a few strings, piano and organ with which to present a full symphonic accompaniment."[6]

For his third Bishopsgate concert, in December 1934, Goodall boosted the orchestra with students from the Royal College. Stung by criticism of the choir, he rehearsed it with fierce determination: "You southern English, you talk and sing as though you've got a potato in your mouth. Get it out!"[7] The programme, even more ambitious than its predecessor, included the first British perform-ance of two difficult pieces for unaccompanied choir from Ernst Krenek's *Die Jahreszeiten*, the British premiere of a neo-classical divertimento by the German composer Max Trapp, whose music had been taken up by both Furtwängler and Bruno Walter, and the first London performance of Cyril Scott's setting of *La Belle Dame sans Merci* for baritone, chorus and orchestra, which had been pre-miered by Beecham at the Leeds Festival the previous autumn. The bass clarinet player, Richard Temple Savage, who later joined the LPO, found that Scott had written notes that were too low for the instrument. "Go and consult the com-poser," said Goodall, indicating a morose-looking figure at the back of the hall. Scott, once known as "the English Debussy," hummed and hawed. "I don't know the compass of the instrument," he said eventually. "Do what you like."[8] For Goodall the incident was proof of a rampant amateurism in English composing. Both *The Times* and the *Daily Telegraph* sent critics. In the latter J. A. Westrup wrote that "Mr Goodall's enterprise in presenting this programme, and the high standard of achievement, deserve the greatest praise." *The Times* said that Goodall "not only understands what this modern music is about, but can make others perform it intelligently."[9]

Goodall's growing reputation as a conductor of contemporary works did lit-tle for his career. In a letter to Maisie Aldridge, a piano student at the college, he described an unsuccessful interview he had had for a job: "One old josser said he heard I did a lot of modern music, as if that was worse than being a murderer." Aldridge had first met Goodall when he conducted the first move-ment of Glazunov's F-minor piano concerto for her at a college concert in June 1934; she was to become one of his closest friends. Goodall's letter to her also described a recent holiday he had had in Denmark, where he had sought out several of the country's leading musicians. (He had actually set out for Finland by sea, in the hope of meeting Sibelius, but had been so seasick that he had to be put ashore at Copenhagen.) The Danish composer Knudagge Riisager had shown him a new concerto for trumpet and strings, "which I may try to do at Bishopsgate in October (it would make Willie Reed go mad!)."[10] In fact Goodall never conducted the concerto. A few months later the Bishopsgate Society decided it had enough of new works and for the 1935–36 season replaced Goodall with an altogether safer figure, J. Pearce Bowden. The first work Bowden conducted was *Messiah*.

Conducting amateur groups was all very well, but what Goodall needed was a date with a professional orchestra. He tried to persuade the BBC to give him a studio concert, but in spite of its enterprise in promoting new works and helping to raise musical standards generally in the country, the corporation had a poor record when it came to providing work for burgeoning conductors. Too many of its concerts went to administrators in its music department like Edward Clark and Victor Hely-Hutchinson, who may have been able musicians, but were not cut out for conducting. The chances of securing an engagement with any of Britain's other professional orchestras were remote. Even established conductors like Eugene Goossens and Basil Cameron were forced to take up posts in America, because they could not make a proper living in Britain.[11] Outside London, only the Bournemouth Municipal Orchestra worked more or less fulltime. The Hallé played for only six months a year, and its members, like those of the City of Birmingham Orchestra, were obliged to take jobs in seaside orchestras during the summer months.

At least two conductors, Reginald Jacques and Boyd Neel, launched their own string orchestras during the decade, but such an enterprise demanded money and abundant optimism. Goodall had neither. However, with the help of his half-sister, Agnes Tetley, and Lady Kathleen Skinner, a stalwart of the St Alban's congregation, he raised a small orchestra of professional string-players for a concert at the Aeolian Hall, New Bond Street, on 3 May 1935. The programme included Mozart's *Eine kleine Nachtmusik*, Sibelius's Romance Op. 42 and *Rakastava*, a suite from Rameau's *Dardanus* and the Max Trapp divertimento. *The Times* congratulated Goodall on his enterprise in giving the Sibelius works – Beecham, the composer's leading British advocate, was not to conduct either of them until two years later – but thought the "small orchestra had hardly enough weight of tone to get the full effect of Sibelius's always interesting writing for strings." In the *Telegraph*, Ferrucio Bonavia said the programme was "adequately interpreted."[12] In short, the reviews were complimentary, but not over-enthusiastic, and Goodall failed to achieve the breakthrough he had hoped for.

He often thought of going to Germany as a répétiteur at one of its innumerable opera houses, a job that could have led to conducting opportunities, but one thing in particular kept him at home, his marriage to a schoolteacher, Eleanor Gipps. She wanted to stay in England, and Goodall respected her wish. Eleanor and her sister had lived in the flat above Goodall in Rowland Gardens and were among the first friends he made after his return to England in 1925. When the two women discovered that he was spending his first Christmas in London on his own, they invited him to join their celebrations. Eleanor, who taught history at a private girls' school, made an immediate impression on Goodall, for she represented a world quite outside his own limited experience. Slim and elegant, and taller than Goodall, she had dark, Italianate looks. Goodall always considered her his intellectual superior: she had read history at Lady Margaret Hall, Oxford, spoke French and German, and had a wide knowledge of literature, painting and the theatre. Among her forebears she could count a general and a governor of New South Wales; Gippsland, a region of some 14,000 square miles in south-east Victoria, was named after him. A zealous convert to Roman Catholicism, Eleanor took Goodall to the Brompton Oratory and to Westminster Cathedral, where the high musical standards set by Sir Richard Terry still prevailed, and introduced him to plays and art galleries (though he was never to show much interest in the visual arts). She also helped him to learn German, smartened up his appearance and ironed out his Canadian accent.

The two soon became engaged, to the surprise of their friends, who considered them a curious match: he, an impressionable, unsophisticated musician; she, an aloof Catholic blue-stocking, who was not at all musical. Goodall always claimed that it was Eleanor who proposed. They married on 2 August 1932 at the Church of Our Most Holy Redeemer, Chelsea, and went to live not far away in a large top-floor flat at 78 Elm Park Road, where there was a maid with white cap and apron. In the music room Goodall installed a long mirror (he had discovered that Koussevitzky owned one) and before a performance practised his conducting gestures in front of it, often late into the night. He told his new wife that one day he too would convert to Roman Catholicism.

Though a shy person, Eleanor Goodall had a more forceful personality than her husband: she took in her stride his eccentricities, set-backs, tantrums and even his strong emotional attachments to other women. Though ambitious for Goodall, she was rarely seen at concerts or the opera. Even in the early days of their marriage she felt ill at ease in the company of musicians and preferred friends who shared her own interests. Most of Goodall's colleagues in the conducting class were not even aware that he had a wife. He never talked about her.

Of all the jobs Goodall took to augment his income from St Alban's none was more curious than the private choir he trained for Lady Delia Peel, daughter of the sixth Earl Spencer and a lady-in-waiting to Queen Mary; her husband, Sir Sidney Peel, was a financial adviser to the Foreign Office. Lady Delia, who had studied piano and cello at the Royal College of Music, had started the choir in the early 1930s as a diversion for her niece, Mary Peel. Keen, but musically illiterate, Mary and her young friends assembled once a week during the winter months to sing madrigals and folk-song arrangements at Lady Delia's house in

Hill Street, Mayfair. Though impressed by Goodall's energy, they were alarmed by his habit of making them sing lines individually, one after another, until they were note-perfect. By the mid-1930s the choir had expanded in size and had even been given a name, the Hill Singers. By now membership was open to any of Lady Delia's friends who enjoyed singing, and Goodall coached them for the annual Kensington Musical Competition Festival. He hated madrigals, and hated folk songs even more – but he liked both Lady Delia and the soup topped with cream that she served at the end of each rehearsal – "a nice change for a patron of Lyons Corner House." Goodall referred to the singers as the "Nobs and Snobs," though never to their faces.

Goodall worked with the Hill Singers on Friday evenings. On Thursday evenings throughout the winter of 1935, and on into the following spring, he coached the amateur Dorking Madrigal Choir for the 1936 Leith Hill Musical Competition, which was presided over by its founder, Ralph Vaughan Williams. Rehearsals were held at an elementary school in Dorking, with the elderly members of the choir crammed into tiny double-desks. The accompanist, who played on the school's old upright piano, was a 19-year-old student from the Royal College, Ruth Dyson, who later became professor of harpsichord there:

> Reggie had a good sense of humour, but most of the time he was strung up – a state exacerbated by our stupidity, mine included. When most people get cross, their beat gets more extended, but his got smaller and smaller. When he was really cross, he conducted with the ends of his fingers only. There seemed to be no bones in them at all.[13]

As was his custom, he picked out individuals: "The lady in the end row. You sing that by yourself. Now the next! And the next!" For a group of amateurs who had joined the choir for evenings of innocent enjoyment Goodall's perfectionism came as a shock. Some of them had nightmares. To general bemusement he would call out instructions in German – "Gebunden, gebunden!" (legato, legato) – even in a madrigal by Weelkes or a chorus from the Verdi Requiem. The secretary of the choir was more than a match for him. She understood what he meant, but interrupted on behalf of those who did not: "Mr Goodall, what is 'gebunden'? Is it a *German* word?" The two of them argued fiercely over the poor attendance record:

> Secretary: You must understand, Mr Goodall, nearly all the members had 'flu last week
> RG: 'Flu? I was working in London last week with a temperature of 103.
> Secretary: We haven't all got your strong suicidal tendencies, Mr Goodall.

In the competition the choir did better than it had in previous years, winning both the part-song and full-chorus sections, and Goodall was asked to return the following year. Only in the sight-reading tests did the choir come nowhere.

It did not bother Goodall. "Sight-reading's something you do at home," he declared, "like cleaning your teeth. I don't want to hear anybody sight-read, not even Kreisler. I'm only interested in hearing what Kreisler has been practising for the past five years."

For long periods Goodall worked with amateur choirs practically every night of the week. He even took on another private choir, the Monday Singers, organised by Sir Maurice Bonham Carter, who had been private secretary to Herbert Asquith and was married to Asquith's daughter, Lady Violet. The singers found Goodall deferential and unsure of himself, except when it came to music. Then, said one, "he was like a fiery little stoat. He wasn't afraid of anyone."[14] There were altercations about the correct way to interpret madrigals, and in the end Goodall was forced to beat what for him was a rare musical retreat. He handed over responsibility for the madrigals to a member of the choir, David McKenna, later chairman of the Sadler's Wells Opera.

When Goodall resigned from St Alban's, Holborn, in June 1936 he lost his only year-round source of income and money became a worry for him. He was very conscious of the fact that had it not been for Eleanor's job as a teacher, he would have been in serious financial difficulty. However in the autumn of 1936 Sir Hugh Allen secured for him the conductorship of the Handel Society, an amateur organisation with a choir of around one-hundred and an orchestra of fifty, which gave two or three concerts a year. Goodall could not abide the music of Handel, but he could not afford to be choosy. "The society may have been antediluvian," he recalled, "but they paid me well." Founded in 1882 to revive the composer's lesser known choral works, the society continued to provide a valuable service into the 1930s, when performances of anything except *Messiah* were still rare. In its fifty-seven years of existence it gave all of Handel's oratorios except *Esther* and *Joseph*, a unique achievement for its time, though standards of performance were usually low. When Goodall took over, the society was enjoying one of its better periods, thanks to the efforts of his two immediate predecessors, Douglas Hopkins, who brought in professional orchestral players as section leaders, and Guy Warrack.

The Handel Society was not unlike Lady Delia's choir writ large. Several of its members also belonged to the Hill Singers or the Bonham Carter choir. "We were gentry, not working class," said one of them. "It was a choir for our friends and relations."[15] A large number of them lived in Eaton Square. The president was Lord Blanesborough, a former Lord Justice of Appeal, the treasurer Lt-Colonel Valentine Vivian, adjutant of the Gentlemen-at-Arms. Several of the tenors and basses were in the Territorial Army and during the run-up to Munich were called out to man defence batteries. Goodall fulminated as he watched some of his best singers troop out in mid-rehearsal to attend evening parades.

He bolstered the woodwind and brass sections of the orchestra with students, among them Richard Adeney as first flute, and the horn-players Norman Del Mar and Livia Gollancz. In an attempt to raise the standard of the string section, he brought in Reginald Morley from the LPO as leader and Cecil Aronowitz as sub-leader, but they were unable to make much impact: too many of the players were of an advanced age and barely competent. Goodall's rehearsal accompanist was Charles Groves from the conducting class. Groves worked hard to improve the Handel singers' articulation. "Remember now," he told them, "L for Lords, L for Ladies." They loved it.

Most of the society's concerts were held at the Royal College of Music, where from 1936 to 1939 Goodall conducted – from memory, as usual – Handel's *L'Allegro ed il Penseroso, Dixit Dominus*, excerpts from *Ariodante* and *Arminio*, Act 1 of *Semele*, the Chandos *Te Deum* and *Joshua*, which had not been heard in England for half a century. Bonavia's review of *Joshua* in the *Telegraph* is striking testimony of the changes in both Handel scholarship and public taste that have taken place in the seventy-odd years since Goodall performed it:

> There is no tradition, no precedent, no convention to guide conductors, singers, or even the critic in search of the most fitting way of presenting this music. The general impression was that Reginald Goodall guided his forces wisely and well, earning our gratitude for showing us the Handelian rarity.[16]

Judged by later criteria, the performance lacked "authenticity," though it was not marked by the excesses of Michael Costa's version of *Judas Maccabaeus*, which Sir Henry Wood conducted for the BBC a few months later, with double woodwind, trombones and plenty of percussion.

To Goodall's relief the society's concerts were not devoted solely to the works of Handel and he had the opportunity to conduct symphonies by Haydn, Beethoven, Tchaikovsky, Franck and Sibelius, as well as one of the earliest performances in Britain of Fauré's Requiem. There was nothing by Wagner. For Goodall his time had not yet arrived.

Goodall made his debut as an opera conductor in April 1936, with a semi-amateur company that performed at the King George's Hall, part of the old YMCA building in Tottenham Court Road. The work was *Carmen* – "Terrible! With me conducting it must have been the end." Otherwise almost nothing is known about the event. The hall's records were destroyed when the building was demolished in 1971 to make way for the YMCA's new headquarters, and it seems the performances were not reviewed. All Goodall could remember about the company was that it was run by a tenor who fancied himself in roles that were well beyond his capability: "He drove me up the wall, but I was paid." It is possible that the company was the British Grand Opera Society, which was certainly appearing at the King George's Hall at around that time. Goodall was asked back to conduct *Cavalleria Rusticana* and *Pagliacci* in February the following year. Robert Bossert from the college, who led the small orchestra, remembered that although at the dress rehearsal Goodall took the final bars of *Pagliacci* at the marked *vivace*, when it came to the performance he caught everyone unawares by conducting them *prestissimo*, with the result that the show ended in musical chaos. Fortunately there was so much noise coming from the stage that few people in the audience noticed."[17]

At 34 Goodall had left it rather late to start a career in opera. After the *Carmen* he applied to join the music staff for Glyndebourne's third season, but was turned down, presumably on the grounds of inexperience; at the college he had considered opera a frivolous activity. It was not at all easy to find operatic work. The Sadler's Wells Opera and the Carl Rosa touring company were the only two permanent operatic organisations in the country. Covent Garden mounted a summer season of international opera and occasionally played host to visiting companies, but for much of the time it was dark. There were no regional companies and no public subsidies for opera of any kind.

Goodall's first fully professional job in opera came about by chance in September 1936. One of his college friends, Robert Irving (later a distinguished ballet conductor), had just started work as a répétiteur with a new venture, the British Music Drama Company, when he was offered the post of music master at his old school, Winchester. Irving accepted it and recommended Goodall as his replacement. Goodall's first task was to prepare the chorus for *Boris Godunov*, which was to open the company's three-week season at Covent Garden in November. The experience gave him a taste for Russian nineteenth-century opera he never lost.

The company had been founded jointly by the conductor Albert Coates, whose own opera, *Pickwick*, was premiered during the season, and the Russian-born producer, Vladimir Rosing. Goodall retained a high opinion of Coates: "He was a big man – not one of those niggling people. He may not have been very exact, but he got a marvellous sound from orchestras. They played for him with *Schwung* [verve]." Financial backing came from F. J. Nettlefold, a senior director of Courtaulds. His wife, the mezzo-soprano Vera de Villiers, featured prominently in the casts; she also figured prominently in the affections of Albert Coates, who subsequently married her. "Opera is music drama," proclaimed Rosing, "it must be acted as well as sung," but his efforts to apply Stanislavskian principles to *Boris* failed to impress the critics. Goodall's chorus was much admired, however, not least by Coates, and he was invited to stay on at Covent Garden for Beecham's month-long winter season, which opened on Boxing Day

1936. In the course of it Goodall conducted the offstage orchestra in *Un ballo in maschera* and was put in charge of the steam-machine for the witch's oven in *Hansel and Gretel*. Norman Feasey, who was also on the music staff, recalled Goodall's nervousness about the steam:

> We used real steam – a wonderful machine – but it was tricky. You had to make sure that the witch, who had been pushed into the oven by the children, had got out the other side before you switched the steam on. The musical cue was a very important one, so I asked Reggie to do it. "I wasted my time at college," he shouted. "They didn't have classes in steam." He wasn't cracking a joke. He was furious.[18]

Between performances Goodall took conducting lessons from Francesco Salfi, the Italian who was in charge of *Ballo*, *Il barbiere di Siviglia* and *Gianni Schicchi*. The highlight of the season for Goodall was Richard Strauss's *Salome*, conducted by Hans Knappertsbusch, who was making his first – and last – appearance at Covent Garden. Knappertsbusch wanted the rise of the curtain to coincide exactly with the opera's opening phrase for clarinet and insisted on having a member of the music staff to give the signal to the stagehands. Goodall watched for Knappertsbusch's upbeat through a spyhole at the side of the stage. "It was," he said, "like doing it for God." Artistically the season had its successes, though financially it was a disaster. London was in the grip of a influenza epidemic and members of the company fell prey to it daily, Goodall included, though it did not stop him working.

Once again he was asked to return to Covent Garden, for the 1937 international season, but he felt that prospects at the Opera House were too precarious. Instead he chose to conduct Richard Addinsell's incidental music for a new West End production of *The Taming of the Shrew*, which was to open in March 1937 at the New Theatre (now known as the Noël Coward). With a cast headed by Edith Evans as Kate and Leslie Banks as Petruchio, it looked a good bet. Evans had recently had a triumph as Rosalind in *As You Like It* at the same theatre, and it was generally assumed she would repeat it with the *Shrew*. The pay was a good deal more than Goodall would have got at Covent Garden, and he calculated that, given a good run, he would soon be able to settle his debts and buy all the records and scores he needed.

The critics savaged the show. In the *Sunday Times* James Agate said he could not imagine why Edith Evans had wanted to play Kate. He poured scorn on Claud Gurney's production, Doris Zinkeisen's designs – "when the revival is over the whole lot can be offered to Sadler's Wells for their next new production of *The Barber of Seville*" – and Addinsell's music, which "at one point combined something reeking of Albeniz and the Seville of happier days."[19] The production limped on for five weeks and then closed.

Simultaneously with the theatre offer, Sir Hugh Allen, as loyal as ever to his protégé, recommended Goodall to the Royal Choral Society, which was looking for someone to assist its regular conductor, Malcolm Sargent.[20] Goodall was asked to attend an audition:

> There was a short list of three and we all took a rehearsal. The test pieces were from *The Dream of Gerontius*. I knew the work and it was music that suited me. I won hands down – the other candidates didn't know how to deal with this Catholic thing. If it had been *Judas Maccabaeus*, I'd have been kicked out almost before I'd started. Sargent was there with Sir Hugh Allen. They said, "That was very good, Goodall." I never got to conduct any of the concerts. Sargent was the big man. The Albert Hall would have emptied if it hadn't been him conducting.

Most of Goodall's work for the RCS entailed taking rehearsals for Sargent, who was in such demand as a conductor throughout the country that he rarely had time to attend to all his commitments. He would pay Goodall to stand in for him at rehearsals with an orchestra in Leicester or the British Women's Symphony Orchestra. In the case of the Royal Choral Society, Goodall applied his well-tried methods:

> I remember rehearsing the end of the Credo in Beethoven's *Missa solemnis* – "Et vitam venturi saeculi." *Allegretto ma non troppo*. I loved that bit, but it's very hard for the tenors – it must have the life of the world running through it. The tenors were very mushy, and I made them sing it singly, then four at a time, then eight, then row by row and finally all together. There was a lot of grumbling and grumping [*sic*]. They hated me. One man said, "We're not supposed to be solo singers." Then Sargent came to rehearse, and they thought, "We'll show the little bastard we can do it," meaning me. And they sang damn well – you've got to give them hell, you see. "You've rehearsed that very well, Reginald," said Sargent. They were furious – Sargent complimenting me in front of them all. [Laughter.] And so he should have done. I'd nearly killed myself! I rehearsed in that way with orchestras too, usually in sections, but sometimes with just the second clarinet, say, or the third bassoon or the tuba. But they liked it – unlike all those singers.

Reviewing the performance, which took place in April 1938, J. A. Westrup picked out the "Et vitam" for special praise, but thought "the choir's constancy and heroism would have had more effect under a conductor who had a better understanding of the work. Dr Sargent's interest seemed tepid."[21] Goodall earned £50 for a year's rehearsals. Sargent was paid £50 a concert.

The one-and-a-half years that remained before the start of the second world war were a turbulent time for Goodall. He was horrified by the prospect of war and full of despair about not getting the jobs he felt were his due. He complained that he felt so tired he could no longer memorise scores. Colleagues noticed in him a volatile mixture of arrogance and diffidence. When things were going well, he became over-excited. When they were going badly, he was acutely depressed. At one point he thought seriously of returning to Canada to take up a post he had been offered in Winnipeg. He grumbled to colleagues that his wife did not always give him the encouragement he needed in his faltering career. He began to regard with suspicion the Jewish musicians arriving in Britain as refugees and became obsessed with the idea that the BBC in particular was giving them jobs that by right were his. Goodall assured colleagues that if Hitler were to find himself in charge of Britain, the BBC would soon get its just deserts. Many found his credulousness disturbing.

By the time Goodall made his final visit to Germany with Reinhold von Warlich in the summer of 1935 the Nazis had an unshakable grip on the country. Goodall noted with approval the growing prosperity, the industrial revival, the building of the autobahns, the fall in unemployment. Even more important for him was the fact that this was the land of Bayreuth and the Berlin Philharmonic Orchestra, of Beethoven and Furtwängler. No matter that the opera houses and orchestras predated the Nazis. As Goodall saw it, musicians were valued figures in Germany – unless, of course, they happened to be Jewish – and in consequence there were opportunities for work undreamed of at home. He reasoned that if the system were introduced into Britain, his life as a musician would be transformed. Although British admirers of Nazism were not that rare in the mid-1930s, Goodall may have been unique in being drawn to the creed for musical reasons.

Some of his colleagues in the conducting class were shocked by his enthusiasm for Germany. Others, like Emanuel Young, took a charitable view: "You have to realise that if the German movement of the time had been Communism, Reggie would almost certainly have joined it."[22] Most regarded Goodall, not as a political fanatic, but as an obsessive, whose views were muddled up with his frustrations over work. A joke went round the college that if Sir Oswald Mosley's British Union of Fascists were to get into power, Goodall would be appointed Minister of Culture. Later in the 1930s, in the aftermath of the Munich debacle, Goodall was to give unstinting support to Mosley's campaign for peace at any price, though he still did not join the BUF. Nor did he ever meet Mosley.

One further element affected Goodall's extreme views. Through Eleanor he was exposed to a particular strand of right-wing opinion not uncommon among middle-class English Roman Catholics at the time. Nostalgic for a society in which the church played a central role, they applauded Mussolini for signing the Lateran treaty of 1929, which guaranteed the sovereignty of the Vatican and made Roman Catholicism the state religion of Italy. The Duce was seen as a moral force for good and a bastion against Bolshevism, which, as the English Catholic press reminded its readers constantly, was responsible for the murder of thousands of Christians in the Soviet Union. Not even the plight of Jews in Germany following Hitler's accession as Chancellor in January 1933 was allowed to deflect attention away from the situation in the Soviet Union, as the English Catholic theological and literary journal, *Month*, made clear in June of that year: "We are more concerned about our own people who in various parts of the world are enduring persecution far more bitter and unjust than that, grave as it is, which at the moment afflicts German Jewry."[23]

Faced with the Antichrist of Bolshevism, which was regarded by extreme elements as Jewish in origin, many English Catholics came to regard Christianity and Fascism as compatible. It was not a view shared by the Roman Catholic hierarchy or the English priesthood generally, but in Ireland there were plenty of clerics, notably Father Edward Cahill, a Jesuit professor of church history and social science with anti-semitic inclinations, who were in favour of the setting-up of a corporatist state with laws enshrined in traditional Christian morality. Goodall absorbed many of these ideas – or, rather, half-absorbed them, for it is doubtful if he understood them properly. Even in old age he appeared to believe that in the 1930s "the Pope was in favour of Fascist countries. I learned about that from Eleanor."

Goodall's friends looked on with alarm as both his views and his behaviour grew more unpredictable. He decided to adopt a policy of being completely candid in everything he said, no matter what the circumstances. The consequences were disastrous. People thought him tactless and rude, among them Betty Humby, who, with William Glock, ran an enterprising series of Sunday night concerts at the Cambridge Theatre devoted to the lesser known works of Mozart, Haydn and Schubert. Goodall had conducted two of the concerts with some success – one in 1937, the other in 1938 – and had been asked back for a third in April 1939, but he fell out with Humby over a choir she had asked him to form, and as a result he had to withdraw."[24] He was invited to take over the choral class temporarily at the Royal College, but was so dictatorial that the students breathed a sigh of relief when their regular conductor, Reginald Jacques, returned. Occasionally Goodall took one or other of the conducting classes, which led him to hope that he might be offered a permanent job at the college, but nothing was forthcoming. Even the Handel Society tried to get rid of him. Fortunately for Goodall, John Cruft, who had been invited to replace him, tipped him off that dirty work was afoot. Goodall was able to fight off the challenge.[25]

In May 1939 Maisie Aldridge wrote to her mother: "He constantly says he's no good. Soon he will have lost all his work and there's nothing else to turn to." Two months later she wrote: "His nerves are in a bad state. He's had almost as much as he can stand. This state of mind has stopped him taking advantage of things that <u>have</u> come his way these last few years."[26] Goodall spent a good deal of his time reading books on music. He marked bits he thought important and scribbled comments in the margins. Clearly he felt that the following passage from Wagner's treatise *Über das Dirigieren* (On Conducting) reflected his own experiences. He underscored it heavily:

> It might be asked: but what do the queer conductors with celebrated names amount to, considered as practical musicians? ... The general public is so ready to take the excellence of their doings for granted, and to accept it as a matter of course, that the middle-class musical people are not troubled with the slightest doubt as to who is to beat time at their musical festivals, or on any other great occasion when the nation desires to hear some music. No one but Herr Hiller, Herr Rietz, or Herr Lachner, is thought fit for this.

Goodall crossed out Hiller's name and substituted Sir Adrian Boult's. He surrounded another passage from the book with exclamation marks:

> I know of no one to whom I would confidently entrust a single tempo in one of my operas: certainly to no member of the staff of our army of time-beaters. Now and then I have met with some poor devil who showed real skill and talent for conducting: but such rare fellows find it difficult to get on, because they are apt not only to see through the incompetence of these celebrities, but are imprudent enough to speak about it.[27]

Since Goodall had no conducting engagements at all in 1939, apart from the Handel Society, he decided to start a rehearsal orchestra, which at least would give him some practice. At Maisie Aldridge's suggestion he advertised for players in the *Daily Telegraph* and got a large response from students, young professionals, out-of-work musicians and some good amateurs. Starting in June, the orchestra met once a week at St Paul's church hall in Onslow Gardens, South Kensington, to play through all the Beethoven symphonies, except the Ninth. Other works were performed as well. Participants paid 2s. 6d. a session to cover costs. Goodall found it a valuable experience:

> It was good for me and good for the players, particularly the young ones who wanted to learn the basic orchestral repertoire before starting on their professional careers. I did the *Dream of Gerontius* – not very well; I didn't have all the chorus. Also the Tchaikovsky violin concerto and the Elgar and Dvořák cello concertos – students wanted to have a go at them. Reginald Morley, who led for me, played the Beethoven concerto. I practically lived in Onslow Gardens. The Handel Society held their rehearsals there, too.

But the orchestra did not provide Goodall with an income. In desperation he applied for the job of chorus coach with the Carl Rosa opera company. Eleanor Goodall was of the opinion that since he did not have much work in London that was worth keeping anyway, he might as well go out on tour. In the event nothing came of the job and Goodall remained in London. To compound his financial difficulties, the lease on the flat in Elm Park Road came to an end and he and Eleanor took a lease on a small house in South Kensington, 4 Thistle Grove, which entailed a good deal of extra expense. They moved in on 31 July 1939. Goodall completed the Beethoven symphonies and then, in late August, embarked on a Brahms cycle. On 1 September Hitler's troops marched into Poland. On 3 September Britain declared war on Germany. Five days later Goodall joined the South Kensington branch of the British Union of Fascists. He thought that Mosley was the only person who could put a stop to what he considered was a senseless war.

CHAPTER 7

Bournemouth at War

O N the outbreak of war London's theatres and concert halls were closed, along with its cinemas and art galleries. The Royal Choral Society suspended its activities and the Handel Society was disbanded for good. Goodall had no paid work of any kind. Eleanor's school was evacuated to Shropshire and she went with it, leaving her husband to his own devices in London, where he took to writing slogans on walls and pavements in support of Mosley's campaign for a negotiated peace; the BUF was not declared a proscribed organisation until July 1940.

Goodall's confused state of mind can be gauged from a letter he wrote to Maisie Aldridge on 22 September 1939:

> No work at college – more staff than they need. Prices are going up more and more. What is all this for – certainly not to protect Poland or we should declare war on Russia – we've done nothing to assist Poland – thousands of lives have been lost – merely because a stupid and ignorant minority would rather anything happen than that we should have any understanding with that country.
>
> I've been listening in to the German news bulletin 9.00pm-9.15 from Cologne or Hamburg. 10.40 a talk from an English person who happens to be in Germany. 11.20 & 12.15 news bulletins.
>
> I have opened the eyes of 5 or 6 people this week to the fact that even this country breaks promises and didn't even keep the Treaty of Versailles – well I must stop now – and go to a B.U. meeting.

The "English person" was presumably the propagandist William Joyce, known to the British public as Lord Haw Haw.

The temporary collapse of London's musical life gave Goodall's Symphony Rehearsal Orchestra an unexpected boost, for a number of leading players from the LSO, finding they had no work, applied to join to keep their hands in, though they drifted away again when Queen's Hall reopened in early October. More players were lost to conscription, and eventually the orchestra had to close down before a cycle of Sibelius's symphonies could be completed. The forces still available were too unbalanced: there were no fewer than seven horns at one rehearsal, but only one bassoon. Goodall started to assist Sargent again, marking up scores for him and attending his rehearsals, but it was the only work he had.

Meanwhile Maisie Aldridge had given up teaching the piano in London and returned to live at her old home at Christchurch. Her father was a leading solicitor in nearby Bournemouth. She was fearful that if Goodall persisted in writing slogans in public places, he would sooner or later fall foul of the authorities. The rehearsal orchestra's leader, Reginald Morley, wrote to her on 22 October about the LPO's first wartime concert in London, which Boult had conducted at Queen's Hall the previous day: "Reggie Goodall was there complete with scores and full of his usual enthusiasm; I suppose he will one day get his chance to be a great conductor, provided he does not let politics overrule him!" Aldridge felt it was essential to get Goodall away from London and the BUF, though it was easier said than done. There was little chance of finding conducting work for him in Bournemouth. A month after the declaration of war, the town council had slashed the size of the Bournemouth Municipal Orchestra from sixty-one to thirty-five players, with no redundancy money for the twenty-six victims.

One of the few sacked musicians with an alternative job was a trumpet-player, Walter Tiller, who played the piano in a trio at the Cadena tea-rooms. There was a faint chance that he and his colleagues might get their jobs back eventually, for the council had promised to reconsider the orchestra's future in March 1940. To enable the players to keep in practice, Tiller organised twenty of them into a small rehearsal orchestra, and persuaded three fellow café musicians to boost the ranks – John Doe, who also played at the Cadena and taught the cello at the Bournemouth School of Music, and two members of a quintet from Brights restaurant, the violinist John Greenstone and the cellist Reginald Giddy. Robert Bossert, a former Municipal violinist, was appointed leader (as a student he had led the orchestra for Goodall's *Pagliacci* in the Tottenham Court Road). There was no question of anyone being paid, but there was always the hope that the orchestra might be offered an engagement. Gordon Bryan, a local composer, agreed to conduct them, but soon dropped out because of other commitments.

Maisie Aldridge read about the orchestra in the *Bournemouth Daily Echo* and wondered how she might help. She discussed the matter with a neighbour from Christchurch, Charlotte Watmough, who said that if Aldridge could organise some initial concerts for the orchestra, she would put up a £100 guarantee against loss. Aldridge telephoned Goodall in London to ask him to conduct. To her relief he agreed to come to Bournemouth. The players welcomed the initiative of the two women, who were appointed honorary organisers. The orchestra acquired a name – the Wessex Philharmonic (thought up by one of Aldridge's sisters) – and, with Goodall conducting, gave its first concert on the afternoon of 8 December 1939 for the boys of Portsmouth Grammar School, which had been evacuated to Southbourne. The programme was repeated that evening at a public concert in Christchurch Town Hall:

Mozart	Overture, *The Marriage of Figaro*
Pergolesi-Barbirolli	Suite for oboe and strings (soloist: Peggy Shiffner)
Haydn	Symphony No 88 in G
Sibelius	*Valse triste*
Elgar	Serenade for strings
Britten-Rossini	*Soirées musicales*

All the players were paid £1, which covered both concerts; Goodall got two guineas. At this stage the word "Philharmonic" was somewhat misleading: with only twenty-eight members the Wessex was in effect a chamber orchestra. Indeed it was smaller than the reduced Municipal Orchestra, which continued to give concerts on Thursday afternoons at the Pavilion under its regular conductor, Richard Austin.

Next, Charlotte Watmough found a home for the orchestra, St Peter's church hall in Hinton Road, which at a squeeze could hold 500 people. The orchestra gave its first concert there at lunchtime on New Year's Day 1940. The programme, which included Mendelssohn's Violin Concerto, with a young German refugee, Gerhard Kander, as soloist, was repeated in the evening, with the addition of Wagner's *Siegfried Idyll*. Goodall told Maisie Aldridge that he had not "got the *Idyll* taped"; he would have to do a lot more work on it.

The borough organist, Percy Whitlock, who as "K. L." wrote music criticism for the *Echo,* noted that "Goodall conducted mostly without scores on Monday and seemed to have things well in hand. With Sargent, he seems to prefer a brisk pace, and also exhibits one or two curious mannerisms in common with Sargent's usual practice."[1] Whitlock did not say what they were. He can hardly have been talking about stick technique, since former Wessex players remember Goodall's beat as being quite unlike Sargent's. "It was always a bit vague," said one, "but you got used to it. You had to."

At first the Wessex Philharmonic was regarded as a temporary organisation, but that changed in April 1940 when the town council finally met to discuss the Municipal Orchestra's future. Far from reinstating players, the council sacked eleven more of them, which reduced the orchestra further to twenty-four members. Richard Austin considered it was now too small to play anything but "teashop music" and resigned in disgust as musical director.[2] The chairman of the entertainments committee, Councillor A. H. Langton, remarked snidely that he thought it customary for the captain to stay on the bridge until the last member of the crew had left the ship.[3]

From that moment on the Wessex increased in size – though it never had more than fifty players – and so did its repertoire. Goodall was appointed principal conductor. The practice of giving two concerts on a Monday in Bournemouth was continued; patrons were encouraged to bring sandwiches at lunchtime, though they were asked not to knit, since it distracted visiting artists. Subscription tickets were introduced and audiences grew, with an unexpected preponderance of young listeners. Concert-goers were encouraged to buy extra tickets, which were left at the box office for servicemen, nurses and railwaymen.

Goodall introduced many works new to Bournemouth. At a time when Benjamin Britten was regarded with suspicion because of his decision to live in America, Goodall gave early performances of *Les Illuminations*, with its original soprano soloist, Sophie Wyss, and the Violin Concerto. On 25 November 1940 he conducted the first performance of Vaughan Williams's *Household Music: Three Preludes on Welsh Hymn Tunes*. A programme note said that the work had been written for the Wessex, a claim hotly denied by the composer, who wrote a letter of complaint to the orchestra.[4]

Goodall also introduced unfamiliar works from earlier periods, for example Bruckner's Overture in G minor, which in May 1940 shared a programme with Brahms's Violin Concerto (with Eda Kersey as soloist) and Schubert's Fourth Symphony. The Schubert was as much a novelty as the Bruckner. Whitlock thought it "an earnest if uninspired work." Having criticised the first flute for playing sharp in the Brahms and the timpanist for being too loud ("factors on the debit side which one has experienced before on listening to this orchestra"), he went on to attack the Bruckner overture:

> Its efforts at playfulness could not really disguise the lymphatic Teutonism of the composer's outlook, and though one might disown any association with the lady who, after a Strauss tone-poem at a recent Pavilion concert, declaimed for all to hear that she "didn't hold with all this Nazi music," one must record the feeling that a whole programme of undiluted Germanic high-thinking was a bit too much for an average Britisher.[5]

It was as well for Goodall that his enthusiasm for Germany was not generally known outside the confines of the orchestra. Some Wessex players were hostile to him because of his views, and wanted him replaced, though they never campaigned against him publicly, and no word of their feelings ever appeared in the local press. According to Richard Adeney, who was principal flautist with the Wessex in 1941, the majority of its members "accepted him as politically ineffectual, and few took him seriously. He wasn't aggressive. He was gentle. He was just in a terrible muddle."[6] Players found Goodall weirdly inconsistent. One moment he was making anti-Jewish remarks, the next he was singling out a Jewish soloist for special praise. Over coffee during rehearsal-breaks, he would extol Germany's virtues – its roads, its schools, its music – to Alfred Friedlander, the Jewish leader of the viola section. Goodall greatly admired Friedlander's warm tone. Friedlander accepted the lectures philosophically. He thought Goodall was crazy.[7]

As far as Goodall was concerned, the sooner hostilities were over – one way or the other – the better. Music could then return to a more normal existence. When the French signed an armistice with the Germans in June 1940, he expressed the hope that the British would quickly do the same. He fired off complaints to public figures about their support for the war. "I've written to the Bishop of Grantham an appropriate letter," he told Maisie Aldridge. "I hope his old C of E goes phut!"[8] (The bishop had suggested in a sermon at Lincoln cathedral that pacifists were chiefly responsible for the war.) Wessex players remember Goodall handing out BUF leaflets in the town calling for a peaceful settlement, which, bearing in mind his position in Bournemouth, was unwise, though not illegal during the early months of the war. Sir Oswald Mosley himself came to Poole, next door, in March 1940 to make a plea for peace before a packed audience; he was not interned until two months later.

Percy Whitlock and one or two others centred on the Bournemouth Pavilion were anxious to see Goodall interned as well, but their efforts to interest the security services in his activities always ended in failure. Whitlock not only doubled as borough organist and the *Echo's* music critic, but also worked as an official in the Bournemouth food control office, in which capacity he kept a keen eye open for fifth-columnists. In June 1941, having been told by a member of the Muncipal Orchestra that Goodall had called the sinking of the German battleship Bismarck "disgusting," he immediately reported the story to a Detective Constable Grose of MI5, who appears not to have taken the charge seriously.[9]

Only once did Goodall land in trouble with the authorities for expressing his views too loudly. Travelling home by trolley-bus after a Monday lunchtime concert that had not gone well, he lectured his fellow passengers on the inadequacies of British musical life, comparing it unfavourably with Germany's. One of his hearers reported him to the police, who took him away in a "Black Maria" van for questioning. The cellist John Doe and the Wessex's treasurer, Leslie Bickel, hurried to the police station, where they assured police officers that in spite of the apparently treasonable views Goodall was expressing, he was in fact harmless; if they could find a way to release him, it would be convenient, for he was due to conduct a concert that evening at St Peter's Hall. Fortunately for Goodall, Bickel was a respected figure in Bournemouth – a former World War I fighter pilot, he was a branch manager of Lloyds bank and a sergeant in the local Home Guard – and the police accepted his promise that Goodall would cause no further trouble. Nothing more was heard of the incident.

Towns hit harder by the war might have reacted less tolerantly. There were plenty of uniforms to be seen in Bournemouth, there was barbed wire on the beaches to deter invaders, and there had been German bombing raids resulting in civilian fatalities, but some detected an air of unreality about the place. In August 1941, as Hitler's forces advanced headlong towards Moscow and Leningrad, three men in German uniform stood around in the middle of Bournemouth and then ordered drinks in a hotel, where their fellow customers, who included British servicemen, failed to take any notice of them. Eventually a member of the Home Guard fetched the police, who identified the "Germans" as British soldiers on an exercise.[10]

The writer J. B. Priestley, who visited Bournemouth in March 1941 to open a week-long festival given by the Wessex Philharmonic (he offered to give £25 to its funds, provided five other citizens did likewise), wrote of the town in *Picture Post*: "It has been bombed a little and air-raid warnings are frequent ... On the other hand, I must add that this large pleasant resort seemed to be doing itself pretty well ... Nobody could call it a bad war in Bournemouth. Its front line aspect is negligible." The furious controversy that followed spilled over into the letters column of *Time and Tide*, where an indignant Bournemouth reader asked if Priesley would have the town show its lights at night so that the Luftwaffe could help it to share the miseries of Coventry and Southampton.[11]

Goodall was not afraid of bombs. Whenever a warning siren sounded during a concert at St Peter's Hall, he carried on conducting, while a steward paraded in front of the platform with a placard announcing a raid. No one ever left. Maisie Aldridge recalls sitting with Goodall on Bournemouth's West Cliff in July 1940, when there was a series of loud explosions below them and chunks of Bournemouth pier hurtled skywards. The central section was being blown up to prevent its use by German troops as a landing stage. Aldridge tried to attract Goodall's attention to the extraordinary sight, but he would not look up from his score of Beethoven's Fourth Symphony, which he was due to conduct that night. He considered the explosions, like the bombs, a tiresome distraction.

Charlotte Watmough, who had borne a good deal of the orchestra's costs during the first four months of its existence, moved away from Bournemouth in May 1940, leaving Maisie Aldridge as the organising secretary. With help from players (and in some cases their wives), she raised funds, arranged out-of-town dates and school concerts, handled publicity and, with assistance and advice from the LPO's secretary, Thomas Russell, secured call-up deferments for particular musicians, including Goodall. However, many players believed they would be better served by a professional manager. Goodall vacillated. He sided with the players over the question, but was anxious not to lose Aldridge, for he valued her musical judgment. There were endless squabbles between the various factions until, in February 1941, the Wessex players turned themselves into a self-governing co-operative. Managers came and went. Aldridge, exhausted by the whole business, returned to teaching, though she continued to deal with the orchestra's publicity and organised accommodation in private homes for visiting artists. She also took on the time-consuming chore of negotiating with the police over foreign nationals who had been engaged by the orchestra. Bournemouth had been declared a prohibited area under the Aliens Order, 1940, and foreigners were not allowed to stay in the town without special permission. This led to some curious decisions by the authorities. In July 1942, for example, the Russian conductor Anatole Fistoulari was given permission to visit Bournemouth to work with the Wessex, but his fiancée, the sculptress Anna Mahler, daughter of the composer, was not, because she held a Czech passport. The Hampshire Constabulary admitted it did not know what the position was in regard to Czechs, despite the fact that they were classified officially as allied nationals.[12]

Fifty years on, it is not easy to assess the standard of the Wessex. It made no recordings and was reviewed in the national press only very occasionally. H. C. Colles, chief music critic of *The Times*, making a rare visit to Bournemouth in September 1940, wrote of an all-Beethoven programme conducted by Goodall: "There were details in the symphony [No.2 in D] which would not pass muster in a gramophone record, but this was good playing, honest of purpose, well controlled in tempo, articulate and expressive." Goodall, said Colles, was "a very capable and musicianly conductor."[13] Colles heard the Wessex again in March 1941, this time under two guest conductors, Sargent and Boult. He noted: "The strings are greatly improved in unanimity and decision. The tone and phrasing of individual wind instruments in solo passages still leave something to be desired, but their ensemble is good and the brass rarely blares."[14]

Because of military call-up, Goodall was faced with a constantly changing membership. Besides professional players, the Wessex embraced students, amateurs and, later on, as players became ever harder to find, military bandsmen from the Marines at Portsmouth and the Royal Tank Regiment at Bovingdon. Sometimes they appeared on the platform in uniform. Goodall's achievement was to weld this disparate body into an orchestra that was capable of giving compelling performances.

John Greenstone, who led the Wessex for a time and later became a founder member of the Philharmonia Orchestra, had this to say in 1987:

> In the Wessex's early days we had some very poor players – we had to put up with the situation – but Reggie worked hard with the orchestra and there were performances I haven't heard equalled since. In Reggie's make-up there is a lot of tragedy. I don't know where it comes from, but I can tell it's there when I compare the way he conducted Schubert's Unfinished Symphony with the innumerable

performances I've done with other conductors. Nobody ever got to the heart of the music like he did. It wasn't a matter of the notes. It was to do with the way he shaped the music. Reggie saw the music through the composer's eyes, whereas a great many conductors only see it through their own eyes.[15]

Greenstone's remark about tragedy is perceptive. Goodall said of the Amsterdam Concertgebouw Orchestra in 1986: "There is a depth to their sound. They can get sadness and tragedy into it. They haven't time to achieve that sort of thing in this country – the way orchestral players work here is disgraceful."

For John Doe, the most important characteristic of Goodall's conducting was "its sheer, absolute honesty," whether he was performing the music of Mozart, Elgar or Tchaikovsky. His Beethoven "had a depth. There was nothing shallow about it, nothing superficial or chromium-plated. His tempi were always steady – not slow. People were inclined to say he was too slow, but I didn't think so. He gave you room to play."[16]

When a new work was introduced into the orchestra's repertoire, the string principals were invited to Goodall's house in St Alban's Avenue to discuss the bowing. Not only did he expect all the players to bow the same way, he expected them to use the same part of the bow. Survivors of those sessions agree that the precision of the string-playing was remarkable. Rehearsals for the full orchestra, held in St Peter's Hall, were long and painstaking. Hours meant nothing to Goodall. Joyce Aldous, the Wessex's timpanist, recalled:

> He never rehearsed in big sweeps. Instead it was like embroidery; he would take two or three bars at a time, or even a single bar, which he would go over again and again until the oboist or the clarinettist or whatever had got it right. However the results were never disjointed, as they can be with certain conductors who work in great detail. For some players, particularly the old-timers, it was very boring – they were driven crackers. Egerton, the oboe-player, used to sit with his head in his hands. Reggie could be a so-and-so, but many of us thought he was the best of all the conductors who worked with us – and I include people like Henry Wood and Boult – because he was a great man for teaching. He taught the orchestra how to play."[17]

Aldous was one of several players who, until they joined the Wessex, had never worked in an orchestra before. She had started her professional career at 15, as the drummer in a cinema band in Weybridge. A year later she went to Bournemouth to play the drums for a women's orchestra that performed in the Royal Exeter Hotel's palm court. Her godmother, she discovered, was married to the Municipal Orchestra's founder, Sir Dan Godfrey, who arranged for her to have a few lessons with its timpanist. In June 1941 Aldous was playing in a band at Bobbys restaurant, when she heard that the Wessex needed someone to replace its timpanist, who had been drafted into the fire service. Egged on by her colleagues, she went down to the orchestra's office in Old Christchurch Road, where she asked if she could apply for the job. "A bloody woman?" exclaimed Goodall incredulously. Aldous, quite used to male prejudice in the musical profession, stood her ground. "I'm sorry," she said, "but I can play." "Right," said Goodall, embarrassed by his initial reaction, "come with me."

They went to St Peter's Hall, where the timpani were kept. After Aldous had tuned them, Goodall handed her a score of Beethoven's *Pastoral* Symphony, which was due to be performed at the next concert. He conducted and sang his way through its fourth movement (the "Storm"), while she played the timpani part. "Fine," he said. "I'll help you, as long as you want to be helped." Aldous got the job, and for a time Goodall went through the programme on the piano with her before each concert. Under his tutelage she became so accomplished that in 1943 she was picked by John Barbirolli as a percussion-player for the reorganised Hallé Orchestra; four years later she became its timpanist, a post she held for twenty years.

Aldous and Greenstone were not the only "café" musicians in the Wessex who went on to play in leading British orchestras. John Doe played in Beecham's Royal Philharmonic, and Reginald Giddy played in both the LPO and RPO before joining the Suisse Romande Orchestra under Ernest Ansermet.

Money was a constant problem for the Wessex. In its early days the orchestra could afford to pay its guest artists only a pittance – often they got £3, plus a rail fare – yet it attracted some of the country's best-known conductors and soloists. Albert Sammons, Henry Holst, Myra Hess, Solomon, Clifford Curzon, Benno Moiseiwitsch, Moura Lympany and Eileen Joyce were among those grateful for a day or two by the sea. Sir Henry Wood conducted four concerts and an open rehearsal for the cost of his hotel bill. Not everyone had a peaceful visit. The pianist Kendall Taylor, arriving in Bournemouth after midnight in September 1940 to find an air-raid in progress, eventually discovered his hostess and her family in a dug-out shelter in the garden, where he joined them until morning. Boult and Sargent received the highest fee, £10, which to most Wessex players seemed a fortune. Richard Adeney, who was principal flute for three months in 1941, was paid just over £2 a week; he remembers it as the only time in his life when he was hungry through lack of money.

The orchestra spent hours haggling with music publishers. On one occasion, Chester's was persuaded to reduce the performing-right on Grieg's first *Peer Gynt* suite by five shillings. Goodall wrote to Maisie Aldridge, "<u>Don't</u> say we performed it again at Talbot Heath or we shall have to pay another fee – and in writing to publishers <u>don't mention</u> that <u>we give 2 concerts</u> [in Bournemouth] as some may charge a double fee."[18] When it suited him, however, Goodall ignored the financial problems and, behind the orchestra's back, ordered scores it could ill afford. Hiring the parts and paying the performing-right fee for Elgar's Cello Concerto in November 1940 came to more than Goodall earned for conducting it. The soloist was Beatrice Harrison, who had recorded the work with the composer. She told Maisie Aldridge that in her opinion no one could touch Goodall's conducting of it.

The orchestra received occasional grants from the newly founded Council for the Encouragement of Music and the Arts (CEMA), forerunner of the Arts Council, to enable it to visit towns like Southampton and Swindon, Newbury and Winchester, Weymouth and Ryde, but there was no extra money for concerts in Bournemouth itself. No help could be expected from the town council, which was antagonistic towards the Wessex – in his first *Times* review, Colles had poured scorn on the council for its philistinism and parsimony.

Finance was not the only problem. Public transport was so haphazard that players often failed to arrive at concerts through no fault of their own. One wind-player, Patrick Dingle, remembers having to play the second trumpet part in a Mozart symphony on the clarinet.[19] Goodall himself once saved the orchestra's honour by standing in for a missing percussion-player at a guest conductor's concert. The chaotic nature of wartime music-making, and the artistic compromises it involved, drove him to distraction. At one concert, furious about some administrative mishap, he charged on to the platform and startled the audience by taking the National Anthem at twice the normal speed. The orchestra could barely play it. One of the few people who had a calming influence on him was Eleanor Goodall, who had joined him in September 1940 and was teaching at the Bournemouth School for Girls. "All right, Reggie," friends remember her saying, as Goodall stormed round the sitting-room, "just sit down." He usually did.

Early in 1942 Bournemouth corporation discovered that the Municipal Orchestra, which had been reduced to playing in the Pavilion's theatre pit and on the pier and Pine Walk bandstands, was actually making a profit. Councillors developed a sudden enthusiasm for orchestral music. The chairman of the beach and Pavilion committee, Alderman A. H. Little, pointed out that Sir Stafford Cripps (then Britain's ambassador in Moscow) had said that the morale of Russia was being kept up by the availability of good music; and, besides, a large number of civil servants in the town were asking for more orchestral music. On 3 March the council voted by 38 to 11 to increase the Municipal Orchestra's grant by £3,000 a year, so that it could be expanded once more to symphonic strength. Some council members smelt a rat. "Whether we like it or whether we don't," declared Alderman F. B. Summerbee, "there's a suspicion that this is coming about as a result of the jealousy that apparently exists between the Municipal Orchestra and the Wessex Orchestra." At a special meeting convened a fortnight later, Councillor R. F. Seward warned that the Wessex would be killed off as a result of the council's "foul stroke."[20]

The readers of the *Echo* who had once castigated the council for reducing the size of the Municipal Orchestra now criticised it for wanting to increase it. The extra £3,000 was all very well, it was said, but the Municipal Orchestra would still number only thirty-six players, or forty-five on special occasions. "It happens," wrote one reader, "that the Wessex strings are particularly good, and if the desire to do the sensible thing exists, the obvious solution is amalgamation ... It does the town no good to have these two orchestras of odds-and-ends and shreds and patches competing. They both suffer from the same trouble and leave much to be desired. Combined, they could give us the real thing." But the council was not interested in a merger; instead, it tried to poach players from the Wessex. Goodall wrote to a friend that he had "never been in a place where there is more talk about music, and less real music."[21]

One of those who followed the correspondence with interest was the composer Kaikhosru Shapurji Sorabji, known, if known at all, for his immensely long but rarely performed piano works. In the *New English Weekly*, he rebuked Bournemouth council for its "municipal meanness" and spiteful attitude towards the Wessex, "which, by dint of immense work, unselfish artistic enthusiasm and musicianly enterprise, [Goodall] has wrought into an instrument of a great deal more than mere promise." The orchestra, he continued, had "generally prevented music from totally expiring from pernicious anaemia in this sea-side town of some 95,000 inhabitants."[22]

Sorabji's view was a little rosy. Having enjoyed a virtual monopoly on orchestral music in Bournemouth for two years, the Wessex had by now grown complacent. The June issue of *Musical Opinion* commented that, with "so competent a permanent conductor as Reginald Goodall, it is puzzling to account for the occasional handing over of the Wessex Philharmonic Orchestra to some guest conductor who hardly commands competence enough to keep time with the band through *God Save the King*! And can nothing be done to brighten up the programmes, some of which ... for sheer tedium could hardly be matched in wartime England?" The players had found that it was cheaper (and easier) to go on churning out the same old chestnuts than it was to rehearse unfamiliar works. Goodall became increasingly worried about the lack of rehearsal time, but could do little about it. Now that the orchestra was self-governing, he had far less say in its affairs. He was its employee.

The newly rejuvenated Bournemouth Municipal Orchestra posed a serious threat to the future of the Wessex, because the town was not large enough to justify two orchestras. With Goodall's support, the players decided that their best hope of survival was to become a touring orchestra. By July 1942 they had virtually abandoned Bournemouth. Maisie Aldridge, who still retained a toe-hold as secretary of the Friends of the Wessex, found that her members were getting restless. Why, they asked, should they continue to support an orchestra that only rarely appeared in the town? The final straw for Aldridge was a letter she received from the Wessex informing her that it was changing its name to the Bournemouth Philharmonic Orchestra, because, it claimed, many of the places it now visited had no idea what or where Wessex was. In October she and her fellow committee members wound up the Friends and returned its funds to the original donors. In doing so, she severed her last link with the orchestra she had helped to found.

Boult, who had been conducting the orchestra in Cardiff, wrote to Aldridge on 23 October 1942 expressing sympathy over the demise of the Friends. He complained of low playing standards and inadequate rehearsal time: "it was quite a job to keep one's temper over the whole affair." By now Goodall was in despair about the rehearsal situation and complained about it constantly to the players' committee, which remained unsympathetic. The orchestra had adopted a punishing schedule, giving as many as twenty-seven concerts a month, with Goodall conducting well over half of them. Sometimes he conducted twice in one day. Not surprisingly the players were often exhausted. Touring in wartime was a hazardous business at the best of times, what with the danger of raids, unpredictable trains and the constant problem of finding accommodation. Players spent many nights on floors in parish rooms or on tables in Salvation Army hostels. In Coventry they bedded down in the hall; Goodall slept in the conductor's room.

Many of the orchestra's concerts at this time were promoted by the impresario Harold Fielding, who in the winter of 1942 mounted "International Music Weeks" in Croydon, Bradford and Blackpool. At Blackpool there were eight concerts in all. Goodall conducted four of them, and at a fifth (conducted by Fistoulari) accompanied his fellow Lincolnshireman, the tenor Alfred Piccaver, on the piano. Piccaver, who before the war had been a leading member of the Vienna State Opera, sang "E lucevan le stelle" from *Tosca*, a ballad by Tirindelli and Eric Coates's *Bird Songs at Eventide*.

The third conductor for the Blackpool week was Rudolph Dunbar. Born in British Guiana, he was the first black conductor to work with the LPO and LSO; he was also London correspondent of the Associated Negro Press of America. Dunbar's programme of Weber, Coleridge-Taylor and Dvořák was punctuated with appearances by the popular piano duettists Rawicz and Landauer, who played among other things the *Warsaw Concerto* and a selection from *Snow White and the Seven Dwarfs*. Rawicz and Landauer also headed the bill for the final Saturday night programme, which drew a crowd of 3,000 to the New Opera House. Goodall conducted the Polovtsian dances from *Prince Igor* and Tchaikovsky's Fifth Symphony, Piccaver sang a pair of arias, and Rawicz and Landauer, whose names on the advertisements were printed many times larger than Goodall's, brought the house down with the *Sleeping Beauty* waltz, a Johann Strauss selection and, once more, the *Warsaw Concerto*.

Although it was not Goodall's idea of a good night's work, not all the players agreed with him. It had already occurred to some of them that they might make a good deal more money if they were to concentrate on light music. One in particular who was keen to abandon serious orchestral concerts was a trombone-player, G. "Pony" Moore, a large man with strong opinions who had long been a thorn in Goodall's side. "I'll squirt it at you," said Moore after one altercation over phrasing.[23]

It had also occurred to some of the players that, whatever direction the Wessex (or Bournemouth Philharmonic) eventually took, it might do well to have a principal conductor with a more prepossessing platform-manner. Not even Goodall's keenest supporters in the Wessex found it easy to defend his habit of shuffling on glum-faced, his baton stuck under his arm, and launching straight into the programme without bothering to acknowledge the audience's presence. Often, at the end of a concert, he seemed reluctant to accept the applause. It was not unknown for players to hang on to his coat-tails to prevent him leaving the platform. He rarely seemed satisfied with his performances.

Early in 1943 Goodall warned the orchestral committee that if he could not have more rehearsals, he would resign. Two of its members, "Pony" Moore and Walter Tiller, saw their chance to be rid of him, though the third member, the cellist Reginald Giddy, stood up for Goodall, arguing that in wartime Britain it would be difficult to find another conductor as good. But Giddy was over-ruled, and by a vote of two to one Goodall was told to go. On 6 February 1943 he conducted the orchestra for the last time in a pair of marathon concerts at Congleton in Cheshire, one in the afternoon, the other in the evening. Between them they comprised Beethoven's *Egmont* Overture, *Emperor* Concerto and *Eroica* Symphony, Elgar's Serenade for strings, Glinka's *Ruslan and Ludmila* Overture, three of Dvořák's Slavonic Dances, Sibelius's Romance in C, and Tchaikovsky's First Piano Concerto and Fifth Symphony; the soloist in both concertos was Louis Kentner. Daisy Gottlieb, "an accomplished musician now living in Congleton," reported in the local paper that, in the *Egmont* Overture, Goodall "made us re-feel the ultimate triumph of the unconquerable," and that after the Elgar Serenade the audience expressed its appreciation "by clapping until it hurt."[24]

Alfred Barker, who was now leading the orchestra, took over the concert that Goodall should have conducted at Birmingham Town Hall on 11 February. "There is no point in pretending that the performances could pass as good," wrote Eric Blom in the *Birmingham Post* the following day; "those who gave them must have known they were not up to Wessex standard – they were at best Middlesex." Such was the melancholy end to Goodall's three years and two months with the orchestra. He had conducted it more than three-hundred times in music by seventy-three composers – which hardly squares with his claim in later years that he rarely accepted concert engagements because he did not know any repertoire (a list of works he conducted with the Wessex is given on pages 216–9). In doing so, he played an important, though forgotten, role in helping to encourage the surge of interest in serious music that came with the war.

George Weldon took on most of Goodall's remaining dates, though the post of principal conductor remained unfilled. The orchestra lurched from one crisis to another. Bournemouth corporation, hostile to the end, was granted an injunction prohibiting the use of the name Bournemouth Philharmonic. The players had no money to launch an appeal against it. Soloists complained that their fees were not being paid. In May, three months after Goodall's departure, the Wessex collapsed under a mountain of debts.

CHAPTER 8

Private's Progress

A FTER THE Wessex débâcle the Goodalls lived in a rented house in
Chelsea, 78 Sydney Street. Eleanor found work at a school in Croydon,
but all Goodall could get was the odd job at one or other of the music col-
leges. The London he had known before the war had changed irrevocably. As
a result of the bombing St Alban's, Holborn, was a ruin, as was Queen's Hall.
Covent Garden opera house was being used as a Mecca dance hall. Many of
Goodall's former colleagues were in the Forces; some had been killed. Reinhold von Warlich was dead. In November 1939 he had committed suicide in his
estranged wife's New York apartment. To the surprise of his pupils, it turned out
that he had been an American citizen since the first world war. The prospect of
another war between his adopted country and the homeland of his forefathers
had proved more than he could bear.

Orchestral concerts in central London were confined to Saturday and Sunday afternoons, but there were at least four of them each weekend. In addition
the LPO gave Sunday evening concerts at its new home, the Orpheum cinema
in Golders Green.[1] Programmes were far from adventurous, but audiences were
on the increase. There were now more opportunities for promising British conductors than there had been before the war, for they faced little competition
from foreign visitors. Goodall, however, found it impossible to find conducting work, in spite of the experience he had gained with the Wessex. He always
maintained that his pro-German sympathies militated against him during this
period, which is no doubt true, but he also failed to grasp a major opportunity
when it was presented to him.

A month before Goodall left the Wessex he was given a Sunday evening date
with the LPO in Golders Green by his old supporter from St Alban's days, Felix
Aprahamian, who was now assistant to the orchestra's secretary, Thomas Russell. With Beecham, the LPO's founder, away in America, the orchestra was
constantly on the look-out for new conductors, and Goodall was in effect being
auditioned. Players like Reginald Morley, who knew and admired his work,
hoped the occasion might mark the start of a long and fruitful association with
the LPO. But it was not to be. The concert, on 10 January 1943, was by no means
a disaster, but nor was it a great success. It consisted of Beethoven's third *Leonora*
overture, Rachmaninov's rarely performed Piano Concerto No. 1, with Kendall

Taylor as soloist, and Sibelius's First Symphony. Goodall was unfamiliar with the concerto and found that the single three-hour rehearsal he had been granted was insufficient for him to master the whole programme to his satisfaction. The orchestra could not give him more time, since it also had to rehearse a completely different programme for an afternoon concert that same Sunday under Leslie Heward at the Royal Albert Hall. The LPO felt that Goodall lacked the technical proficiency to cope with the exigencies of wartime concert-giving and did not ask him back.

Goodall had appeared once before in London under Aprahamian's auspices, on 24 September 1942, when he had directed a small chamber ensemble at the Wigmore Hall in music by the group of French composers known as Les Six. The programme, which Aprahamian had devised for the French National Committee, was an unusual one for Goodall – Honegger's *Rapsodie*, Durey's *Images à Crusoë*, with Sophie Wyss as soprano soloist, Tailleferre's *Image* for eight instruments, Poulenc's *Le bestiaire* and *Mouvements perpétuels*, and Milhaud's *Machines agricoles* – but he had the support of some of the best instrumentalists in the country. Practically all of them were serving either with one of the Brigade of Guards bands or with the RAF Central Band and RAF Symphony Orchestra based at Uxbridge:

Flute I	Geoffrey Gilbert
Flute II	Gareth Morris
Oboe	Peter Newbury
Clarinet	Bernard Walton
Bassoon	John Alexandra
Horn	Dennis Brain
Violin I	Leonard Hirsch
Violin II	Gerald Emms
Viola	Max Gilbert
Cello	Kathleen Moorhouse
Double Bass	Adrian Beers[2]

The celesta player in the Durey and Tailleferre was none other than Benjamin Britten, who had returned to England from America earlier in the year. The following day Britten wrote to Pears about the concert:

> I was at the Wigstein playing the Celeste last night. [The Wigmore was called the Bechstein Hall until 1917.]
>
> Quite nicely, but it's a pukey little instrument – I nearly pushed it over trying to make a noise on it! I found counting the bars a trial tho' – Dennis Brain helped me, and we got on alright, except one spot when I had (in the Durey) to do the same for about 12 bars & forgot to count them. However, when Reginald Goodall started looking angry, I decided to stop![3]

Goodall and Wyss were paid five guineas; the rest, including Britten, two. None of the reviews commented on the conducting.

Goodall's employment problem was eventually solved by the Ministry of Labour and National Service, which early in April 1943 sent him his call-up papers. As principal conductor of the Wessex Philharmonic he had been granted deferment of military service on the grounds that he had been usefully engaged in helping to boost the nation's morale. Now that he was out of a job there was no reason why he should remain a civilian, and just ten weeks after leaving the Wessex he presented himself at No. 13 Primary Training Centre, Squires Gate Camp, St Annes, Lancashire.

14591742 Private Goodall got off on an unpromising start, as the complete set of entries from his diary for the first two weeks makes clear:

17 April	Joined army. Absolute hell
18 April	Sick all day in Hut
19 April	Sick all day & night. Hospital
23 April	This day of all days [Good Friday] spent in drilling and shooting. Inoculated twice
24 April	vaccinated, ill
25 April	ill all day [Easter Day]
26 April	Cpl Church, Bayonet
30 April	vaccinated
1 May	ill again

Stories of Goodall's military incompetence began to filter back to London. During weapons training, it was said, he had pulled the safety-pin out of a live hand-grenade, which he had then failed to throw. As his fellow recruits hurled themselves to the ground, the instructor had snatched the grenade from Goodall's hand and tossed it out of the trench just before it exploded.

After a month's initial training Goodall was transferred to the Royal Army Ordnance Corps and posted to No. 1 Command and Supply School at Saltburn-by-the-Sea on the north Yorkshire coast, where he qualified as a storeman. His surviving letters to Eleanor reveal that, like Wozzeck, he found it hard to come to terms with barrack-room life – the noise, the bullying, the snoring. He was depressed by the philistinism of his colleagues. "How I long to be back in music," he wrote on 31 May. "I get so frightened that I'll get right out of it – just as I was beginning to get on."

The timpanist Joyce Aldous wrote to him with news of the musical world. Following the dissolution of the Wessex she and a number of other players had been absorbed into a new touring orchestra, the National Philharmonic (not to be confused with Sydney Beer's National Symphony Orchestra), which had been formed by Harold Fielding. Early in June 1943, Aldous wrote to Goodall to say that she had persuaded Fielding to let him conduct the orchestra during his forthcoming leave. Would he agree to do it? Unsure about the answer, Goodall wrote to Eleanor on 18 June: "I feel that I ought to spend my time seeing what I can do about getting out of this ordinance work into some army music – apart from the fact I want to spend all the time I can with you – much as I would love to conduct again – an odd concert is only disturbing & would cut into any arrangements."

Eleanor must have persuaded him to accept Fielding's offer, for on 25 June he travelled to Swansea, where the following day at the Empire Theatre he conducted a popular Saturday-night programme consisting of Eric Coates's *Knightsbridge March*, Saint-Saëns's G-minor piano concerto and Addinsell's *Warsaw Concerto*, both with Eileen Joyce as soloist, Borodin's Polovtsian dances and Elgar's first *Pomp and Circumstance* march, with the packed house singing the words of *Land of Hope and Glory* in the trio-section. For the audience it was an emotional occasion.[4] Goodall's feelings about it are not recorded.

After spending three days in London he went straight to a new posting, No. 7 Battalion, RAOC, at Chilwell, just outside Nottingham. "I'm so hopelessly depressed & miserable," he wrote to Eleanor on 21 July, "& it's all so useless, hopeless & stupid – when you think what I could be doing." His one relaxation was reading – Shakespeare's plays, Mozart's letters – but "people hate to see one read, the corporal in our hut always gives me a fatigue to do if he sees me reading; this morning ... although I had been on duty all night, I did my duty of sweeping the floor and then tried to read the morning prayers; but at once he had me scrubbing the table." His fellow privates enjoyed strewing his books around the hut. Reading, Goodall observed, "always seems to annoy non-readers."

Musicians who visited Chilwell to entertain the troops returned to London with stories of Goodall's odd behaviour. On one occasion, having been ordered to provide bedding from the stores for troops in transit, he apparently put the palliasses and blankets, not in the barrack huts, but outside in the rain. He seemed to be on the verge of a nervous breakdown. Fortunately for Goodall a sympathetic colonel arranged for him to see a psychiatrist in Nottingham. Then, on 24 August, he was transferred to Southport in Lancashire for treatment at the North West Regional Neurosis Centre. The following day he was interviewed by an army psychiatrist, Dr Tronchin-James, who was not sure what he should do about the case. Needing advice about Goodall's professional background, the doctor telephoned a friend of his, Joan Ingpen, who was working in London for the music division of ENSA, which provided entertainment for the services. He asked her if Goodall was any good as a musician. If he was, he said, he would recommend him for a discharge. If he wasn't, he would keep him in the army. Ingpen told Tronchin-James that although she had never heard Goodall conduct, she understood that he was very competent. Goodall got his discharge.[5] "Very good Dr," he wrote in his diary. "Thank you BVM."

On 19 September, after 188 days of service life, Goodall was released on "ceasing to fulfil Army physical requirements." He breathed a sigh of relief and so, no doubt, did the army. His constant prayers to the Blessed Virgin Mary that he might be released (always recorded in his diary) had been answered, and it was time to repay the debt. Goodall had long felt the need for the final authority of Rome, and the day after he got back to London he visited Father Kenneth Dale-Roberts of the Brompton Oratory. On 19 December, after three months of instruction, he was received into the Roman Catholic Church.

The doors of the musical world, however, were still closed to Goodall. Strong opposition to him in the BBC's music department may have stemmed in part from his pre-war claims that the corporation was run by a Jewish cabal. He had last tried to obtain work with the BBC in August 1939, when he had had an interview with Sir Adrian Boult, then director of music as well as chief conductor of the BBC Symphony Orchestra. According to Goodall, Boult had been unhelpful: he had seemed more concerned with Goodall's educational background (always a sensitive topic) than with his musical achievements. Goodall regarded Boult's attitude as being typical of a man who had been educated at Westminster and Christ Church, Oxford.

On 3 October 1943 Goodall again approached Boult, who by now had given up the post of director of music to concentrate on the symphony orchestra:

> I am writing to ask if the BBC would be able to use my services as a conductor.
>
> For the past seven months I have been in the army and have now obtained my discharge, and previous to that I was as you know with the Wessex Philharmonic for three years.
>
> I should be most grateful for any advice or help you can give me, as I find that the Wessex orchestra has disbanded during my service in the army, and after the break caused by my call-up it is difficult to make a fresh start.

Two days later Boult replied from Bedford, the BBC orchestra's wartime home:

> Many thanks for your letter, which I am passing on to London, where all these things are now arranged.
>
> I am afraid that we have a very long list of conductors now, and expect that they will find it difficult to add to the number, but however that may be I very much hope that you will be able to get some work in some way, though at the moment prospects do not look too good. I should think perhaps a most hopeful possibility might be ENSA or CEMA, though of course there is not much actual conducting in either of these. If I can help you in regard to introductions to these do let me know.

It is hard to escape the conclusion that Boult was being deliberately evasive: the list of people who conducted the BBC orchestra in late 1943 and 1944, particularly at its lunch-hour concerts in Bedford, includes a number of routineers, whose names have long been forgotten.

Aubrey Beese, personal assistant to the BBC's new director of music, the composer Arthur Bliss, wrote to Goodall on 23 October:

> Your enquiry about the possibility of securing a conducting engagement with the BBC has been passed on by Sir Adrian Boult to the Director of Music.
>
> Mr Bliss would be glad to know when you are next conducting at a public concert so that if possible a representative from the Music Department may attend.

Goodall replied to Beese on 1 November:

> Since my return from the army I have found it impossible to obtain a single conducting engagement so I'm unable to let you know when, if ever, I shall be conducting next. Would it be possible to arrange a private audition for me?

It took Beese two months to react. On 30 December he offered Goodall cold comfort:

> Although your suggestion (that a special audition should be arranged for you) was considered here, it was felt that such a practice would be quite impossible owing to the very heavy pressure on our time, and to the fact that it would not be right to allow such a priviledge [sic] in one case without granting it in all.
>
> I am sorry, therefore, that the suggestion in my letter of October 23rd still stands, – namely, that if you secure a conducting date anywhere we will do our best to send a representative, if we have one available, at a reasonable distance. Need I say that I very much hope you will be successful in securing such engagements, and regaining any ground you may have lost through being in the Army.[6]

At this point the correspondence stopped, at least for the time being. Goodall, who had not lost his sense of humour, told Maisie Aldridge in an undated letter:

> I've tried the ballet, ENSA, the Phil, the LSO, the Scottish, the Northern Phil, Boult and the BBC (the same reply I had 5 years ago – a big waiting list. I can't believe that, for I think I'm right in saying that everyone in England has now conducted the BBC except perhaps Miss Hankins).

Elsie Hankins was principal of the Bournemouth School of Music.

Goodall was unemployed for a year after his discharge from the army. He spent most of the time studying scores. The impasse was eventually broken by an old colleague from the Royal College, whom Goodall happened to bump into by chance at Chester's, the music publisher. He mentioned to Goodall that there was a job going on the music staff of the Sadler's Wells Opera. The company had been touring ever since the autumn of 1940, when the Sadler's Wells Theatre, its London base near the Angel, Islington, had been commandeered as a rest-home for bombed-out families. At this particular moment the company was finishing a seven-week season at the Princes Theatre (now called the Shaftesbury) in London. Its director was the soprano Joan Cross. Goodall knew her slightly. Before the war he had conducted Mozart's concert aria, *Bella mia fiamma*, for her at one of the Cambridge Theatre concerts; later, she had sung a group of operatic favourites with the Wessex Philharmonic. He assumed that she, like everyone else, would rebuff him, but he telephoned her none the less. To his surprise she said she would arrange a meeting for him with the company's musical director, Lawrance Collingwood.

Collingwood was sympathetic to Goodall's plight, but told him he was looking for a répétiteur, not a conductor. Goodall said he was desperate for work and would be grateful for anything that involved music. Collingwood signed him on and told him to meet up with the company in Birmingham the following Monday.

CHAPTER 9

Enter Grimes

GOODALL joined the Sadler's Wells Opera on 24 September 1944. The company lacked both the vocal and technical resources to stage large-scale operas, which few theatres on the touring circuit could have accommodated anyway, but it had in its repertory nine well-contrasted works ranging from *Cosi fan tutte* to *Hansel and Gretel*. Maintaining musical standards was a constant struggle: Lawrance Collingwood's two assistant conductors, Muir Mathieson and Boyd Neel, both lacked operatic experience; and because of the depredations of military call-up, he and Joan Cross had to make do in many cases with principal singers who were either unsuitable or inexperienced. Even seasoned artists found it difficult to survive the pressures of constant touring. Cross was the company's most distinguished singer, but because of her administrative duties (she had been running the company since June 1941), her stage appearances were by necessity limited in number. "War conditions have hit the opera of Sadler's Wells harder than the ballet," wrote a critic on *The Times*, "and standards of performance have been adversely affected by touring more in singing than in dancing. A prima ballerina can sustain a company but one soprano does not make a season – she cannot sing Gilda tonight, the Countess tomorrow, Gretel at Christmas, and Mimi at matinées. Male dancers are not so scarce as tolerable tenors. Yet here is the opera company still in being ..."[1]

The company's orchestra, numbering thirty-two players, was workaday (many of the country's best players were in the services), while the chorus contained veterans, particularly among the men, who in more propitious times might have been pensioned off long before. The provincial press tended to praise performances indiscriminately, though sometimes more rigorous critical standards were applied. Eric Blom, reviewing *Madam Butterfly* in Birmingham, wrote that although the opera was beautiful to look at, and the production first-rate, the "orchestra lacked body, warmth and passion, sometimes even accuracy; and none of the singing came anywhere near greatness."[2] But there was a positive side to the company's activities. New audiences for opera were being tapped, and they were turning out to be large and appreciative. "This week's visit to the Theatre Royal would have seemed an undreamed of treat to Norwich music-lovers in the days of peace," wrote the *Eastern Daily Press*; "but the war has turned things upside down (and not always for the worse)."[3]

Eric Crozier, who in 1943 produced a lively *Bartered Bride* for the company, has pointed out that "so long as the war lasted, some drop in musical standards was inevitable. Tyrone Guthrie [stage director and administrator of the Vic-Wells organisation throughout the war] and Joan Cross ... agreed that it was necessary to offset this musical decline by presenting opera to its new provincial audiences as a well-acted and visually attractive entertainment. This was the origin of the often-heard complaint in the profession that the Wells form of opera was 'over-produced.'"[4]

Goodall's knowledge of opera was very limited in 1944. Indeed he knew only three of the works in the company's repertoire, *Hansel and Gretel*, *The Barber of Seville* and *Gianni Schicchi*; he had worked on them during his brief period at Covent Garden before the war. The rest he had to learn quickly as the company moved on to Leeds and then Newcastle-upon-Tyne. At first his name did not even appear in the programmes.

On 30 October 1944 the company reached the Theatre Royal, Glasgow, where the Scottish Orchestra provided extra players for the pit and members of the amateur Glasgow Grand Opera Society boosted the ranks of the chorus. Collingwood suddenly found himself short of conductors and gave Goodall *The Barber of Seville* on 1 November. Goodall said he did not feel ready for it, but Joan Cross overrode his objections. It was the first time he had conducted a professional performance of an opera. The cast included Peter Pears as Count Almaviva and Edmund Donlevy as Figaro; the Rosina was Rose Hill, who years later achieved much wider fame in the television comedy series, *'Allo 'Allo*. The recitatives were replaced by dialogue. "Imagine it," said Goodall, looking back on the occasion, "the *Barber* at *Götterdämmerung* speed!"

He may have been only half-joking: the *Manchester Guardian*, reviewing a *Barber* conducted by Goodall three months later, noted that in the Act 2 finale the singers "showed a constant tendency ... to get ahead of the conductor's beat".[5] Five days after his first *Barber*, Goodall conducted *Gianni Schicchi,* with Donlevy in the title-role and Edith Coates as Zita; it shared a bill with *Il Tabarro* under Collingwood. There were a lot of empty seats: wartime Glasgow was not interested in Puccini's one-act operas. Cross thought Goodall's conducting at this stage "routine, but all right."

When the company returned to London in December 1944 for a seven-week season at the Princes, Goodall conducted his first *Bartered Bride* ("a step forward," said Cross) and followed it a fortnight later with *Hansel and Gretel*. By now he was described in the programme as chorus master. Two months later he was promoted to assistant conductor. He added *Il Tabarro* to his tally, and then *Rigoletto*, which he conducted for the first time on 8 March 1945, at the Lyceum Theatre, Sheffield. John Hargreaves sang the title-role, Tom Culbert was the

Duke, and Linda Parker the Gilda. The composer and critic George Linstead, writing in the following day's *Sheffield Telegraph*, had praise for Hargreaves, but did not mention Goodall; as for the rest, there "was no obvious pleasure in the singing of Verdi's coloratura and such well known arias as 'Caro nome' and the much traduced 'La Donna è Mobile' had a pallor not in keeping with the traditions of Italian opera. The ensembles, however, were finely drawn."

Far more to Goodall's taste than *Rigoletto* was the concert he gave the following night at Sheffield's City Hall, when he conducted the Hallé Orchestra for the first time. His badgering of the orchestra had paid off at last. Barbirolli, a conductor Goodall esteemed, had written to him some ten months earlier with a promise of a date with the Hallé in the not too distant future. But far from filling Goodall with hope, Barbirolli's letter had merely fuelled his paranoia. He wrote to Maisie Aldridge:

> Barbirolli said "All my friends speak so highly of your work." Either this is baloney or he's letting me down lightly – but it shouldn't take all these months to have a date if Weldon & Fistoulari can have one within two months. It really does embitter one.

The Sheffield programme, which began with the *Bartered Bride* overture, included four works Goodall particularly liked: Elgar's Violin Concerto (with Ida Haendel), Beethoven's Eighth Symphony, Debussy's *L'après-midi d'un faune* and the prelude to *Die Meistersinger*. Linstead wrote that in the symphony there was "speed, high spirits and plenty of humour in the playing. Only in the last movement did one feel that the conductor could have thrown his cap a little higher in the air." As for the Wagner, which Goodall had never conducted before, "he carried off the music with an élan which left some of us breathless but glowing."[6]

After the Sheffield concert, the Hallé asked Goodall back for further dates in September, November and December 1945, as well as in March 1946, when one of his Manchester programmes included Brahms's Violin Concerto, with the gifted French player, Ginette Neveu, who only three years later died in an air crash. The *Guardian's* chief music critic, Granville Hill, thought her interpretation "revealed a depth of insight that was astonishing in so young an artist." Goodall, he said, accompanied "in a manner that was broad yet sensitive in style and carefully balanced with the solo music." The *Guardian's* general verdict on Goodall was favourable: he "showed that he is versatile and that he is authoritative in his treatment of the orchestra and of the music he selects ... [He] won conspicuous success." George Linstead, reviewing another concert with the Hallé in Sheffield, wrote that Goodall was "fast establishing his position as one of the leading young British conductors."[7] Goodall was often described in reviews at the time as being young. He certainly looked it, though he was already in his forties.

On the day after Goodall conducted his first *Barber* in November 1944, the show-business reporter of the Glasgow *Evening News* revealed in an article based on an interview with Joan Cross that the Sadler's Wells company had plans for a "new English opera, 'Peter Grimes', now being scored by Ben Britten." It is doubtful if many people outside the company took in the significance of this item of news. A month later, when the company was at the Bristol Hippodrome, the 31-year-old composer himself talked about *Grimes* to a reporter. "It is founded," he said, "on a poem by George Crabbe, who hailed from the same part of the country as I do (East Anglia). It is the story of a rather eccentric fisherman and a school-mistress in a fishing village on the East Coast."[8]

Britten had known nothing of Crabbe's work until the summer of 1941, when he read an article about the Aldeburgh-born poet by E.M. Forster.[9] Britten and Peter Pears were in California at the time, and Forster's description of the flat, melancholy marshes of the Aide estuary filled the composer with a yearning for his native Suffolk. He resolved to return to England. In Los Angeles, Pears bought a second-hand copy of Crabbe's complete works. Forster had mentioned in particular *The Borough*, a series of poems in rhymed couplets about the harsh realities of life in Aldeburgh in the eighteenth century. The subject of one poem, Peter Grimes, a violent fisherman haunted by the ghosts of his murdered apprentices, seemed suitable for operatic treatment, and Britten and Pears started to construct a scenario. Neither had much experience of opera: Britten's sole venture to date, *Paul Bunyan*, an operetta to a text by W. H. Auden, had proved a critical disaster at its premiere at Columbia University in May 1941. However, when the conductor Serge Koussevitzky learned of the *Grimes* project, he arranged for the opera to be commissioned in memory of his wife, Natalie. It was intended that the premiere should be given at the Berkshire Festival at Tanglewood, where Koussevitzky's Boston Symphony Orchestra played each summer.

When Britten and Pears eventually returned to England in the spring of 1942, they were registered as conscientious objectors. At first Pears concentrated on recitals, but in December he was auditioned for the Sadler's Wells Opera by Cross, who, against the advice of her music staff,[10] engaged him as a principal singer. Britten often came to Pears's rehearsals and performances, particularly when the company was in London, and used his visits to familiarise himself with the technicalities of opera production. By the autumn of 1943 the text of *Grimes* had been more or less hammered into shape by the composer and his librettist, the playwright and journalist Montagu Slater; Eric Crozier gave a good deal of practical advice. Britten began to compose the music in January 1944. Some months later he learned that, because of transport difficulties, the Tanglewood premiere would have to be postponed until after the war. Koussevitzky waived his right to the first performance.

When, in a dingy Liverpool studio, Britten played the prologue and Act 1 to Cross, Collingwood and Guthrie, they agreed immediately to take the piece, though its premiere would have to wait until the company returned to Sadler's Wells Theatre, since *Grimes* demanded a largish stage and a decent-sized orchestra pit. Britten's publishers, Boosey & Hawkes, wanted to keep the opera for the reopening of Covent Garden, but Britten believed it would make a more powerful impact in a smaller theatre, even though, says Crozier, he "deplored the low musical standards of the Wells in general and of its orchestra in particular."[11] After a good deal of discussion the publishers gave in.

By December 1944 it seemed likely that the company would be back in London for good by the following May or June. Despite the continuing V1 flying bomb and V2 rocket attacks on Britain, a sense of optimism was sweeping the country: the first German city, Aachen, had already fallen to the allies. Detailed planning for a production of *Peter Grimes* could begin at last. Originally Britten had thought he might conduct the opera himself[12]; now he wanted Goodall to do it. Not only had Goodall proved himself an able colleague before the war, he had also championed the composer's music during the Wessex years; his wide experience as a choral conductor may also have worked in his favour.

It is a measure of Britten's regard for Goodall that he should have chosen him in preference to Collingwood's assistant, Boyd Neel, who in the public's mind was more closely associated with the composer's music. Neel had not only commissioned and conducted the premiere of Britten's *Variations on a Theme of Frank Bridge*, but had also conducted the first performances of *Les Illuminations* and the Prelude and Fugue for strings, which had been written specially to celebrate the Boyd Neel Orchestra's tenth anniversary. Any worries that Collingwood himself might have wanted to conduct the new opera were soon dispelled; he thought it should be entrusted to a younger man. (Similarly, Guthrie raised no objection when Britten said he wanted Eric Crozier as producer.) But instead of leaping at his opportunity, Goodall at first insisted that he was not qualified to handle such an important assignment. Once more he was overruled by Joan Cross.

Since Britten had modelled several characters on actual members of the company – Ellen Orford on Cross, for example, and Auntie on the mezzo-soprano Edith Coates – casting was in some cases a foregone conclusion. Grimes himself was written for Peter Pears, though Britten had not always envisaged him in the part. An early list of characters drawn up by the composer in June 1942 has

Grimes down as a baritone. This is not so surprising as it might at first appear, for in the early 1940s Pears's voice, though beautifully placed, was very light with an unimpressive top. Because it didn't project well in big theatres, it is unlikely that Pears would have been acceptable in a role like Grimes at Tanglewood, with its seating-capacity of 6,000. Sadler's Wells, with 1,650 seats, was more suited to him.

Pears's best parts were Ferrando in *Così fan tutte* and Vašek in *The Bartered Bride*; Rodolfo in *La Bohème* and the Duke in *Rigoletto* were, strictly speaking, not for him, though he sang them quite often. The Duke's high B flats in the last act filled him with alarm, and he split one or another of them with such regularity that he became known in the company as "the cracking good tenor". "Must he be murdered?" sang Edith Coates as Maddalena after one particularly disastrous B flat in Bristol. "Say sister," exclaimed an American GI in the front row, "you've got something there!"[13]

Pears may have been a butt for company jokes, but his colleagues found him friendly and good-natured. Britten, on the other hand, was regarded with suspicion. Most singers assumed that, when they returned to Sadler's Wells, the theatre would reopen with something big and splashy, with company favourites in leading roles: *Il Trovatore*, perhaps, with Joan Cross as Leonora and Edith Coates as Azucena (though the company did not have a tenor who could have coped with Manrico). However, it was becoming increasingly clear that the chosen work was going to be something very different – a new work from a British composer who had yet to prove himself in the theatre.

Initial discontent turned into resentment when vocal scores for the first act were handed out in February 1945. As might have been expected, the plum roles of Grimes himself and Ellen Orford had gone to Pears and Cross, though at first Ellen was to be shared with another company soprano, Elizabeth Abercrombie. Britten then decided he only wanted Cross; Abercrombie's colleagues were indignant. Edith Coates's role as a bawdy landlady was pronounced an insult to her standing as one of the longest-serving and most respected members of the company – though there is no evidence that Coates, celebrated throughout the profession for her racy good humour, took this curious line herself. Some company stalwarts, for example the baritone John Hargreaves, were left out of the cast altogether. Hargreaves, a combative Lancastrian, became the malcontents' standard-bearer.

The choice of conductor was greeted with particular surprise, for the company had assumed that the job would go to Collingwood. There were singers who barely thought of Goodall as a conductor. In the twenty weeks he had spent with the company, he had conducted no more than nine *Barbers*, six *Schicchis* and a few performances of *Tabarro*, *Bartered Bride* and *Hansel and Gretel*. As a coach, as well as a conductor, he was held by some members of the company to pay far too much attention to the actual notes in the score for comfort. Singers who had acquired slovenly habits during the war years took offence when he accused them of inaccuracy. Goodall did not particularly like the *Barber*, but felt that if it had to be performed, it might as well be done properly. In this he reckoned he had Wagner on his side. The following passage in Goodall's copy of *Über das Dirigieren* is heavily marked:

> It was only at a suburban theatre at Turin (i.e. in Italy) that I witnessed a correct and complete performance of the "Barber of Seville;" for our conductors grudge the trouble it takes to do justice even to a simple score such as "Il Barbiere." They have no notion that a perfectly correct performance, be it of the most insignificant opera, can produce an excellent impression upon an educated mind, simply by reason of its correctness.

However, in his quest for textual correctness, Goodall sometimes seemed in danger of losing sight of the *Barber*'s inherent sparkle. He gained the reputation of being a poor accompanist with no feel for the ebb and flow of an Italian line. He did not dismiss the criticism; indeed he was the first to admit that he had no real sympathy for Rossini's, or even Verdi's, music. But he knew that singers who would not, or could not, sing accurately in the Italian repertoire would be lost when they came to the complexities of *Peter Grimes*. If his uncompromising attitude was resented by many of the singers, it none the less won the admiration of Britten, Cross and Collingwood. Goodall was grateful for their support, the strongest he had received professionally since he had left St Alban's, Holborn. He concentrated on his work and stayed out of company disputes.

Ensemble rehearsals for *Grimes* started on 22 March 1945 in Liverpool. The entry in Goodall's diary is laconic: "1st act of PG rehearsal." Britten played the piano. (Goodall also made a note of the suit he had bought that day at Burton's for £4 17s 6d and 26 clothing coupons.) The entry for the following day is equally brief: "B.B. played Act III Grimes" (the composer had completed the score the previous month). As rehearsals progressed, opposition to *Grimes* within the company became more strident. It was attacked on grounds of cost, the time it took to rehearse and the "cacophony" of its score. The baritone Tom Williams, who had been cast as the sea-captain, Balstrode, suddenly pulled out, claiming that the part was impossible to learn. He was replaced by a young ex-miner, Roderick Jones, who had been snapped up by Cross in 1944 after his discharge from the Navy on medical grounds

The atmosphere became more rancorous by the minute. Britten and Pears were sneered at as "Joan's pansies". There were complaints, understandable enough at a time when the nation was poised for a great military victory, that the composer, producer and leading tenor of the opera chosen to reopen Sadler's

Wells should all have been conscientious objectors.[14] Britten did not help matters when he insisted that members of the cast should not accept concert engagements during the rehearsal period, thus cutting off a source of income that was commonly used to supplement meagre salaries.

Cross herself was accused of putting on *Grimes* solely so that she could have a leading role in it. This was unfair, because she had originally turned down Ellen Orford on account of her administrative duties; it was Britten who had put pressure on her to change her mind. The accusation was also absurd, for if she had chosen to reopen Sadler's Wells with *Il Trovatore*, and cast herself as Leonora, then presumably there would have been no complaints. It is a tribute to Cross's strength of purpose that she never lost her nerve, though she did hand over the direction of the company to Tyrone Guthrie in an attempt to defuse the dispute.

The situation was exacerbated when singers got wind of a plan for the Sadler's Wells Opera to become the nucleus of a new national opera company to be based at Covent Garden once the war was over; Sadler's Wells Theatre would be used for an opera school under Cross's direction. The Sadler's Wells board and the committee set up to advise on the Opera House's future (the musicologist, Edward J. Dent, was a member of both bodies) were in broad agreement on the matter. The Sadler's Wells singers were filled with alarm, justifiably so, for redundancies would be inevitable if the scheme were to go through; many voices would prove too small for the wider spaces of Covent Garden.

A document in the Opera House archives, headed "Notes on a Programme for Covent Garden" and dated April 1945, declares that few of the singers and orchestral players at Sadler's Wells, and none of the music staff with the exception of one assistant conductor – presumably Goodall in the light of what happened later – would be of any use to the new organisation. Joan Cross, on the other hand, "can sing certain roles better than anyone in the country, and her advice and knowledge would be of considerable assistance." Eric Crozier was thought to be a man worth watching. Collingwood, the company's principal conductor since its foundation in 1931, was to be offered a sinecure.

The notes are unsigned. Their most likely author is David Webster, former general manager of Lewis's department store in Liverpool and chairman of the Liverpool Philharmonic Orchestra, who had been appointed Covent Garden's administrator as early as August 1944, though as yet he had no house to administer, for Covent Garden was to remain a dance hall until October 1945. Webster turned up constantly during the Sadler's Wells Opera's 1944 Christmas season at the Princes Theatre to spy out the land. Singers noted that he seemed to be on very friendly terms with Cross and Guthrie. What, they wondered, was he up to? No one seemed able to calm their anxieties, least of all Cross and Guthrie, who by now were involved in official discussions about the takeover. The split between management and singers widened dangerously. Cross's critics claimed later that if only she had behaved in a less autocratic manner and taken the company into her confidence, a good deal of trouble might have been avoided. Those sympathetic to Cross wondered why she never tried to rally the substantial support she enjoyed in the company, particularly among its young members. Goodall thought it prudent to stay on the sidelines.

Given the tensions, it is remarkable that the preparations for *Grimes* proceeded as efficiently as they did. The older men of the chorus found the music impenetrable. The company's new chorus master, Alan Melville, battled on doughtily, convinced that the opera was going to be a smash-hit, though few of his colleagues shared his confidence. The rebels predicted an almighty flop; even Guthrie was unsure about the outcome. Goodall, however, rarely thought of the opera in terms of failure or success. His one concern was to secure the best possible musical result. Characteristically, he grumbled to Maisie Aldridge that *Grimes* was being put on in a rush. In fact it was rehearsed for an unprecedented eleven weeks. Britten attended many of the sessions and Goodall consulted him constantly about details. Crozier noted his childlike hero-worship of the composer. Some found Goodall nervous and on edge when Britten was present, but more confident when he was away.

From Liverpool, the company travelled to Hammersmith, Wimbledon and Birmingham, rehearsing *Grimes* as it went in church halls, hotels, a gymnasium, anywhere where there was a piano. Goodall coached the orchestral players, sometimes in groups, sometimes in pairs, sometimes individually. It was a gruelling schedule, for the company was also giving eight performances a week. The premiere at Sadler's Wells was fixed for 7 June 1945. Exactly one month earlier, on Monday 7 May, the Germans surrendered. That day the company started a two-week season in Wolverhampton. Streets in many parts of the town were bedecked with Union Jacks, an effigy of Hitler was burned on a bonfire, and thousands danced in the open air. Goodall noted in his diary, "After 5½ yrs of unnecessary hell & war unconditional surrender," the only comment about the war he ever made in it. The company spent VE-day rehearsing *Grimes* in Wolverhampton's Civic Hall.

Guthrie was also in Wolverhampton, but his mood was far from celebratory. He foresaw, correctly, the splitting-up of the Vic-Wells empire. Ninette de Valois was determined to take the Sadler's Wells Ballet to Covent Garden, the opera company was rent with schism, and the Old Vic drama company, now run by a triumvirate of Laurence Olivier, Ralph Richardson and John Burrell, was showing every sign of wanting to break away from the Vic-Wells aegis. "The fact," wrote Guthrie, "that it was during my regime that their courses began to diverge I count the most serious failure of my professional life."[15] But at least all three companies had survived the war, in itself no mean achievement.

The Wolverhampton visit ended on 19 May. Wartime touring was over. In four years and seven months the Sadler's Wells Opera had visited no fewer than fifty-seven different towns and cities, not to mention garrison theatres for ENSA. Back in London, Goodall left nothing to chance. To get the feel of the opera as a whole before the dress rehearsals took place, he asked Alan Melville round to Sydney Street, where Melville played the whole score of *Grimes* on the piano, while Goodall conducted. In the theatre, Goodall was at last able to work with the full orchestra, which had been specially augmented to fifty players. He asked Philip Blake, an old friend from the College conducting class whose advice he valued, to sit in on the final rehearsals. Goodall was particularly unhappy about the timing of the townspeople's great cries of "Peter Grimes! – Peter Grimes! – Grimes!" in the manhunt at the end of Act 3 sc. 1. He knew that the longer he dared make the pause between each cry, the greater would be the impact. At first he kept losing his nerve and putting down the chords too soon. "Wait," whispered Blake at his side, "Wait … wait … wait … now!"

Many of the streets surrounding Sadler's Wells had been bombed, but the theatre itself was not badly damaged, though it needed a good deal of restoration. Thanks to the profits made by the Sadler's Wells Ballet during the war years, the debt on the building had been wiped out; in addition, CEMA had offered to guarantee the reopening season against loss. But without the ballet company to share the expenses, the future of the theatre itself was very uncertain. Existing artists' contracts, Goodall's included, had come to an end on the final day of the Wolverhampton visit. The governors announced that new contracts would be issued, but only for the six-week London season; there was no guarantee of work once it was over. The news caused consternation. The company's two Equity representatives, John Hargreaves and Elizabeth Abercrombie, formed a committee of singers to confront the governors, who were told in no uncertain terms that the company as a whole had no wish to go to Covent Garden, that turning Sadler's Wells into an opera school was poor reward for the years of wartime struggle, and that in the opinion of the committee it was essential to keep alive a company in a smaller house where young singers could start their careers before going on to the Royal Opera House.

What the committee did not know was that by now at least one of the Sadler's Wells governors, the composer and director of the Royal College of Music, Sir George Dyson, had got cold feet about a move to Covent Garden.[16] The board seemed taken aback by the vehemence of the singers' views, and two governors in particular, Edward Dent and the chairman, the Earl of Lytton, expressed pleasure that the company's loyalty to Sadler's Wells was so strong.[17] The singers were mollified. A demand that they should be allowed to run the company themselves was dropped, as was a threat to boycott the London season. On 7 June, the day *Grimes* opened, Dyson informed Webster that as far as he and his fellow governors were concerned the plan for the Sadler's Wells Opera to go to Covent Garden was dead.[18]

The first night of *Peter Grimes* took place amid great nervousness from everyone, including Guthrie. "Whatever happens," he said to Joan Cross, shortly before curtain-up, "we were absolutely right to do this piece."[19] Guthrie also worried that the theatre's central chandelier, back in place for the first time since the air-raids, might come crashing down on the heads of the musical world assembled in the stalls below – Ralph Vaughan Williams, Sir George Dyson, William Walton, Michael Tippett, John Christie of Glyndebourne, Yehudi Menuhin (in Britain to give concerts for American forces), Albert Coates. The house was sold out, "with more evening clothes and fur wraps than have been seen in the theatre since the war began."[20] The queue for the gallery had started to form at 10 p.m. the previous evening. Britten ("a young man with disordered hair," reported the *News Chronicle* the next day) paced up and down at the back of the stalls during the performance. He was too nervous to sit down.

In the pit Goodall hurled himself into his task with uncustomary abandon. Eyewitnesses recall him leaping into the air at climactic moments. "If you looked at Reggie too much," said one member of the audience, "you became hypnotised; you couldn't look at the stage. I remember the singer Rose Hill turning to me during the storm scene. 'If he's not careful,' she said, 'he'll do himself an injury.'"[21] The orchestra, thought Cross, "were probably a very moderate band individually, but that night they pulled out all the stops for Reggie Goodall and I count him the supreme *Grimes* conductor."[22] Goodall judged the cries of "Peter Grimes!" to perfection. On each one the townspeople advanced a step nearer the audience and then paused menacingly. After the final "Grimes!" a woman in the stalls was heard to gasp, "It's too much … I can't stand it." "I knew I was home," said Goodall.

The applause at the end rolled on and on. Afterwards there was a first-night party at the Savoy, but no one present remembered Goodall attending it. Cross believed that as soon as the curtain came down for the last time he caught the No. 19 bus back to Chelsea to brood about the evening.[23] Doubtless the fact that the intricate round in the pub scene, "Old Joe has gone fishing," had gone badly adrift was a matter of deep irritation for him. (Asked once why he always looked so miserable when taking curtain-calls, he replied that all he could think about

on such occasions were the mistakes that had occurred during the performance.)
By the time Guthrie reached the Savoy, "in a state of psychic and physical collapse," the party was dispersing and he returned home for a dried-egg omelette
and chocolate made with dried-milk.[24]

The next morning's newspapers must have given the opera's detractors in the
company food for thought, since the reviews were almost unanimous in hailing
Grimes as a turning-point in the history of English opera. There was only one
widely expressed criticism: that it was hard to hear the singers' words. "It is a good
omen," wrote Frank Howes in *The Times*, "that this first-fruit of peace should
declare decisively that opera on the grand scale and in the grand manner can still
be written. Expectations ran high and were not disappointed." Reviewers were
lavish in their praise for Joan Cross and Goodall (though opinions about Pears's
contribution were more divided). "In Mr Reginald Goodall," said Howes, "the
company has discovered an operatic conductor with a talent for dramatic music,
and his piloting of orchestra and chorus through a complex score was the chief
factor in the opera's successful performance." Two days later William Glock wrote
in *The Observer*: "Reginald Goodall's conducting I liked very much; he seemed to
combine an experienced control of stage and orchestra with a musicianly enthusiasm which sometimes rose to the level of evangelical zeal." Desmond Shawe-Taylor
was equally enthusiastic in the *New Statesman and Nation*: "The performance was
a triumph for Sadler's Wells. Seldom are composers so well served as was Britten
by the conductor, Mr Reginald Goodall, and the entire cast." In gratitude, Britten gave Goodall the complete composition sketch of the opera, inscribing it: "to
Reginald Goodall – a souvenir of the splendid work, & great understanding over
the 'first performance' – June 7th 1945."

Six days before the premiere Goodall had resumed his correspondence with the
BBC's music department:

> When some time ago I wrote to ask you if you would offer me a job as conduc-
> tor you replied that you would like someone from the BBC to attend a concert
> conducted by me.
>   On Thursday next June 7th I am conducting the first performance of Benjamin
> Britten's new opera "Peter Grimes" at Sadler's Wells – though this is not a
> symphony concert it will no doubt serve your purpose, as the only symphony
> concerts I conduct at present are for the Hallé orchestra in the north.

Julian Herbage, the BBC's music programmes organiser and something of a
grandee in the department, had already been asked to prepare a report on the
premiere for the corporation's new director of music, Victor Hely-Hutchinson.[25]
Now, as a result of Goodall's letter, Herbage was asked to include a detailed
comment on the conducting. Herbage's two-page memorandum, written on

the day after the premiere, typifies the insularity and condescension endemic in the BBC's music department at the time. He had harsh words not only for Britten – "until he enters more intensely into his drama and characterisation and until he purges his style of many of his trivial and eclectic elements, he will not make a real success in the operatic field" – but also for Goodall:

> Much praise has been lavished on Reginald Goodall, the conductor. Certainly he had heavy odds to contend with in an indifferent orchestra, and certainly he kept things together and moving. I did not feel, however, that he showed signs of being any more than the normal competent operatic conductor, and I would certainly like to hear some of the music again in better surroundings with a better orchestra and a more experienced man on the rostrum.[26]

Fortunately, the opera was not without its supporters within the BBC. Shortly after the premiere, Herbage's young assistant, Basil Douglas, sent two confidential memos to the director of music, in which he praised both opera and conductor, and urged the BBC to relay *Grimes* in its entirety.[27] Hely-Hutchinson's deputy, Kenneth Wright, was seriously worried about the department's procrastination. A memo he wrote to his superior on 13 June lets slip the fact that, although by then there had been three performances of the opera, neither Hely-Hutchinson nor the conductor Stanford Robinson, who was responsible for opera broadcasts, had attended any of them. *Grimes*, said Wright,

> ... is the kind of musical event of importance which in Paris or Brussels would never be allowed to pass unrepresented in the local broadcasting; and Director Collaer [director of music, Belgian radio] was most anxious to know if and when the opera, in whole or in part, would be produced by us. I would suggest that to wait until Programme C [the Third Programme] comes along will look either like lack of confidence in the most important of our young composers, or the kind of timidity in our programme building of which we are not as yet suspected by our continental colleagues.

Wright's warning must have made an impression, for a decision to broadcast a complete performance was taken at last. Initially the BBC wanted to pre-record the opera, so that it could be fitted more easily into the tightly organised radio schedules (at that point there were only two domestic programmes, the Home Service and the General Forces Programme). But the Sadler's Wells orchestra turned down the money offered for the recording, and eventually the BBC arranged to broadcast the opera live from the theatre on 17 July. Sadly for posterity, the orchestra stipulated that no recording of the performance should be made.

The relay, in the Home Service, was judged a success. Hely-Hutchinson told Guthrie it was "most memorable."[28] French and Swiss radios broadcast Act 1, and the BBC overseas services transmitted all or part of the opera to Europe,

North America and Africa. A listener survey in Britain revealed that fifty-three per cent of those who tuned in liked the music very much; fifteen per cent disliked it. Only Goodall was unhappy about the enterprise, though for a non-musical reason. He complained to his old sparring partner at the BBC, Aubrey Beese, that in its billing for the broadcast, the *Radio Times* had printed Eric Crozier's name in capital letters, while his own had been featured much less prominently. Beese, now music productions manager, sent a memo about the incident to Hely-Hutchinson:

> While I was trying to pacify Reginald Goodall ... he made some general references which I think I ought to pass on to you. Pretending to give the impression that he didn't really mind, he said that that was "just the B.B.C.", and that he had given up trying to deal with us. He referred back to a letter (which I think I may have signed for the then D. M.) replying to a request from him to conduct one of our Orchestras. It was all said in parenthesis, but I gathered that he felt rather sore that no notice had been taken of him; and he considered that his Cambridge Theatre concerts and his work at Sadler's Wells etc., had entitled him to some notice.
>
> As far as I remember, when he did ask for a conducting date a long time ago [Goodall's last letter to Beese was dated 1 November 1943], we sent the usual formal request that he should let us know when he would be conducting so that someone might go and hear. Whether he ever wrote again, or whether anyone ever went to hear him, I do not know.[29]

Hely-Hutchinson wrote to Goodall expressing regret about the billing: "It is obviously absurd that the producer should be presented to a wireless audience as a more important person than the conductor."[30] He added a vaguely worded promise that Goodall would be offered engagements "from time to time" in the future. A copy of the letter was sent to Julian Herbage. Beese added a note to it: "Would you try and get Goodall in fairly soon? I think we really should put him in in view of the excellent work he did over 'Peter Grimes'." Nothing happened for several months.

Unlike the BBC, the British Council was quick to recognise the opera's worth. Brian Kennedy-Cooke, in charge of the council's arts and science division, discovered that Decca was planning to record excerpts from *Grimes* with Goodall and the Sadler's Wells cast. He proposed that the Council should put up extra money to enable the company to record the whole opera. Decca was delighted. The idea was put to the Council's music committee. A majority of its members, including Sir Adrian Boult, Arthur Bliss, Dame Myra Hess and Ralph Vaughan Williams, gave it their unqualified approval. Edward Dent, on the other hand, advised "waiting until time has shown whether [*Grimes*] is likely to become an international repertory opera or not. I hear that there are chances of its being performed in Stockholm, Zurich & Basle: also in U.S.A. But with all admiration for its originality and power I am doubtful whether it will obtain lasting popularity even in England." The composer William Walton opposed the project, which, he said, should be discussed "at a calmer moment when the wildly hysterical & uncritical eulogies & general 'ballyhoo' have somewhat abated, & the true merits of the work can be properly assessed."[31]

Dent and Walton were outvoted, however, and plans were made to record the opera during the fortnight beginning 27 August. The first hint of trouble came in a letter Tyrone Guthrie wrote to the council on 9 July. He asked if it might be possible to record *Grimes* within the space of a week, rather than a fortnight. "The governors," he said, "have been approached by ENSA with a suggestion that the Sadler's Wells Opera Company go overseas, and they are anxious that this offer be, if possible, accepted as well as your offer to record *Peter Grimes*. I should add that ... [the] ENSA offer is not yet absolutely definite." The tour was due to start on 3 September, the half-way point in the proposed sessions. Decca replied that the recording could not possibly be completed in less than two weeks.

What Guthrie did not reveal in his letter was that the ENSA tour had been set up behind his back. Without informing either Guthrie or Cross, John Hargreaves had approached Walter Legge, ENSA's music liaison officer, with the proposal that his organisation might sponsor a visit by the company to the British forces in Germany. Legge, who in 1938–9 had acted as Beecham's assistant artistic director at Covent Garden, was delighted to have the chance to manage an opera tour. The Sadler's Wells governors gave the enterprise their blessing, and in doing so severely weakened Guthrie's authority. Hargreaves and his followers were jubilant, claiming they had secured the survival of the Sadler's Wells Opera. Perhaps they had; even at the time the situation was not clear-cut. Guthrie tried without success to arrange a compromise over dates that would allow both recording and tour to take place. The "rebels" said that if there really was a plan to record the opera – which most of them doubted – then it could happen when the tour was over.

The London season ended on 21 July with a performance of *Grimes*; like its eight predecessors, it was sold out. The following day the company left for a three-week visit to Belfast, where Goodall was responsible for three performances of *The Bartered Bride* and five of an opera he had only recently conducted for the first time, *Madam Butterfly*. Joan Cross sang her last Cio-Cio-San for the company. The Pinkerton was a new recruit, James Johnston from Belfast, a tenor with a strong lyric-dramatic voice of the kind that had not been heard at Sadler's Wells since before the war. That the split between the two factions was as wide as ever can be gauged from a letter Britten wrote to Pears on 1 August: "I do so hope this lousy tour isn't being too hellish for you – don't take any notice of those ludicrous fools – they couldn't matter less. Just sing as well as you can, & spend the time with Joan and Laurence [Lawrance Collingwood] and Reggie – & think about next week when you'll be here [in Suffolk]."[32]

Goodall spent the Belfast visit in a state of high anxiety. He had wanted to join the ENSA tour, but had not been invited to do so, because, it was reported at the time, "a remark made by him in a fit of temper" had been repeated to Walter Legge.[33] Presumably the remark was critical of Legge's sudden involvement in the company's affairs. Now Goodall was worried that his outburst had spoiled his chances of being given a new contract by the company once the tour was over. The management tried to reassure him (not with much success) that he was "an extremely valuable person."[34]

The company returned to London on 12 August. Guthrie, exhausted by the power struggles, resigned as administrator of Sadler's Wells and the Old Vic "to concentrate on literary and experimental work for the theatre." Joan Cross also resigned, not, it seems, without a push from the governors;[35] Pears and Crozier went too. The baritone Edmund Donlevy reflected the depression felt by many when he wrote of the "elements of quarrelsomeness, overweening ambition, envy, fear of unemployment, hysteria, etc, etc, which have appeared in so many guises during the last six months or so which have done more to damage the artistic standard of the company's work than anything else could possibly have done."[36]

In spite of the upheavals, the British Council had not abandoned its plans to record *Grimes*, though by now it had decided to dispense with the Sadler's Wells orchestra and chorus, as well as most of the original singers, and use instead the National Symphony Orchestra, a special chorus of forty and "the best cast that can be got together," headed by Pears and Cross. Goodall was to conduct.[37] Recording sessions were arranged for late September, but had to be postponed until November when it was discovered that the BBC, anticipating the needs of the Third Programme, had put under contract most of the professional chorus singers in London for full-time work; they could not be released for the recording period. An amateur choir was out of the question, for there was no time to train it. London's only other professional chorus, that of the Sadler's Wells Opera, would be away in Germany; and there was no guarantee that it would agree to take part anyway. David Webster was approached, but he could not help; as yet, Covent Garden had no chorus.

To keep things on the boil, the Council arranged to record the Sea Interludes and Passacaglia from *Grimes* in early November with the National Symphony Orchestra. Goodall was offered 100 guineas to conduct, but when the dates for the recording were changed, he had to withdraw, because the new sessions clashed with concerts he was giving with the Hallé. Britten himself agreed to take over. Fate took a hand once more. The composer fell ill on the day of the recording, and it proved impossible to find a substitute conductor. Decca wondered if it might be possible to revive the idea of recording the complete work with the original Sadler's Wells forces, but by now the British Council was losing heart. On 11 December, Evelyn Donald of its music department informed Decca that it had decided to abandon the project for good: "If we recorded this coming summer ... we might find ourselves with a recording which might compare unfavourably with a new production of the work."

"*Grimes,*" said Joan Cross in 1987, "was the company's greatest triumph, yet it was a catastrophe, too."[38] But though the Sadler's Wells Opera was down, it was far from out.

CHAPTER 10

From Berlin to Lucretia

S IR GEORGE DYSON himself took over responsibility for the Sadler's Wells Opera until a new director could be appointed. He spent most of the summer of 1945 trying to mend fences and instil some discipline into the company. He arranged for a new season to begin at Sadler's Wells on Boxing Day and asked the baritone and producer, Clive Carey, to run it. Carey, who had been associated with the Sadler's Wells company and its Old Vic predecessor since the 1920s, was reluctant to become involved, but Dyson eventually prevailed on him to accept. There was a good deal of argument with singers over contracts. Dyson warned that if they would not agree to the terms offered, "then we shall have to face the fact and disband." It was, he said, impossible to cope with "the nightmare of division" much longer.[1]

Dyson called for higher standards in singing and playing, and urged CEMA's successor, the Arts Council, to give the company a grant rather than a guarantee against loss – "It would then be possible to estimate our resources."[2] In an act of reconciliation with the previous regime he persuaded Lawrance Collingwood (who had declined to join the ENSA tour) to stay on as musical director and wrote to Pears and Cross, inviting them to appear as guest artists in a revival of *Peter Grimes* during the new London season. Pears replied almost immediately. He would do it, he said, provided Goodall and Crozier were also involved.[3] There was no problem as far as Goodall was concerned, since he was anxious to remain with Sadler's Wells. Cross and Crozier also agreed to take part.

The company sailed for Hamburg, the first stop on its tour, on 28 August, only four months after VE-day. Germany was in chaos. Dyson told George Chamberlain, general manager of Sadler's Wells Theatre, that he had heard that "Legge is, as we expected, virtually assuming that he can do anything he likes with anybody, and he rides roughshod, as we all know. I think Hamburg will teach the company a lot about the problems of management."[4] Dyson was to be proved right. Performances took place in the Hamburg Schauspielhaus, which had been commandeered by the British occupying forces as a garrison theatre. The logistical problems were formidable. The scenery was stuck in Hull docks, and at first the company had to make do with a hotchpotch of sets and costumes from the Hamburg State Opera, the Schauspielhaus itself, and even from the Lübeck opera, forty miles away. When the Sadler's Wells scenery did arrive, a week late, it was found to be badly damaged. Further complications arose from singers falling ill as a result of inoculations against cholera and yellow fever; casts had to be changed constantly. None the less the company enjoyed a success with its military audiences. Houses were full to capacity.

It soon became apparent that Legge did not have enough conductors to support a two-month tour. During the three weeks spent in Hamburg, the work was shared between the New Zealander Warwick Braithwaite, Robert Ainsworth, who had been Covent Garden's pre-war chorus master, Walter Susskind, a talented young Czech from the Carl Rosa, and John Barbirolli, who was responsible for two performances of *Madam Butterfly*. But because of commitments at home, Ainsworth, Susskind and Barbirolli had to leave before the next stop on the tour, Detmold. Only Braithwaite was left. Legge had little alternative but to bury the hatchet and send an SOS to Goodall, who was in Southport with the Hallé.

Goodall agreed to join the tour in Detmold. On his return from Lancashire, he reported to ENSA's headquarters at the Theatre Royal, Drury Lane. There he was kitted out with 1 army uniform with ENSA shoulder-flashes (ENSA artists enjoyed second-lieutenant status, though they did not wear badges of rank), 1 cap, 2 shirts, 4 collars, 1 tie, 1 pair of shoes, 1 trench coat (all re-issues), 2 pairs of socks (new) and 1 mug. Thus equipped, and in possession of a permit from the Allied Expeditionary Force to enter the zone of occupation, the former Private Goodall was flown by RAF Transport Command to Detmold, to await the arrival of the company from Hamburg. He was surprised to find himself being saluted, not only by British NCOs and other ranks, but also by German policemen; ENSA personnel were often mistaken for genuine officers. Goodall was not at all sure how he would cope when faced with the ruins of a defeated Germany. Almost at once he landed himself at the centre of a controversy.

During the visit to Hamburg, a twenty-strong group from the Sadler's Wells company had travelled by army truck to give a concert for survivors of the Belsen concentration camp, which the British had liberated the previous April. The camp itself had been burnt to the ground to prevent the further spread of typhus, and as many as 19,000 of its former inmates were now living in crowded conditions at the former SS Panzer training school, two kilometres away. A large number of them were too ill with tuberculosis to be moved. The Sadler's Wells singers noticed that many in their audience were still so traumatised by their experiences that they found it hard to concentrate on the programme.[5] The accompanist was Susskind, whose mother had spent six months in Belsen. She was fortunate; she had survived the epidemics, starvation and maltreatment that had claimed so many lives. (Belsen, unlike Auschwitz, was not an extermination camp; most of its inmates died of neglect.) A large notice at the camp gates said that 10,000 – actually 13,000 – unburied corpses had been found when the British arrived; a further 13,000 people had died there since, "all of them victims," said the notice, "of the German new order in Europe."

The concentration camp's commandant, Josef Kramer, and forty-four members of his staff were on trial at Luneburg, and by chance the whole court was at Belsen on the day of the concert to collect further evidence. The Sadler's Wells group looked on as British military police marched the accused into the camp. The actor and barrister Leo Genn, now a lieutenant-colonel and an assistant prosecutor at Lüneburg, pointed out Kramer – handcuffed to the Belsen doctor, Fritz Klein – and the 21-year-old Irma Grese, notorious head of the labour squads. Before going to Belsen all three had been at Auschwitz. They were subsequently executed.

Two days after the concert the entire Sadler's Wells company stopped at Belsen during their journey south to Detmold. Although the barrack huts had been destroyed, the mass graves testified to the camp's terrible past, as did mounds of shoes and striped prison clothing that had once belonged to inmates and had still not been cleared away. When the company, greatly affected by the experience, reached Detmold, Goodall was there to meet it. In the canteen, he reacted to stories of the visit with bizarre insensitivity. Belsen, he maintained, was a British fabrication, a propaganda stunt cooked up by Denham film studios. Some members of the company ignored his views ("Oh God, there goes Reggie again"). Others were greatly upset by them. Others still found the incident a useful excuse to bait him mercilessly and belittle him at every turn.

Goodall was fortunate in having loyal friends in the company, who did their best to protect him. They found it hard to fathom out his limitless capacity for self-deception, and could only imagine it to be the result of either bravado or eccentricity, rather than anything more sinister. The fact was that Goodall, the most pacific of men, could not admit – even to himself – that the nation he admired above all others had been capable of acts of such inhumanity, that the Nazis had acted as cruelly as the Bolshevists he execrated.

Those who took the trouble to break through Goodall's carapace of shyness and unsociability were often surprised to find an amiable and engaging companion, who loved jokes and good gossip. He particularly enjoyed the company of the young dancers who appeared in *The Bartered Bride* and other operas. One of them, Romayne Grigorova, remembers him on the tour as being "a jolly fellow, who enjoyed life to the full."[6] There were parties and pranks. One night Goodall joined the dancers in the bar for cherry brandies and drank so many that he had to be put to bed (he never had a good head for alcohol). Another night the ballerinas sewed up the sleeves and legs of his pyjamas. Next morning at breakfast they waited for a reaction from him, but none came, neither a smile nor a cross word. Where, they wondered, had he slept?

After a week in Detmold the company moved to Berlin. Walter Legge delivered a lecture about behaviour during the 100-mile journey through the Soviet occupied zone. Under no circumstances, he said, was anyone to show any kind of emotion if challenged by the Russians. At the Helmstedt checkpoint, Mongolian-looking troops with sub-machine-guns manned the barrier. According to the account of the tenor Powell Lloyd, they were the cause of some "odd behaviour on the part of one of our number who was anti-Russian, a Catholic and very pro-German [i.e. Goodall]. He had to be forcibly restrained as he was putting his tongue out at the coach window and giving 'thumbs down' signs."[7]

Only when Goodall got to Berlin was the reality of Germany's humiliation finally borne in on him. Many parts of the city still resembled a battlefield, with wrecked tanks, overturned cars and the remains of barricades littering the streets. Because of shortages of medicines, soap, even hot water, it was proving almost impossible to keep epidemics in check. The city's death-rate was five times higher than normal; dysentery and typhoid were rife. Everywhere gangs of women with long-handled shovels and wheel-barrows toiled to clear the rubble, which teemed with rats. In the Tiergarten, Berliners scavenged for sticks and brushwood, anything that might be stored for winter fuel. The food situation was desperate. There was a plague of rabbits, but shooting them was out of the question: a German found in possession of a firearm could be sentenced to death. The British officer in charge of local food production tried to encourage Berliners to use snares, but "curiously," lamented the *British Zone Review*, "the Germans had no idea of trapping rabbits."[8]

Despite everything, theatrical life went on. The Berlin State Opera's historic home in the Unter den Linden, now in the Soviet sector, was a shell, but its company was very much alive, playing against drapes at the Admiralspalast theatre in the Friedrichstrasse. Goodall, Powell Lloyd and several others, all of them in uniform, went there to hear Gluck's *Orfeo ed Euridice*, sung in German by a magnificent cast: Margarete Klose in the title-role, Tiana Lemnitz as Euridice, Rita Streich as Amor. The last time any of the Sadler's Wells party had heard Lemnitz was in London before the war, when she had sung Eva in *Die Meistersinger*; Lloyd had taken the small role of Augustin Moser. Lemnitz had been a member of the pro-Nazi faction among the German singers at Covent Garden. Now – and the irony was not lost on the British artists – she was being fêted amid the ruins of Hitler's capital in a theatre that was answerable to the Soviet authorities. Her singing, said Lloyd, was "better than ever."[9]

The Sadler's Wells company performed in the British sector, at the Theater des Westens, temporary home of the Deutsches Opernhaus (now the Deutsche Oper), whose own theatre in Charlottenburg had been bombed. Strict orders from the military not to fraternise with the local population had been ignored from the start of the tour, for without the close co-operation of the German stagehands, electricians, scene-shifters, dressers and orchestral players (the Sadler's Wells orchestra did not go on the tour) it would have been impossible to get the six operas in the repertory on to the stage. In any case, the company considered the orders an affront to human dignity, particularly since most of their German helpers were half-starved. Goodall, who conducted two perform-ances of *Rigoletto* in Berlin, discovered that members of the Deutsches Opern-haus orchestra were playing in the pit for nothing more than the price of a meal. He gave them what he could: chocolate, cigarettes, tea, soap.

The contrast between the players' lives and his own in Berlin shocked him. Like other senior members of the company, he was staying in some style at the nearby Hotel Savoy, which was used exclusively by British officers. Though the rooms had no locks on the doors – they appeared to have been machine-gunned – the food was excellent and there was plenty of cheap drink. The din-ner menu for 6 October 1945 was:

> *Potage cultivateur*
>
> *Bouchées Magda*
>
> *Médaillon de bœuf soubise, pommes de terre macaire*
> *Pommes de terre copeau, Choux-fleurs à l'anglaise,*
> *Haricots verts sautés*
>
> *Crêpes confiture*
>
> *Canape au fromage – café*

To Berliners it would have been a banquet.

The other four performances during the Berlin week were conducted by Suss-kind, who by now had returned from England (Braithwaite had gone home for good after Detmold). The company had three more weeks in Germany left: two of them in the spa town of Bad Oeynhausen, which served as 21 Army Group's headquarters, the final one in Düsseldorf, where on successive nights Goodall brought the tour to a close with *Rigoletto, Madam Butterfly, La Bohème* (which a week earlier he had conducted for the first time) and *The Bartered Bride*. On 28 October the company flew back to London.

In the course of one year Goodall's fortunes had changed dramatically. His career was now flourishing as never before. After only a short pause, he returned north for more dates with the Hallé, and then went to St Matthew's church, Northampton, to conduct a broadcast concert of three works written specially for its choir, Britten's *Rejoice in the Lamb*, Edmund Rubbra's *The Revival* and Lennox Berkeley's *Festival Anthem*. With the National Symphony Orchestra, he made his first gramophone recording, of Tchaikovsky's *1812* Overture, which Decca issued on 78s in America as well as Britain. He also recorded two Beethoven overtures, *Coriolan*, dark and brooding, and a blazing *Leonora No. 1*, which for some reason were rejected for publication, though test pressings have survived. In addition he was appointed musical director of the Sadler's Wells Opera-Ballet, newly created by Ninette de Valois to fill the vacuum left at Sadler's Wells when the main ballet company went to Covent Garden.

The Opera-Ballet (direct ancestor of the Birmingham Royal Ballet) was an amalgam of the professional dancers who took part in Sadler's Wells opera productions and students from the Sadler's Wells Ballet School; the *corps de ballet* was drawn almost entirely from the school. De Valois intended that it should act as a stepping stone for young dancers and choreographers to the senior company at Covent Garden and in this she was strikingly successful. A high proportion of those who took part in the first short season went on to attain distinction as dancers, choreographers and administrators. They included the 16-year-old Kenneth MacMillan, Anne Heaton, who was only 15, Nadia Nerina, Alan Carter, Peter Darrell, Joan Harris, Alexander Grant, Barbara Fewster and Pauline Wadsworth. The company's two principal dancers were June Brae, a pre-war favourite at Sadler's Wells, and Leo Kersley. The ballet mistress was Peggy van Praagh, later artistic director of the Australian Ballet.[10]

The suggestion that Goodall should go to the ballet came from Lawrance Collingwood, who said that de Valois had been very impressed by his conducting of *The Bartered Bride*. At first Goodall was doubtful – "I said I was not a ballet person" – but Collingwood told him to try it for a while and see what happened. In fact Goodall found the experience congenial: for a start he did not have to see so much of his old persecutors in the opera company; he was also to a certain extent his own master. Classes and rehearsals began in December, with the first night scheduled for 8 April 1946, half way through the opera season. Performances were arranged for Monday evenings and occasional Saturday afternoons.

Goodall attended most of the rehearsals and often played the piano for them, sometimes four-handed with the regular company pianist. He worked closely with the choreographers of the season's two new ballets, Andrée Howard's *Assembly Ball*, danced to Bizet's Symphony in C, and Celia Franca's *Khadra*, which used music from Sibelius's incidental music to *Belshazzar's Feast*. Reviews spoke of the company's youthful enthusiasm and high spirits. Goodall enjoyed the intensity of the rehearsals and noted with amusement that he got more respect from the dancers than he did from most singers in the opera company. Leo Kersley, who danced the Master of Ceremonies in *Assembly Ball* and the Lover in *Khadra*, thought that "this co-operation, right from the start, helped make the new ballets all very much of a coherent whole ... Reggie neither spoiled [the young members of the company] nor talked down to them but simply took them as they were."[11]

As well as the two new works, there were six ballets revived specially for the season: de Valois's *Promenade* and *The Gods go a'Begging*, Act 2 of Ivanov's *Casse-Noisette* (a particular favourite of Goodall's), Fokine's *Les Sylphides* and *Le spectre de la rose*, and Frederick Ashton's *Façade*, with Ashton himself dancing the role of the Dago in the tango. Goodall conducted all of them, except *The Gods go a'Begging*. For good measure he gave Weber's *Oberon* overture as curtain-raiser to *Le spectre*, which uses the same composer's *Invitation to the Dance*.

Goodall spent only one season with the ballet company, but he looked back on it with affection:

> I liked the ballet people. Dancers are dedicated – not like all these singers! Well, a lot of singers. I used to go to the rehearsals, of course. That's what they liked about me. I didn't just go in at the last minute and chop it out. You have to know how to accommodate dancers, otherwise you can ruin the whole thing. A pretty little dancer would turn round to me and say, "Could I have a little more time, please, on that beat, Mr Goodall?" And I'd say, "Certainly, dear."

He was not as accommodating as that with singers.

The new Sadler's Wells opera season had opened on 26 December 1945 as planned. Because of his ballet commitments, Goodall was not listed as an official conductor for it, but he conducted more than forty performances none the less, as well as thirteen triple-bills of ballet. First came a revival of *Rigoletto*, followed by eleven performances of *Peter Grimes*, which was again a big success with the public; on the first night an admiral sporting three rows of medals was spotted in the standing places.[12] The *Times* critic reported that Goodall "once more showed his ability to unleash and control the forces that move through this powerful score."[13]

In *Rigoletto*, Goodall worked hard to get expression into the playing of what he called disparagingly the "rum-ti-turn" accompaniments. He even asked Britten, a Verdi admirer, to go through the score with him and give him ideas.[14] A *Times* review of one performance, with Redvers Llewellyn (recently released from the RAF) as Rigoletto, James Johnston as the Duke and a young Australian, Vera Terry, as Gilda, reflects the rising vocal standards in the company:

> With all its deficiencies in the details of the production, the performance, which was ably directed by Reginald Goodall, revived one's almost extinguished hopes of once more hearing opera sung, as it should be, by singers capable of communicating the drama to the audience chiefly by the quality of their vocal tone.[15]

Dyneley Hussey in *The Spectator* was impressed by Terry's acting and the quality of her voice, but thought she still had a lot to learn:

> She must, for instance, obey the conductor in matters of tempo; if she disagrees with him, let them settle their difference beforehand, off the stage. In this instance I thought Mr Goodall in the right.[16]

Goodall seemed incapable of getting a bad review at this time, though the BBC continued to hold a low opinion of his work. He finally achieved a studio concert with the BBC Orchestra on 29 December 1945. There was only one three-hour rehearsal, but he was familiar with the works in the programme – the *Hebrides* Overture, Haydn's *Surprise* Symphony, the *Siegfried Idyll* and three dances from *The Bartered Bride*. Eric Warr, unsuccessful as a conductor, but an able administrator at the BBC, delivered the *coup de grâce* to any hopes Goodall might have had of further engagements:

> A note from Denny yesterday about the quality of this performance reminded me that I had placed the recording of it in various overseas broadcasts and also that I had, in fact, listened to the broadcast on Saturday afternoon. It was a bad performance. The orchestra's tone was sour and its intonation frequently poor, and the Siegfried Idyll was dull and insensitive. I have replaced the programme.[17]

Fortunately for Goodall, he had plenty of other irons in the fire. During rehearsals for the *Grimes* revival he was asked by Benjamin Britten to conduct the premiere of his new opera, *The Rape of Lucretia*, which was to be the sole offering at Glyndebourne's first post-war festival in July 1946.

Glyndebourne's owner, John Christie, had wanted Beecham to re-open the festival with a season of *Carmen, Figaro* and *Die Zauberflöte*, but the plan had collapsed in November 1945 after disagreements between the two men over repertory, singers and orchestra. There were also problems about finding a chorus and getting Glyndebourne ready in time; during the war it had been used as a home for evacuee children. Rudolf Bing, Christie's general manager, first heard that Britten was writing a new opera from Eric Crozier, whose support he had enlisted in an abortive scheme to amalgamate Glyndebourne and Sadler's Wells.[18] Britten, disillusioned by his experiences with a conventional opera company, had decided that his next stage work would involve much smaller forces than *Grimes* – a cast of only eight, an ensemble of twelve instrumentalists and no chorus. Because *The Rape of Lucretia* demanded a relatively small budget to put on, it seemed to Bing the perfect answer to his impelling need for a festival production. John Christie, impressed by the success of *Grimes*, agreed that Glyndebourne should accept managerial and financial responsibility for it.

On 7 January 1946, Bing wrote to Goodall, saying he was happy to confirm Britten's wish to have him as musical director. But a week later, after meeting

Goodall for the first time, Bing changed his mind. He wrote to Christie's wife, the soprano Audrey Christie:

> I am afraid [Goodall] is what John would call "a little man." This may be of course an unfair judgement but one cannot help forming an opinion if one talks to a man. I said so to Britten over the telephone this morning and I cannot help feeling that for this particular work, and with the lack of other really suitable conductors, Hans [Oppenheim, a member of the pre-war music staff at Glyndebourne] would be by far the best choice ... [*Lucretia*] is very much on chamber music lines and will require more than anything else superb coaching and superlative workmanship, and of all musicians working in this country only Hans can do it ... If [Britten] insists on having Goodall and if we can get him – which incidentally is not at all certain – that is the end of it and we must hope for the best, but I will resist for all I am worth ...[19]

Bing could be forgiven for misjudging Goodall's personality – Goodall may well have been at his most diffident and monosyllabic during their meeting – but he was demonstrating surprising ignorance, or it may have been prejudice, when it came to Goodall's musical abilities, since "superb coaching and superlative workmanship" were precisely the qualities that Goodall could bring to the enterprise. Christie, however, accepted Bing's verdict and so, apparently, did Britten. The post of musical director was taken away from Goodall and given instead to the Swiss conductor, Ernest Ansermet, who enjoyed a substantial reputation as an interpreter of contemporary music. Ansermet's appointment went some way to satisfying Christie's wish to inject a more international flavour into the proceedings, which he found a bit cosy and English for his taste.

Goodall was made Ansermet's assistant, with the promise that he would be given performances to conduct both at Glyndebourne and on the tour that was to follow the festival. He was also made responsible for picking the members of the orchestra. It has often been claimed that Goodall conducted *Lucretia* on alternate nights at Glyndebourne. In fact he was allotted only four of the fourteen performances. If he felt that the decision to replace him as principal conductor was a slap in the face, he did not admit to it, though it must have hurt none the less. Assembling the orchestra proved a harder task than anticipated. Some of the players Goodall wanted, including all four members of the Hurwitz String Quartet, were still in the army when he auditioned them. The quartet's leader, Emanuel Hurwitz, and its viola player, Kenneth Essex, were released in time for the premiere, but their two colleagues, Jordan Lauland and Terence Weil, were not, and were replaced by two future Amadeus Quartet players, Peter Schidlof and Martin Lovett.[20]

For producer, Christie was keen to have Carl Ebert, who with the conductor Fritz Busch had been one of the twin artistic pillars of pre-war Glyndebourne.

This time Britten stood firm and insisted on the job going to Crozier. There was no argument over Glyndebourne's first choice for the title-role, Kathleen Ferrier. Christie had wanted her as Carmen, though in Beecham's opinion, "no contralto has ever succeeded in doing anything with the role but make a complete ass of herself."[21] Lucretia seemed a more suitable role for her stage debut.

Because the fourteen performances were being given in the space of only sixteen days, the opera was double-cast. Nancy Evans was the second Lucretia, while Peter Pears and Joan Cross shared the roles of Male and Female Chorus with Aksel Schiøtz and Flora Nielsen. The soprano role of Lucretia's maid, Lucia, was shared by Margaret Ritchie and Leslie Duff, who before the war had both sung in Goodall's Bruckner performances at St Alban's, Holborn. Rehearsals began at Glyndebourne on 10 June. Sadler's Wells released Goodall to work in Sussex, though to Bing's annoyance he had to return to London for ballet performances and the occasional opera. Bing felt that some singers, Ferrier included, needed all the coaching they could get in view of their inexperience in opera.[22]

Goodall was remembered by colleagues at Glyndebourne that season as a solitary, shadowy figure, who rarely mixed with them during the breaks in rehearsal. "He was a loner," said Leslie Duff. "He never opened his mouth to give an opinion about anything except the music. I felt that there was something wrong in his life, that he wasn't particularly happy."[23] Goodall admired Ansermet, and got on well with him, but was prickly when it came to the management, which was understandable, given that Bing had been responsible for his demotion. Bing's assistant, Moran Caplat, found that "dealing with Reggie was never easy; he seemed to feel he was not being given the respect that was due to him."[24] Respect was a pre-occupation of Goodall's. Together with twenty-five other members of the company, he was put up in the main house, where he was allotted the room once occupied by Childs, John Christie's butler. The choice was no doubt accidental, but to some it seemed symbolic. Eric Crozier recalled asking Goodall what his ambition was. "Working in a theatre where they are performing Wagner and just being part of it," he replied.[25]

The Rape of Lucretia did not enjoy the general critical acclaim that had greeted *Peter Grimes*. Britten's music was widely praised, but reviewers found Ronald Duncan's libretto pretentious and the Christian moralising tacked on to the story absurd, a criticism still levelled at the work more than sixty years later. The nine-week tour took in Manchester, Liverpool, Edinburgh, Glasgow, Sadler's Wells Theatre and Oxford, a remarkable sixty-one performances in all. Goodall conducted thirty-two of them; the remainder went to Hans Oppenheim, who had been appointed head of music staff at Glyndebourne. Bing's hopes for a box-office success to match that of *Grimes* were not fulfilled.[26]

At Glyndebourne, audiences had been healthy, but on tour, especially in the north of England and Glasgow, they were derisory.

The tour ended on 28 September. Two days later the company sailed for Holland, where, at the invitation of the Dutch Wagner society, it gave six further performances. Goodall conducted twice in Amsterdam (where Britten himself conducted the first night) and once in The Hague, but his time in Holland is best remembered by some for a fracas in an Amsterdam nightclub, where he was attracted to a Dutch woman sitting at the next table. The more Goodall pressed his suit, the angrier the woman's four male companions, all from the Dutch East Indies, became, until it seemed that one of them was about to pull a knife on him. Moran Caplat hustled Goodall into the street to safety.[27]

On 11 October, Goodall conducted a studio performance of *Lucretia* for the BBC's Third Programme, which had been inaugurated only twelve days earlier. The BBC had wanted to broadcast the opera direct from Glyndebourne, but had been stymied by the fact that the second act clashed with the nine o'clock news in the Home Service.[28] (In the case of *Grimes*, the news had fitted exactly into the interval between its second and third acts). As far as the BBC was concerned, there was no question of changing the time of the news for *Lucretia*: there would be a national outcry. Nor was Glyndebourne prepared to delay the start of the second act: members of the audience would miss the last train back to London (because of petrol-rationing, few travelled to the festival by car). Since *Lucretia* was thought too highbrow for the only other domestic radio channel, by now renamed the Light Programme, the opera had to await the arrival of the more flexible Third. As a result of its procrastination, the BBC was beaten to the post by Dutch radio, which on 4 October relayed a performance of *Lucretia* conducted by Oppenheim from the Amsterdam Stadsschouwburg.[29]

Considering that John Christie had lost £11,000 on *Lucretia*[30], and was not keen on either the opera or its composer (Britten, for his part, detested Christie), it is to his credit that he was prepared to accept another work from the same source for the next festival. However he made it clear to Britten and Crozier that he would not underwrite any more tours.[31] Composer and producer reacted swiftly. Because they considered touring an important element in their plans, they decided to form their own company, and wrote to Christie offering to perform at the festival, but not under Glyndebourne's management; they would come as guests. They also offered to buy John Piper's sets for *Lucretia*.[32] Relations between the two sides became frosty, though by the end of the year Bing had grown conciliatory, and it was confirmed that the Britten-Crozier company, at first called the New London Opera Group, would present a new work by Britten, as well as a revival of *Lucretia*, at the 1947 festival. Glyndebourne itself would mount a production of Gluck's *Orfeo*, with Kathleen Ferrier in the title-role.

Orfeo opened the festival on 19 June. On the following evening the Britten-Crozier company, now billed as the "English Opera Group Ltd who come as visitors to Glyndebourne," gave the premiere of Britten's new comic opera, *Albert Herring*, with the composer himself conducting. A fortnight later Goodall – who by now had joined the staff of Covent Garden – conducted the first of three performances of *Lucretia*, to which Britten and Duncan had made a number of revisions. Seven of the instrumentalists were new, as were several of the singers, and Goodall constantly interrupted rehearsals for corrections. When things went wrong musically, Goodall was much given to shaking his fists in the air or dashing up on to the stage, where he "literally jumped up and down" with fury. Some of the younger singers found his tantrums distressing.[33] Crozier was maddened by what he considered time-wasting (and money-wasting) behaviour.[34]

Feelings ran high off-stage, too. The Junius, Denis Dowling, one of several newcomers not long demobilised from the Forces, was astonished to be warned by the English Opera Group management not to talk about the war in front of Britten and Pears, for fear of upsetting them. Travelling to Glyndebourne by train for the start of rehearsals, Dowling found himself in the same compartment as Goodall, who soon fell to talking about Wagner and Germany. He claimed that much of the anti-German feeling prevalent in Britain had been fuelled by government propaganda. Dowling was appalled. As a lieutenant in the 58th Light Anti-Aircraft Regiment, he had entered Belsen within days of its liberation and had acted as liaison officer between the camp and British divisional headquarters. He had seen bodies being bulldozed into the mass graves. "If I had had a different temperament," said Dowling, "I would have hit Reggie. I remember asking myself, what sort of a set-up is this? Here were these conscientious objectors, and they had a pro-Hitler man coming along as conductor. They seemed able to shut things out of their minds altogether. There was a very funny atmosphere at Glyndebourne. People were frightened of each other. I was riled, but like others I was restarting my career after the war. You kept your mouth closed."[35] Dowling was not the only ex-serviceman at Glyndebourne who felt he was living in cloud-cuckoo-land.

In 1947 the BBC more than made up for its past dilatoriness by broadcasting both *Albert Herring* and *The Rape of Lucretia*, not once, but twice. In addition, arrangements were completed for HMV to record an abridged version of *Lucretia* immediately after the festival was over. HMV had wanted to make the recording the previous year, but three of Britten's first choices for it, Pears, Ferrier and Ansermet, were all under contract to Decca.[36] By 1947 only Pears had switched to HMV, and it was decided to go ahead with Nancy Evans and Goodall instead of the other two. (Ferrier recorded the Glyndebourne *Orfeo* for Decca.)

Because of the commercial risk involved, HMV approached the British Council for financial help. The chairman of the council's music committee, Arthur Bliss, was in favour of the recording, but believed the opera would have to be cut by almost half because of probable expense. William Walton thought Bliss's estimate too generous; in his opinion, four 78 rpm sides (about sixteen minutes of music) were sufficient. Walton also opined that the composer was not always the best judge of his own work when it came to choosing extracts – which caused Steuart Wilson, the Arts Council's music director and a member of the Covent Garden board, to suggest that Britten should nominate someone to choose the bits for him.[37] In the end good sense prevailed, and sixteen sides, about two-thirds of the opera, were recorded.

The *Gramophone Record* thought the result "a veritable triumph" and "by a long way the most important contribution to recorded English opera the gramophone has yet given us." *The Gramophone* devoted almost a page to a review by Alec Robertson. Joan Cross, Peter Pears, Nancy Evans, Margaret Ritchie and Denis Dowling were picked out for special mention, and there was "a word of praise for Reginald Goodall's fine handling of the orchestra."[38]

No sooner had the recording been completed, than the English Opera Group took *Albert Herring* and *Lucretia* to Holland and Switzerland, under the auspices of the British Council. Goodall conducted *Lucretia* in Scheveningen and Amsterdam, and then, on 14 August, at the Lucerne Festival. Between Amsterdam and Lucerne he returned to London to rehearse the repertory for Covent Garden's forthcoming tour of the provinces. Britten wanted him to stay on in Lucerne to conduct *Herring* on 18 August[39], but Goodall was due in Glasgow the following night to conduct his first *Turandot* (with Eva Turner) for the new Covent Garden opera company, which he found a far more seductive prospect. Goodall never appeared with the English Opera Group again, nor was he invited to conduct the premiere of any of the composer's subsequent operas. "Ben thought I should have stayed with him," said Goodall, "but joining Covent Garden was a big thing for me. I didn't want to abandon it." Ironically, Britten had helped Goodall to get the job at Covent Garden in the first place by recommending him to David Webster.[40]

Even if the composer had not taken umbrage, it is unlikely that Goodall would have stayed with the English Opera Group much longer. For a start he did not share Britten's predilection for small-scale opera: he felt that if *Albert Herring* was a portent of things to come, then it was time for him to withdraw anyway. He found *Herring* "silly – that's the word, silly; that prissy Englishness would have been knocked out of Ben if he had studied abroad. His entourage persuaded him to do that sort of thing, you know." Although Goodall was greatly moved by parts of *Lucretia*, in particular the final section, starting with Lucretia's entrance and her confession to Collatinus, he missed in it the sonorities that Britten achieved with the larger orchestra in *Grimes*. "Ben had anguish in him," he said. "Grimes expressed it."

The thread of overt homosexuality that runs through the later operas seemed to Goodall too self-conscious: "I always felt that being a homosexual worried Ben a lot. Stupidly! Yes! He was too much of an East Anglican [*sic*]. He had that East Anglican guilt." Goodall's felicitous portmanteau-phrase, "East Anglican," may not appear in any dictionary, but it conveys his meaning successfully. He found Britten's puritan streak unnerving and often told the story of the night he and Margaret Ritchie arrived back late at Glyndebourne after dining at Lewes. Britten and Pears ("they looked so tall") were standing by the fireplace. "Reggie!" said Britten disapprovingly, as though addressing some naughty schoolboy. "Where have you been?" Goodall preferred a headier approach to life and art.

CHAPTER 11

Covent Garden

G OODALL'S invitation to join the staff of the Covent Garden Opera –
as assistant conductor to the musical director, Karl Rankl – had come in
September 1946. His salary was to be £35 a week, double what he was getting
at Sadler's Wells. His contract with the Sadler's Wells Opera still had eleven
months to run, but the company agreed to release him "for anything as important as that, because ... it may be a long time before you get the chance again."[1]
Goodall moved to Covent Garden on 11 November, hopeful that at last he
might be able to escape Verdi's clutches and concentrate instead on the German repertoire, and on the works of Wagner in particular. He was to be disappointed. During the first season there were no operas by Wagner and only one,
Der Rosenkavalier, by Richard Strauss. Not unreasonably, Karl Rankl, an Austrian by birth though British by adoption, chose to conduct it himself.

Critics and audiences were delighted that Covent Garden was being used for
opera again, but were generally disappointed by the *Carmen* that Rankl conducted on the opening night, 14 January 1947, with Queen Mary and members
of the Labour government in the audience. "We all wish the new Covent Garden Trust success, " wrote Philip Hope-Wallace in *Time and Tide*," but that must
not stop me from describing their first effort ... as a dire penance for anyone who
really loves this epitome of the Gallic spirit, this gem of the French lyric stage."[2]
Like the rest of the repertory, *Carmen* was sung in English, a policy that was to
be pursued until the end of the 1950s, though exceptions were soon to be made
for *Tristan* and *The Ring*. It was agreed that foreign artists could be called in
for certain roles – provided they sang them in English – but "politically" it was
considered important that there should not be too many of them.[3]

Carmen was followed sixteen days later by another French opera, Massenet's
Manon. This time Goodall conducted. The theatre was freezing. The coke for the
heating boilers had not been delivered, and the audience, long inured to shortages of all kinds, sat in their overcoats and hacked away bronchitically. Hope-
Wallace thought Goodall "conducted with real feeling for tempi and nuance,
with affection and delicacy," a view shared by the *Times* critic, who wrote that
"texture and tempo were right, details of the playing made their mark; the music
had its proper sweetness without cloying." There was less enthusiasm for Frederick Ashton's production and for the principal singers, who included a young
American, Virginia McWatters, as Manon and the veteran English tenor Heddle

Nash as des Grieux. Desmond Shawe-Taylor found them "frankly inadequate, Mr Nash sounding dog-tired and Miss McWatters supplying a top-dressing of near coloratura which failed to redeem a middle register of the musical comedy order; I know she is pretty, but prettiness is not enough."[4] The twelve performances did poor business. Goodall thought *Manon* suited him: "Harmonically, French music is far more interesting than Italian. It's closer to German music."

Goodall pleaded with Webster not to give him anything by Verdi to conduct, but to no avail. His second new production of the season was *Il Trovatore*. Ironically Goodall emerged from it with some credit, though nobody else did, apart from the Azucena, Edith Coates. The unfortunate Manrico, the English tenor Arthur Carron, who had spent the war years at the New York Metropolitan, came a vocal cropper in the "Miserere" and from the gallery earned the first post-war boos to be heard at the Opera House. Already the policy of performing the repertory in the vernacular was causing difficulties. There were not enough experienced British singers to staff one permanent opera company in London, let alone two; and in any case, many of the best artists still saw their careers in terms of oratorio rather than opera.

After the London season the company went on tour to Glasgow, Liverpool, Manchester, Birmingham and Croydon. Goodall conducted numerous performances of *Carmen, Trovatore* and Puccini's *Turandot*, the cause of his break with the English Opera Group:

> I conducted a lot of Puccini's operas. I much preferred him to Verdi, chiefly because of the harmonies, the colours, the whole texture of Puccini's music. Verdi is all on the top line – all melody. For me that's not interesting. Take "La donna è mobile." It's just a tune. You can't do anything with it harmonically. Now play the basic notes of the *Tristan* prelude, the opening phrase. It may not seem to mean much at first – but add the harmony and it speaks everything. It evokes a mood. That's what I like about Wagner.

The only Verdi opera Goodall claimed to like was *Otello*, though he never conducted it.

Rankl endured a hail of brickbats during his five seasons as musical director at Covent Garden, both from the press and from individuals like Beecham, who branded his appointment "the mystery of mysteries."[5] Goodall, however, took a positive view of him: "Rankl knew the workings of a German theatre. He established the right number of répétiteurs and instilled a sense of discipline." He may not have been in the class of Furtwängler or Bruno Walter, but recordings that have survived of him conducting Act 1 of *Tristan* and part of *Götterdämmerung* at Covent Garden suggest he was a conductor to be reckoned with in the German repertoire. He created an excellent chorus, for which he held auditions all over Britain, and an efficient orchestra, which he built round the nucleus of the Sadler's Wells Ballet orchestra. A nervous man, he had an alarming and unpredictable temper, but in 1946 he was one of the few musicians in the country with sufficient practical experience to build up an opera company from scratch. A pupil of Schoenberg, he had been musical director of opera houses in Wiesbaden, Graz and Prague before the war, as well as assistant to Otto Klemperer at the Kroll Oper in Berlin. Rankl was not Jewish, but he had a Jewish wife, and he came to Britain as a refugee in 1939. Webster's decision to make him musical director was shrewd, even if it did not always seem so at the time.

With Goodall's appointment, Webster took a much greater risk. Rankl needed an *erster Kapellmeister*, a senior staff conductor who could turn his hand to anything from taking over a performance in an emergency to helping out with the day-to-day administration. In this respect Goodall was hardly the right man. True, he had enjoyed a major success with *Peter Grimes*, but his knowledge of the general operatic repertoire was very limited. Before going to the Opera House he had conducted only ten operas professionally, two of which, *The Barber of Seville* and *Rigoletto*, he had no wish to conduct again. It was not a promising situation. Rankl assumed, wrongly as it turned out, that Goodall would grow into the job.

During the first three months of the company's second season, which opened in October 1947, Goodall conducted revivals of *Turandot, Trovatore* and *Carmen*, as well as performances of a new production of *Grimes*, which he rescued after a dismal first night under Rankl. *Grimes* was brought back later in the season, in preparation for guest performances at the Monnaie in Brussels and the Paris Opera. By now Richard Lewis and an American soprano, Doris Doree, had replaced Peter Pears and Joan Cross in the roles of Grimes and Ellen Orford. Britten found the revival under-rehearsed and in some cases miscast. He sent Webster an angry letter, which ended: "The fact that the performance might be said to have 'come off' was due to the untiring energy of the conductor – Reginald Goodall."[6]

Goodall travelled ahead of the company to rehearse the Monnaie orchestra, which was to play for the performances in Brussels. He reported back to Britten in a letter chock-full of the dashes he preferred to other forms of punctuation:

> Le Grand Hotel
> Brussels
> Wednesday June 2nd/49 [actually 1948]

My Dear Benjamin,

I arrived here early this morning to commence the rehearsals for Grimes – only last night they gave Albert Herring at the Opera which unfortunately I missed – but I thought you would like to know of the great success it had and the intelligent appreciation & love of your music.

I had a talk with the man who translated "Albert Herring" – he likes the music of it even more than Lucretia – he finds it more "spiritual" and at the same time more "tonal" for the public – instancing the C major fugue (is it a Fugue? – but you wouldn't know would you!) also he finds the orchestration fuller as the piano is more integrated with the orchestra than in Lucretia.

I had my first rehearsal with the orchestra and was very surprised & pleased that they played it so well and with such understanding – the strings are particularly good with glowing tone but unfortunately the trombones are weak – the 2nd and 3rd especially so – and that makes it difficult to get a right sonority in all the main passages – the 1st bassoon has a lovely vibrato – he sounds like a saxophone – you can imagine it in "I had to go from pub to pub" we farely [*sic*] lurch along.

Please remember [me] to Peter – I wish he was singing it here – Reggie

The formal "My dear Benjamin" rather than the usual "Dear Ben" indicates a wariness in Goodall's approach to the composer, while the air of sycophancy that pervades the first two paragraphs suggests that Goodall was trying to make amends for his known dislike of *Albert Herring*. The joke about the fugue comes as welcome relief.

A month later Goodall recorded a series of excerpts from *Grimes* for Columbia, with Pears, Cross and the Covent Garden orchestra, but the composer, who supervised, refused to allow the results to be released. According to the Earl of Harewood, who attended the sessions, Britten was unhappy about Pears's contribution when he heard the test pressings. He thought Pears neither sounded authoritative enough, nor showed sufficient vocal maturity in the role.[7] It was a view shared by many critics at the time. Fortunately the composer relented in 1972 and allowed eight of the historic 78 r.p.m. sides to appear on LP. For the critic Alan Blyth they seemed "to represent the work at white heat, straight off the stage, in a way not equalled even by [Colin] Davis. Goodall makes the score even more immediate than either Davis or the composer and obtains electric playing from the Royal Opera House Orchestra."[8] Finally, in 1993, all eleven sides appeared on CD. Goodall, hearing them in old age, thought Pears's singing of the mad scene "marvellous," though he confessed he had never been entirely convinced by the tenor's portrayal of the tormented East Coast fisherman. To Goodall's ears, Pears sounded too polite and middle-class for the role: "There was something about Pears; he had a style. But I liked Jon Vickers's Grimes. It was more manful, a more operatic performance."

No one disputed Goodall's mastery in *Grimes*, but his conducting of other operas in the repertory caused uneasiness among the Covent Garden trustees, who felt he was making too little impact on both press and public. Rankl also came in for continuing criticism. In December 1947 the board discussed the possibility of employing a guest conductor for six months in the season, perhaps the celebrated Italian, Victor de Sabata, or the 39-year-old Herbert von Karajan. The trustees were aware that Rankl was paranoid about guests (for fear they might prove better than him), but felt he could not object to an outsider taking over the Italian repertoire, since he himself had shown no particular interest in it. However one trustee, the ubiquitous Steuart Wilson, argued strongly against the proposal, "both on the general ground that any change in conductors at Covent Garden at this stage was unnecessary, and also, in particular, expressing doubts of the ability and standing of Karajan."

The board returned to the matter a month later. Wilson now said that if any-one were to be called in as a guest conductor, it should be Stanford Robinson of the BBC's opera department. His fellow trustees did not agree with him. They preferred another capable but routine BBC conductor, Clarence Raybould, who, it was suggested, might "eventually replace Mr Goodall." In March it was proposed that Raybould and yet another candidate, Warwick Braithwaite, should be asked to conduct trial performances, though Raybould fell out of the running when he demanded equal status with the musical director.[9]

Given the board's view on Goodall, it is odd that he should have been asked to conduct a new production that season of another Verdi opera, *La Traviata*. It opened in April 1948 and did nothing to enhance his reputation. The direc-tor was Tyrone Guthrie, the Violetta Elisabeth Schwarzkopf, who had recently joined the company from the Vienna State Opera. Like the rest of the cast she sang in English. Schwarzkopf's reviews were mixed; Goodall's were poor. "The music," wrote Desmond Shawe-Taylor, "showed many signs of careful rehearsal (e.g. the unusually effective off-stage effects), but Reginald Goodall's handling of the score was prim, and deficient in Italian sparkle and impulse, especially in the vivacious first act."[10]

On 22 April, in the middle of the *Traviata*s, Goodall took over a single performance of *The Mastersingers* from Rankl, with a cast of British singers. It was the first time he had ever conducted an opera by Wagner, and might well have been the last, because six days after it he wrote to Rankl to say that he wanted to apply for a vacant conducting position with the Sadler's Wells Bal-let: "I like my work with the opera company but I feel there is not the need for me – and with the ballet company as there are only two conductors I should have a regular number of performances each week."[11] Goodall did not get the job. It went instead to Warwick Braithwaite, who was promised a number of opera dates as well.

Braithwaite's appointment gave rise to an unfortunate misunderstanding. On 5 August 1948 several newspapers reported that he was to join, not the ballet, but the opera company. This, said *The Times*, followed the resignation of Reginald Goodall, who had "recently completed two whole opera seasons with the Covent Garden company, and is now, it is understood, anxious to extend the scope of his work." Goodall, normally an assiduous reader of *The Times*, was on holiday with his wife at Killarney and missed the item. The first he heard of it came in a letter from the Opera House:

5 August 1948

Dear Goodall,

I was most surprised as you probably were to read in the "Times" this morning that you were supposed to have left Covent Garden!

Needless to say the information did not come from my office and I am having it corrected right away.

Yours sincerely
David Webster

Goodall was anxious to discover the source of the rumour, but it was never revealed. Corrections were slow in coming and he had to resort to solicitors to secure them. Braithwaite's arrival did nothing for his self-confidence. Nor did the emergence as a regular conductor of a member of Covent Garden's music staff, Peter Gellhorn, who had Rankl's ear. Gellhorn was appointed "assistant to the musical director." Goodall, a hopeless company politician, was unable to cope with the highly competitive situation. At Covent Garden there was no Lawrance Collingwood or Joan Cross to stand up for him. Rankl was too busy defending his own position to help and was in any case disappointed that Goodall had not proved more adept. Webster had the trustees breathing down his neck about both Rankl and Goodall. Goodall was not without friends at Covent Garden – the composer John Gardner, for example, a member of the music staff until 1952, was unwavering in his support – but they were not in positions of sufficient authority to promote his cause.

During the 1948–49 season, the company's third, Goodall was given thirty-four performances to conduct, but perversely (since by then there cannot have been anyone at the Opera House, from Webster to the stage-doorman, who was not aware of his strengths and weaknesses) thirty-three of them were of operas by Verdi – *Traviata*, *Trovatore* and *Aida*. The thirty-fourth was of *Grimes*. Goodall looked on unhappily as Braithwaite shared *The Mastersingers* with Rankl, and Gellhorn conducted performances of *Fidelio* and *Rosenkavalier*. His spirits lifted briefly when the Hamburg tenor Rudolf Schock came to sing Alfredo to Schwarzkopf's Violetta. "Two Germans!" said Goodall. "It suited me, who wanted to turn everything into Wagner. The Italians would have nearly died. I hated the rum-te-tum. I hated Verdi. Schwarzkopf was lovely. Very distinguished. I was terrible. I've apologised to her since then."

For the title-role in *Aida* he had another star from the Vienna State Opera, the flamboyant Bulgarian soprano, Ljuba Welitsch. "I didn't like the opera," said Goodall, "but Welitsch was like a tiger on heat. She was wonderful." However, singers of Welitsch's calibre were the exception rather than the rule, and Goodall felt that too often he was being palmed off with mediocre performers:

> I remember rushing up to Webster's office one day to complain about some awful soprano they'd given me. He was sitting behind his desk. I said, "She's impossible; she's just a raw voice." Webster raised his eyebrows. He said, "Reggie, I'm surprised about that. We think she has distinct possibilities." She never made it. I know when a voice is no good.

The more frustrated Goodall was by events, the more withdrawn and unco-operative he became. In Leeds during the 1949 tour he declined to take a curtain-call after *Grimes*, despite repeated calls from the audience for him to do so.[12] The stage manager reported back to Webster in London that Goodall had "emphatically refused to do this, although we took in all nine curtain calls in the hope that he would appear." It had not been an isolated incident, he said. Goodall had refused to take a call at his last four performances. Could Webster do something about it?[13]

Webster wrote to Goodall at Birmingham, the company's next port of call:

11th April 1949

Dear Reg,

We would all feel very much happier if you would take the odd curtain call from time to time!

I do not know whether you just hate the business of appearing on the stage, but the public like to see the conductor and say "thank you" in one way or another and I think it would be good if you could take the calls.

Yours sincerely,
Best wishes,
David Webster

It was not simply a matter of modesty on Goodall's part. He was distressed by the standard of many of the performances, which all too often were under-rehearsed. Some thought he complained too much.

During the Birmingham visit Goodall conducted a performance of *The Mastersingers*. The orchestra was much reduced in size, while the guild processions in Act 3 were cut completely, because they could not be fitted on to the Theatre

Royal's stage, which was much smaller than Covent Garden's. As a result the orchestral interlude between the act's two scenes ran straight into the Dance of the Apprentices. The join was clumsy, both musically and dramatically. To compound the problems, the first clarinet, Richard Temple Savage, claimed that Goodall's tempo for the dance was too slow and refused to play it. The row that broke out between the two men afterwards was not patched up for four years.[14] The performance went unreviewed, in spite of the fact that the Eva was Elisabeth Schwarzkopf. (The local critics had attended a performance earlier in the week under Rankl, with Blanche Turner in the role.) Two years later Schwarzkopf was to sing Eva at the re-opened Bayreuth Festival.

Meanwhile the Covent Garden board was still wondering what was to be done about Goodall. James Smith, who was both chairman of Sadler's Wells and a Covent Garden trustee, reported that he had inquired about the possibility of work being found for him at Sadler's Wells, but had been told that there was no chance of a regular opening.[15] In July 1949 Webster called Goodall into his office and told him that his services as a conductor were no longer required. He could stay on as a coach if he liked. Goodall agreed to do so; he felt he had little alternative. His pay was cut from £35 a week to £20, a drop of forty-three per cent. On 29 July Webster confirmed the new arrangement in writing, adding that he thought it "very likely indeed that we will ask you to do odd performances in the Pit and we will try to find you a little extra on those occasions." The blow to Goodall's pride (and pocket) was painful, though, as he later admitted, it was a relief not having to put up with "all the baloney and hoo-ha" any longer: "At Covent Garden they thought conducting was the apex. But I discovered that working on an opera and preparing singers could be just as satisfying."

In the event Goodall conducted *Traviata* and *Grimes* during the 1949–50 season. The Verdi, with very much a second-division cast, was not well received by the press. "It is easy to forgive a wrong note or two when the music is played with gusto," wrote the critic of *The Times*; "last night the orchestra's performance under Mr Reginald Goodall showed a painful deficiency in both spirit and ensemble."[16] The following season Goodall did not appear in the pit at all. His career as a conductor seemed to be over. John Gardner said in 1987, "If I had been asked about Reggie thirty-five years ago, I would have said he was finished. They had beaten him, trampled on him. He didn't even put up a fight. That he might resurface one day seemed impossible."[17]

Rankl's humiliation was even more complete than Goodall's. In January 1950 the board accepted a proposal from Webster that the celebrated Austrian-born conductor, Erich Kleiber, should be invited to Covent Garden as a guest. Rankl knew nothing of the plan until the end of February, when the Machiavellian

Webster dealt him a double blow. Having told Rankl that Kleiber would be coming for three months in the winter, Webster then said that the post of musical director was to be abolished at the end of the following season. In future there would be two principal conductors, each responsible for his own productions. Webster hoped very much that Rankl would agree to be one of them.[18] Presumably he also hoped that Kleiber would be the other, though no name was mentioned. For Rankl it was a bitter pill, but he decided to swallow it.

Kleiber's first opera, in December 1950, was *Rosenkavalier*, which in itself was a slight for Rankl, since it had been one of his own successes at Covent Garden. The audience sensed that something special was about to happen, for, as Desmond Shawe-Taylor noted, "the cheers which swept round the house when Dr Kleiber made his first appearance were more than a welcome to a distinguished visitor; they sounded uncommonly like the cheers of a beleagured garrison at the sight of the rescuing force."[19] Kleiber's impact on orchestra, chorus and principal singers was palpable. "Those who think the role of conductor greatly exaggerated," wrote the critic Martin Cooper, "would be hard put to it to find an explanation of the vastly improved finish, resonance, balance and vitality; and if they heard the same orchestra playing *Manon* and *Lohengrin* under their accustomed conductors [Braithwaite in the first opera; Rankl in the second], they could hardly doubt that Kleiber has already effected a regeneration."[20] It seemed that the veil of mediocrity that had hung over so much of the opera company's work was being lifted at last. Next, Kleiber conducted a new production of Tchaikovsky's *Queen of Spades*, followed by revivals of *Rigoletto, Carmen* and *The Magic Flute*. Goodall worked on all of them as a répétiteur.

Rankl's self-esteem was dented further when he learned from Webster that later in the season his arch-critic, Beecham, was to make a belated return to the house for *Die Meistersinger*.[21] Then came news that during the following season Kleiber would conduct the first staging in Britain of Alban Berg's *Wozzeck*. Kleiber was a logical choice for the opera, since he had conducted its premiere in Berlin in 1925, but, as Webster well knew, it had long been an ambition of Rankl's to conduct it himself. Rankl recognised that he had been driven into a corner. In April 1951 he resigned from the company, though he worked on until the end of the season. The board agreed that he should be awarded a special grant of £1,000. Rankl's last appearance as musical director was not at the Opera House, but on tour at the Empire Theatre, Liverpool. The opera was *Rosenkavalier*. After it, Rankl accepted a lift from Emanuel Young, who had recently joined the music staff. He got into Young's car and wept.[22] Rankl never conducted at Covent Garden again. A year later he became chief conductor of the Scottish National Orchestra and was then appointed musical director of the opera company in Sydney. He died in 1968.

Kleiber not only boosted the house's reputation; he also played a significant part in restoring Goodall's self-confidence, by asking for him as his assistant on *Wozzeck*. Goodall's task was to coach the singers and prepare the orchestra before Kleiber arrived for the main production rehearsals. The appointment ruffled a lot of feathers among the music staff, notably those of Norman Feasey, the senior répétiteur, who had first worked with Goodall during the Coates-Rosing season at Covent Garden in 1936. "When Kleiber came," Goodall recalled, "he was considered an important figure – and he knew he was one. He was very famous and was looked on with fear and trembling. When he chose to have me, it was a bit of a surprise for some people. They were furious."

Wozzeck was an immense undertaking for a company that was still relatively inexperienced. Nothing was left to chance. Most roles were double-cast, though the German soprano Christel Goltz was contracted to sing Marie (in English) at all six performances. In June 1951, seven months before the premiere, Goodall flew to East Berlin for five days to read through the score with Kleiber, who was conducting at the Staatsoper. Webster asked Goodall to locate the sets for the original production, but it turned out they had been destroyed, and Covent Garden commissioned new designs from Caspar Neher. Two months later, in order that he might gain experience of *Wozzeck* in the theatre, Goodall was sent to the Salzburg Festival, where Karl Böhm was conducting a new production of the opera, also with Neher's designs and Goltz as Marie. Goodall attended the final rehearsals and the first night. On his return to London he assured Webster that Covent Garden could do it very much better.[23] He then set out to prove it. During the next five months hardly a day went by when he did not have four or five coaching sessions with the singers, most of whom were readily available, since they were either based in London or were members of the resident company. (Goodall never ceased to lament that after the company strength was decimated in the 1970s it was no longer possible to work in this way; for *The Ring* the Opera House could barely field a trio of Rhinemaidens or Norns from its own resources, let alone a team of Valkyries.)

In November, Goodall began sectional rehearsals with the orchestra, so that by the time Kleiber arrived in December, the opera was in a fair state of preparedness. Kleiber was delighted to find that his faith in Goodall had been justified, while Goodall was grateful to Kleiber for rescuing him from threatened obscurity. Flunkey-like, he stuck close to Kleiber throughout the stage rehearsals. Sumner Austin was the official producer, but Kleiber himself was responsible for many details in the staging. Goodall took notes, conducted the orchestra while Kleiber checked the balance from the back of the auditorium, and passed on instructions to singers and stage staff. No doubt Kleiber recognised that Goodall was someone who could be bossed about.

The production was greeted as an important step forward for the company, and Goodall was justifiably proud of his part in it. Kleiber returned to the Opera House once more, in 1953, when Goodall assisted him on a new production of *Elektra*, as well as a revival of *Wozzeck*. Webster's dream of having Kleiber as Covent Garden's musical director came to nothing. He could offer neither enough money nor the conditions Kleiber demanded.

If Goodall had still been on the conducting staff, he would not have had the opportunity to work on *Wozzeck;* instead he would have been tied up with the umpteenth revival of *Traviata* or *Trovatore*. Nor could he have immersed himself in *The Ring*, as he did for the first time in May 1951, when he worked as a répétiteur on two cycles conducted by Rankl, with a cast that included Hans Hotter as Wotan, and Set Svanholm as both Siegmund and Siegfried. There were no fewer than three Brünnhildes: Anny Konetzni for *Die Walküre*, Astrid Varnay for *Siegfried*, and Kirsten Flagstad for *Götterdämmerung;* it was the last time Flagstad sang the role at Covent Garden. Goodall worked with several of the company singers, including Constance Shacklock, Barbara Howitt and Rosina Raisbeck as the Norns, Edgar Evans as Froh and Otakar Kraus as Alberich. He maintained that he learned more from these early sessions than the singers ever did.

The chief répétiteur for the cycles was Norman Feasey, at the time a far more experienced Wagnerian than Goodall; before the war he had worked on *The Ring* at Covent Garden with both Furtwängler and Beecham. Feasey was a popular figure at the Opera House, and by 1951 had become well entrenched as the house's main Wagner coach. He and Goodall became lifelong rivals, who never ceased to pour scorn on each other's work. The Dutch tenor, Hans Kaart, studying the role of Siegmund, was once startled to have the pages ripped out of his score by an irate Goodall, who shouted, "You've been working with Feasey!"[24] Feasey's view of Goodall, shared widely at Covent Garden, was uncompromising:

> John Gardner was very cross with Covent Garden for mishandling Reggie in the operas he was given to conduct and so on. I don't think it did. I think Reggie was his own worst enemy. Nothing was ever right for him. For example, if you offered him a Verdi opera, he'd say, why can't you give me Puccini? He was a strange mixture of uncertainty about himself and arrogance. His first performances were often the best. Then he'd start thinking about it. He'd think himself into a stupor. And he was impractical to a degree. He had an invisible beat. The leader of the orchestra told me of a *Traviata* with Reggie. It has a very quiet opening on strings. Reggie leaned down and whispered, "I've begun." Nobody had seen a thing. He hates the word "technique," but there's no harm in it if it's not pre-eminent. You must be sure that you're visible. That's common sense. I played the celesta for him in *Wozzeck* – a nightmare.[25]

None the less it was Goodall, and not Feasey, who was sent by Webster to represent Covent Garden at the first post-war Bayreuth Festival in July 1951. He heard *Parsifal* and *The Ring* under Hans Knappertsbusch, and *Meistersinger* under Karajan. Goodall's almost childlike delight at being in the holy of holies for the first time in his life is captured in a postcard, full of dashes and containing contradictory comments on the journey, that he wrote to his wife Eleanor almost as soon as he got there:

[28 July 1951]

Had a wonderful journey here – lovely day – very nice room with Frau Bader-schneider and here I am Saturday 6 pm sitting facing the Festspielhaus – what emotion as I came up the hill and thought of the feet that had trod here – RW – Cosima – Richter – Muck. I was rather bored with coming yesterday – but everything is so lovely in this country one can't help losing all one's grumpiness. I'll write you as soon as I get some note paper. Love Reggie

The next morning he attended Furtwängler's rehearsal of Beethoven's Ninth Symphony, which was to open the festival. That night Goodall dashed off another card to Eleanor:

[29 July 1951]

I went this morning to Villa Wahnfried & visited Wagner's grave. This evening Furtwängler did the 9th Symphony. What a wonderful occasion, the orchestra from all over Germany (no spivvy showiness) just great & wonderful understanding of all Beethoven said. I had supper afterwards in a lovely cafe out of town just by the Festspiel Haus[26] – Monday. Now we prepare for Parsifal – starts at 4 pm. What a pilgrimage – and ends at 11 pm!! Reggie

Goodall returned to the festival the following year. In some ways the second visit was even more intoxicating than the first. This time he was there for twelve days, and at the invitation of the composer's grandson, Wieland Wagner, attended rehearsals as well as performances. At a *Parsifal* rehearsal he was introduced to Knappertsbusch, who remembered him from Covent Garden in 1937, when Goodall had given the signal for the curtain to rise on *Salome*. Knappertsbusch invited him to sit in the orchestra pit for *Parsifal*. Goodall was also in the pit for Wieland Wagner's new production of *Tristan* under Karajan.

Goodall missed the 1953 festival, but was back in 1954 and then returned every year until 1962. He treated the visits as his summer holidays. Eleanor preferred to go to Ireland; sometimes Goodall joined her there for a few days after Bayreuth, sometimes not. "Reggie is in his element here," reported Covent Garden's technical director, John Sullivan, who was at Bayreuth in 1954, "he really wants to go up the hill on all fours."[27] Others remember Goodall leaping to his feet during a rehearsal for Act 2 of *Götterdämmerung* and shouting "Bloody marvellous!" as Hagen's vassals erupted on to the stage. He took many of his meals in the Bahnhof restaurant, where he made passes at the waitresses, who fended him off with apparent good humour and welcomed him back the following day. He spoke to everybody in his curious-sounding German, which he always pronounced as though it were English. The result was akin to Churchill's French, and all who heard it marvelled that such a committed Germanophile could have mastered the grammar, but not the sound and inflections of the language. It was particularly remarkable in view of his ability to teach British performers to sing so expressively in German.

Goodall was enthralled by Wieland Wagner's revolutionary – and controversial – productions, which, by abandoning naturalistic effects in favour of sets stripped to their bare essentials, threw unusual emphasis on both music and dramatic situation. Ernest Newman, the veteran English critic and Wagner scholar, wrote of the 1951 *Parsifal* that "we were conscious, for the first time, of the characters as Wagner must have seen them in his creative imagination, and the music, with nothing intruding now between it and us, spoke to us with a poignancy beyond the power of words to express."[28] Curiously, since his name became synonymous with post-war Bayreuth and with the *Parsifal* in particular, Knappertsbusch hated the production; he stayed away from the 1953 festival, claiming that Wieland Wagner's work as a producer came "close to parody".[29] Goodall, however, shared Newman's verdict that the composer's grandson was a "young genius." Wieland's 1956 production of *Meistersinger* gave many critics and members of the audience apoplexy, but not Goodall. He spoke of it rhapsodically: "In the second act he didn't show the streets of Nuremberg but evoked the spirit of [Richard] Wagner's creative vision. Just two lovely laurel trees suspended in a purple-blue light, and the music all breathing the magic and beauty of a midsummer night; the birds, the quintessence …,"[30] Goodall tried to persuade David Webster to invite Wieland Wagner to London, but without success. The ever-cautious Webster, claiming that London was not ready for such productions, turned down an offer from Wieland himself to stage *Tristan* at Covent Garden.[31]

Following Rankl's departure, the musical directorship at Covent Garden was left unfilled for four years. Many were considered for the post, including Sir John Barbirolli, Rudolf Kempe, Josef Krips and, an interesting choice, Benjamin Britten, but for one reason or another none of them took it on, though both Barbirolli and Kempe made frequent appearances at the Opera House during the interregnum. Warwick Braithwaite's contract was not renewed, but Goodall survived. He even made a brief reappearance in the pit during the 1952 provincial tour for *Turandot* and *Tosca*, the first operas he had conducted for two years.

He also conducted *Manon* for the Dublin Grand Opera Society. Meanwhile Covent Garden gave several newcomers a chance to conduct, notably a former hornplayer, Edward Downes, and John Pritchard, a protégé of Fritz Busch's at Glyndebourne. Downes was a familiar face to Goodall: as a 19-year-old student at the Royal College of Music, he had played (without the college's permission) in the Sadler's Wells pit for the first run of *Peter Grimes*. He had also played in numerous performances of *The Rape of Lucretia*.

At the beginning of 1953 Goodall conducted a single *Boris Godunov* at Covent Garden, followed by performances of *Fidelio* both in London and on tour. It was assumed with some confidence at the Opera House that the season would reach a triumphant climax in June with the gala-premiere of Benjamin Britten's new opera, *Gloriana*, written specially to mark the coronation of Queen Elizabeth II. Two months later the production was to be taken to Bulawayo in Southern Rhodesia (now Zimbabwe) for the Rhodes centenary celebrations. John Pritchard was chosen to conduct the premiere, but was not available to go to Africa. Webster half-hoped that Britten himself might conduct the Bulawayo performances, but the composer had other commitments. Britten wrote to Webster suggesting Vilem Tausky, Walter Susskind and Norman Del Mar as possible alternatives. "I will go on thinking," he concluded, "and send you postcards from time to time as ideas occur." Goodall's name was not mentioned.[32] Ideas cannot have occurred very often, for in the end it was Goodall who was given the job.

The gala, attended by the new Queen and Prince Philip, took place on 8 June, six days after the coronation itself. The audience – white tie and decorations *de rigueur*, even in the gallery – assumed that it was in for a modern *Merrie England*, but got instead the story of the bald, ageing Elizabeth I and her love for the young Earl of Essex. Given the occasion, many thought the subject tasteless. "The audience was cold, and rightly so," reported Beverley Baxter in the next day's *Evening Standard*. The applause lasted barely long enough for the singers to take a curtain-call. The music critics did not take kindly to the opera either, though reactions might have been more favourable if John Pritchard had known the opera better. Prodigiously gifted, but famously indolent, he had not left himself enough time to learn the score thoroughly. "A firmer hand would have made it more taut," wrote the critic of *The Times*. Goodall conducted two performances of *Gloriana* at the tail-end of the season, in order to familiarise himself with the opera before conducting it in Bulawayo. The *Times* critic thought it "fared better as a dramatic piece" in Goodall's hands than it had under Pritchard.[33]

The Rhodesian visit was hailed by the *Daily Herald* as the "biggest airlift ever in the world of entertainment."[34] In late July five piston-engined airliners flew the 200-strong company from Blackbushe in Hampshire to Bulawayo, a town of 40,000 inhabitants, "set in an unpopulated desolation of scrub and grassland." The *Herald* reporter estimated that it would take two days to reach Rhodesia (now it might take 24 hours), but Goodall's plane took four days, with stops in Nice, Malta, where repairs caused a 24-hour delay, Wadi Halfa in northern Sudan ("burning hot," Goodall noted in his diary), Khartoum, Juba, Nairobi and Tabora in Tanganyika (now Tanzania). Sets and costumes went by sea to Cape Town, from where they were taken by train to Rhodesia.

People came from all over white-man's Africa to visit the centenary exhibition and attend the operas in the Theatre Royal, a single-storey, hangar-like structure, holding up to 3,050 people, which had been thrown up specially for the occasion. Seats at the back were reserved for Africans, who for the first time in Rhodesia were allowed to join a white theatre audience. Goodall conducted *Gloriana* there no fewer than eight times. The other operas in the repertory, *Aida, La Bohème* and *Figaro*, were conducted by Barbirolli, Downes and Gellhorn respectively. When the company eventually got back to England, David Webster wrote to Britten:

> 4 September 1953

> I did send you a telegram from Bulawayo saying how fine Goodall was with Gloriana, very much better than our other gentleman and the performance itself was very striking. We had a very good house for the first, I gather not quite so good for the others, but I am told that the enthusiasm of the people who went was very considerable indeed, particularly the younger generation. I can't wait to do it here. Personally I'm awfully happy about having Goodall do Grimes, and if necessary Budd before the end of the season. Equally when we come to revive Gloriana again and if you don't do it yourself I think he should.

Britten was due to conduct *Peter Grimes* at Covent Garden in November, but was suffering from acute bursitis in his right arm. He replied to Webster on 6 September:

> I am so glad to hear about Reggie Goodhall [sic] in Gloriana. I had already heard golden things from Cranko & Joan Cross about him (stupidly, no telegram ever arrived from you about it). It is in more ways than one a relief, because I am afraid my arm is no better in spite of rest & medical treatment. So it looks as if he might have to do Grimes too.

John Cranko, who had choreographed the dances for *Gloriana*, was re-staging the *Grimes* at Covent Garden in adaptations of Tanya Moiseiwitsch's existing sets. Britten's arm did not clear up in time and Goodall replaced him as conductor. On the day of the first night, 14 November, Britten sent Goodall a telegram: "NO NEED FOR GOOD WISHES HAVE UTMOST CONFIDENCE

IN YOUR GREAT MUSICALITY AND GIFTS = BEN." The *Times* critic
reported two days later:

> The sea, i.e. the orchestra, was again, as at the first performance, in the sympa-
> thetic hands of Mr Reginald Goodall, who held the packed house just as spell-
> bound in the eloquent salt water (and other) interludes as when the curtain was
> up, and who achieved excellent balance between stage and orchestra pit without
> wasting any point in the composer's uncannily vivid scoring.

Erich Kleiber's wife, Ruth, wrote to Goodall from Cologne: "We were thrilled
to read of your wonderful success with Peter Grimes ... we couldn't be happier
if you were our son."[35]

Webster, as benevolent as he was ruthless, was delighted to have his faith in
Goodall restored. He may have felt let down by his wayward *Kapellmeister*, but
he had retained an affection for him none the less. He was even heard to remark,
"There's no doubt that Reggie has a touch of genius."[36] Goodall had mixed feelings about Webster. Asked if he got on with him, he once replied, "Yes, well no.
I did what he asked. He had a flair." He recalled being summoned to Webster's
office after the *Grimes*:

> Webster said, "Reggie, I think it's time for you to make a comeback" – he used
> to talk to me like that. And I said, "I don't want to make any comeback." I don't
> know what started him on that. But he offered me *Walküre* on the tour, and I
> said I'd do it.

> He didn't give me second-rate singers. It was a damn good cast; it must have
> cost a lot.

The "damn good cast" was headed by three Germans – Anny Konetzni as Brünnhilde, Hans Beirer as Siegmund and Ludwig Hofmann as Wotan (the opera was
sung in German) – while the three remaining principals were from the Covent
Garden company, Sylvia Fisher as Sieglinde, Edith Coates as Fricka, and Frederick Dalberg as Hunding. There was very little rehearsal, but the British singers
had sung their roles at Covent Garden the previous autumn under Fritz Stiedry,
and Goodall was familiar with their work. Konetzni no longer had a high C for
the war-cries, but, like Hofmann, she was immensely experienced: she had sung
the role for Furtwängler. Goodall could hardly believe his luck.

There were four performances in all. The first was at the Davis Theatre, Croydon,
on 5 March 1954. In the audience was a young South African-born critic, Andrew
Porter, whose review for *Opera* proved crucial for Goodall's future career:

> This was a performance of a different class from those we were offered at Covent
> Garden last season. Lucky Croydon, Cardiff, Birmingham and Manchester, to
> have the chance of seeing and hearing what we in London were denied, a Wag-
> ner performance which by any standards today was exceptionally good.

First, since this was in some ways the revelation of the evening, the conductor and orchestra. Reginald Goodall, I was told, had never conducted *Die Walküre* before. Yet overnight, with this performance, he placed himself in the forefront of our Wagnerian conductors. The first act was not quite so good as the rest: it flowed a little too slowly. But never once did Mr Goodall interpose anything between us and the music. His reading of the second act was magnificent, and his third act superb. It sounded like the great music it is (which it never did under Stiedry). Mr Goodall's conception is broad, warm, flowing and profound. On the strength of this *Walküre* he should certainly be offered the second *Ring* at Covent Garden ...

In all seriousness, I must declare that never – from the Bayreuth orchestra, the Vienna Philharmonic, the Philharmonia – have I heard orchestral tone so consistently sumptuous and thrilling as that of the Covent Garden Orchestra on that evening. I know that it was not at full Wagnerian strength; I know that some of the regular players were in the Covent Garden pit with the ballet company. This was one of those unexplained miracles that sometimes happen – Mr Goodall, the Davis architect, my placing in the theatre (block F, row S, seat 35) conspiring to bring it off, and most of all the fact that the Covent Garden Orchestra is a magnificent one. I was not alone in observing this orchestral splendour. (I am told that once, on an earlier tour, there was [a] *Turandot* under Mr Goodall so magnificent that it is still mentioned among the company with a kind of awe.)

The whole third act was a revelation. It started with exciting singing from the Valkyries, all of whose names should go on the record: Rosina Raisbeck, Hella Toros, Edith Coates, Jean Watson, Joan Sutherland, Monica Sinclair, Constance Shacklock and Gita Denise. Their cry of *Weh!* rang out with thrilling effect ...[37]

From Croydon the company moved on to the Empire Theatre, Cardiff, where Goodall conducted *Walküre* and *Tosca*, as well as *Gloriana*, with Joan Sutherland in the role of Lady Penelope Rich (the *Lucia di Lammermoor* that was to launch her international career was still five years away). Only *Tosca* was well-attended. Ironically, since it was the work that had got him back into Webster's good books, *Gloriana* and its Elizabethan dance-rhythms held little interest for Goodall. He had wanted to conduct instead the company's new production of *Der Freischütz*, which was being unveiled in Cardiff rather than London. To his chagrin it had been given to Edward Downes. Webster came from London for the first night and sat in the front row of the circle with senior members of his staff. Goodall joined them. The proceedings opened with *God Save the Queen* and *Mae Hen Wlad Fy Nghadi* (Land of my Fathers). As was the custom in Cardiff, Downes swung round to conduct the audience in the chorus of the Welsh anthem. "Fucking showman!" exploded Goodall, in a voice heard some distance away.[38] He was always a great four-letter man.

In Manchester, Hilde Konetzni, sister of Anny, sang the role of Sieglinde in place of Sylvia Fisher, who had been given time off to marry the company's

Italian coach, Ubaldo Gardini. The first act took on a new, surging intensity. Konetzni changed the production drastically, spending much of the act on her knees. Webster found the result most moving. What, he asked afterwards, had given her the idea? Konetzni explained that she had lost a tooth and was desperately trying to find it before another member of the cast stood on it. She had managed to retrieve it before the act ended. The drama was witnessed by Edward Downes, who, as prompter, had been hiding behind the ash tree. The theatre did not have a prompt-box.

The final stop was Birmingham, where Britten went to hear *Gloriana* under Goodall. Lord Harewood, who was also at the performance, maintains that the composer was disappointed by it – he thought it lacked crispness. At that point, says Harewood, Britten lost faith in Goodall as an interpreter of his music.[39] Most probably he had detected Goodall's lack of enthusiasm for the opera.

No sooner was the provincial tour over than Goodall and the Covent Garden company took *Peter Grimes* to Germany for two performances at the 1954 May festival in Wiesbaden. The Hessische Staatskapelle played in the pit. Goodall's conducting, wrote a Wiesbaden critic, "was as sinewy as it was compelling and precise ... In the interludes the careful shading and illustrative colouring of the orchestral sound was gripping ... At the end of the performance, which lasted more than three hours, tempestuous and renewed applause brought the English guests back to the stage again and again."[40]

Four years passed before Goodall worked on *Grimes* again. In 1958 the composer had just started rehearsals for a complete recording of the opera for Decca at the Walthamstow Assembly Hall, when he pulled a muscle in his shoulder while shaving. Such was the pain he had to stop conducting. At Britten's suggestion Goodall was called in to rescue the situation. Goodall conducted the rehearsals and test recordings, and then Britten grasped the baton and conducted the final takes as best he could.[41] It seems the composer did not manage quite all of them. Peter Pears, who sang the title-role, claimed that Goodall recorded part of the beginning of Act 2, because "Ben was, almost literally, prostrate."[42] When the sessions were over, Britten wrote to Goodall:

Dec. 20th 1958

My dear Reggie,

I shall never forget your kindness & generosity in coming to help me out on the last days' recording of Peter Grimes. It was typical of you – also typical was the way you conducted the piece, without any preparation at all. I am most grateful to you – & send my thanks along with best Xmas wishes to you & your wife –

Yours ever
Ben

Goodall's reply was characteristic:

31.12.58

My Dear Ben,

I appreciated your letter very much indeed – and it was lovely to be with you again on "Peter Grimes" – and to hear Peter singing the Mad Scene so wonderfully.

I felt what I did was woefully inadequate – but I hope it was some help to you all the same.

Yours ever
Reggie

Goodall's career was to last for another thirty years, but, apart from two performances of *Peter Grimes* in 1962 for the Bordeaux Opera with a French cast, he never conducted any of Britten's music again. He retained a deep respect for Britten as a creative artist, but never revised his opinion of *Gloriana* and showed little interest in the works that followed it. "I'm sorry," he said, "but you can't get going in that sort of music". Goodall told the writer and musician Hans Keller that for him, now that he had immersed himself in Wagner's world, Britten's music lacked something. What was that? asked Keller, who admired both Goodall and Britten. "In the first place harmony, a feeling for the basic harmony," Goodall replied. "Harmony has rhythm to it, propels music along ..." He said he wished Britten had written more works like *Grimes*, "because it has power and depth and emotion, which *Gloriana* hasn't for me."[43]

CHAPTER 12

Galley Years

DAVID Webster was impressed by Goodall's *Walküre*. "Reg," he said, "I think we'll ask you to do a *Ring* cycle next season." It did not materialise. Both cycles in the 1954–55 season were given to Rudolf Kempe, *Generalmusik-direktor* of the Bavarian State Opera, who was being wooed by Webster – fruit-lessly, as it turned out – to be musical director at Covent Garden. Goodall assisted Kempe on *The Ring*, but did not share the general enthusiasm for his Wagner conducting:

> For me, it was cold, detached and without depth, but they were mad about him at Covent Garden. Some think [Bernard] Haitink is a bit like Kempe, but his conducting is much warmer. Kempe's was very efficient, but it had no weight or power. He didn't pull you out of your seat.

Kempe soon realised that Goodall was out of sympathy with his approach and for one production had him replaced by an assistant brought over specially from East Germany. Goodall, full of disdain (and jealousy), christened the newcomer Herr Liebfraumilch.

Goodall may not have been given a *Ring*, but that season he did conduct reviv-als of *Wozzeck*, *La Bohème*, *Turandot*, *Manon* and Walton's *Troilus and Cressida*. His handling of *Troilus* was widely held to be an improvement on that of Sir Mal-colm Sargent, who had conducted its premiere at Covent Garden seven months earlier: to the composer's chagrin, Sargent had not learned the score properly.[1] Goodall considered *Manon* something of a retrograde step. Adele Leigh, who sang the title-role, remembered him arriving for the first rehearsal, banging the score down on the piano and saying crossly, "They've given me *this*!"[2] The high-point of the season for him was *Wozzeck*. Audiences were thin, but it was a criti-cal success. William Mann reviewed the first night for *Opera*:

> This was the tenth performance of *Wozzeck* at Covent Garden ... and the first which Erich Kleiber has not conducted. Yet orchestrally it was hardly inferior to the previous nine: partly because the Covent Garden Orchestra knows the opera well by now (should I say "still"?), having learned it under the best possi-ble conductor; partly because Reginald Goodall, who conducted, excels in such music, feels it deeply, and commands the performers – it is gratifying to see that his great gifts are now being aptly used at Covent Garden. The performance did not have the calculated gruesome lucidity of Kleiber's, but it was shot through with compassion, and did not want for precision nor clarity in any of the most complex scenes.[3]

The final *Wozzeck* was on 13 November 1954. Just over a fortnight later Goodall heard that Furtwängler had died. He telephoned friends to talk of his sense of loss. Goodall barely knew Furtwängler – he had met him only once or twice during visits to Salzburg in the early 1950s – but he looked on him as a potent source of musical revelation. Furtwängler could be idiosyncratic, said Goodall (he was surprised by some of Furtwängler's tempos for *The Ring*); what mattered was that music seemed to flow out of him as though it were being created, not recreated.

In all, Goodall conducted thirty-one performances during the 1954–55 season, the most he had been given for six years. The following season he conducted twenty-two, the majority of them on tour. They included his first *Tannhäuser*, as well as performances of *Die Walküre* in Liverpool and Birmingham, this time with Otakar Kraus as Wotan, and Sylvia Fisher as Brünnhilde. The London critics went to Birmingham to hear *Walküre* at the Theatre Royal, which proved as unsuitable as ever for Wagner. Peter Heyworth wrote in *The Observer*:

> Everything was loaded against the performance ... Extended on the floor of the stalls, the orchestra contrived to be big enough to drown the singers while remaining too small to produce the rounded quality of sound the music calls for. If there had been any rehearsal there was no sign of it, the lighting was eccentric, the action took place on a precipice rather than on a ramp and two of the three sets had to be jammed on to a stage clearly too small for them. Such are the hazards of an operatic tour in Great Britain ... Reginald Goodall's tempi were at first laboured and unsteady. But from the opening of the second act he seemed to feel his way constantly deeper into the heart of the music, so that, although the orchestral playing remained rough, he finally succeeded in giving a profoundly felt and meditated performance.[4]

Goodall took over the *Tannhäuser* from Kempe. Some players claimed they found his beat hard to fathom after experiencing the German conductor's faultless technique. There was the odd perilous moment, but there were also passages of great power. For Edward Downes, "no other conductor I've heard could build up the big *concertato* in the second act like Goodall. It was partly a matter of timing – not releasing the climax until the tension was almost unbearable."[5]

Goodall enjoyed the camaraderie of touring, which continued until the early 1960s, when it was dropped because of high costs, which led to poor production standards. The 200-strong company – management, music staff, principal singers, seventy members of the chorus, an orchestra of sixty-five, along with costumes and eighty tons of scenery – travelled in specially chartered trains. The majority stayed in theatrical digs, but Goodall preferred the comfort and quiet of a good hotel. He was not the most worldly of men, but he had a certain style: he liked to shop at Harrods and Peter Jones; his favourite drink was champagne. Once, in Manchester, John Gardner persuaded him to forsake the four-star Midland and share his digs instead. The experiment was not a success. When Goodall put his shoes outside his bedroom door, it was Gardner who bore the landlady's wrath. "Will you tell your friend Mr Goodall that I don't clean shoes!" she said. Goodall complained that there was not enough food. "Who does he think he is?" exploded the landlady. "I've had bigger M.D.s [musical directors] than him here. Eric Robinson for one." Robinson ran a popular television show, *Music for You*. Goodall enjoyed the put-down. The next time he visited Manchester he returned to the Midland.[6]

Goodall's supporters assumed his days of neglect were over, but all he was given during the 1956–57 season were the last two nights of a new production of *The Mastersingers*, with James Pease as Hans Sachs, Erich Witte as Walther von Stolzing and Joan Sutherland as Eva. The earlier performances had been conducted – none too successfully – by the company's new musical director, Rafael Kubelik. But it was not Kubelik who was responsible for Goodall's return to the wilderness: he and Goodall had a mutual respect and liking for each other. Rather the fault lay with the management, for Webster's new-found enthusiasm for Goodall had soon petered out. The "comeback" lasted for only two seasons.

Though the press continued to laud Goodall's achievements, feeling against him remained strong in a house that preferred compliance to unconformity. There were complaints about his bad temper and bloody-mindedness, moods governed by depression and frustration. There were accusations from certain singers, not always unjustified, that he buried his head in the score and never gave them cues, and there were jokes about his turn-out – his tails never seemed to fit – and even the occasional whisper, usually inaccurate, about his Mosleyite past. One story had it that he had been interned on the Isle of Man. As far as Webster was concerned, Goodall did not match up to the glamorous image he was trying hard to create for the house. More damaging for Goodall, there was a widespread feeling that he lacked the quickness, ease and fluency of technique that made life simple in a theatre that had to cope with a complicated schedule of rehearsals and performances. Goodall's refusal to compromise, particularly over rehearsal-time, was looked on with admiration by the younger members of the music staff, but with exasperation by those responsible for the day-to-day running of the house. Thus the notion that Goodall was fit for nothing much apart from coaching became enshrined in Covent Garden lore.

All Goodall was given to conduct during the 1957–58 season was a revival of *The Mastersingers*. His state of mind can be judged by a letter he wrote to David Webster not long after rehearsals had begun. In it he complained that the Beckmesser, Geraint Evans, had been given time off by Covent Garden to rehearse two major roles, Falstaff and Figaro, at Glyndebourne. As a result, he said, Evans would miss the final week of rehearsals for *The Mastersingers*. The letter continues:

> This in addition to all the other troubles with Meistersinger makes me realize I'm utterly incapable of coping with the situation. (This week we have no Eva, Walter, Beckmesser, Sachs, Pogner.)
>
> It needs a far more forceful personality to handle the almost impossible rehearsal situation – I must have a certain quiet & repose – so may I please ask you to release me from conducting Meistersinger.[7]

His request was not granted, and the five performances went ahead as planned. The cast, of British and American singers, was not exceptional, but the critics were unanimous in their praise of the conducting. David Cairns wrote in the *Times Educational Supplement*:

> The riches of this score are inexhaustible. But it takes a great conductor to unlock them. This is just what Mr Reginald Goodall ... has done ... On the opening night he ignored Wagner's directions about the speed of the chorale, and for about two minutes the opera dragged. Thereafter he scarcely put a foot wrong. Indeed, the marvellous thing about this *Mastersingers* was the utter naturalness of it; Mr Goodall's tempos were judged to such perfection that the music seemed to create itself. Yet it was intensely lyrical, never merely relaxed and ambling; time and again he drew from the orchestra tone which blended a fascinating diversity of detail, and phrasing of heart-searching breadth and beauty (in this, as well as in the majestic steadiness of the fugue in Act 2, he recalled Knappertsbusch at his best), while the climaxes were punctuated with admirable finality. By any standards this was an exceptionally fine interpretation, in its way fully worthy to be set beside Signor Giulini's *Don Carlos*. Whether recognised or not, Mr Goodall's *Mastersingers* is a landmark in the post-war history of Covent Garden.[8]

Covent Garden cannot have regarded the revival as any such thing, because the following season Goodall was limited to five performances of *Salome*, with the German soprano Helga Pilarczyk in the title-role. It was the only time he conducted an opera by Richard Strauss, and the result was not particularly successful. David Cairns put his finger on what was wrong, when he wrote that "Strauss has a right to expect brilliance on his own level, and this he too rarely got. Mr Goodall seemed to be burrowing down in search of a profundity that had never entered the composer's head."[9]

In the 1959–60 season Goodall appeared just once, on 6 October 1959, when he took over a performance of *Die Walküre* from the East German conductor, Franz Konwitschny, who had been recalled to Berlin at short notice for a concert marking the tenth anniversary of the founding of the German Democratic Republic. Goodall thought Konwitschny's *Ring* was "wonderful – it had great depth – but Covent Garden treated him as nobody." The official view of Konwitschny may have been influenced by the fact that he drank generous quantities of hock during the intervals of *The Ring*, a habit that caused numerous eyebrows to be raised at the Opera House, though not Goodall's. As always Goodall found the combination of fine musicianship and a larger-than-life personality irresistible. Goodall loved Konwitschny's insouciance, though he did not have the nerve to match it himself. During the long, exposed passage for the first violins after the hero has passed through the fire in the final act of *Siegfried*, Konwitschny stopped conducting and instead sat listening to the music. When he had conducted the passage at rehearsal, it had not gone well. In performance it went perfectly – the players were so terrified about having to do it without him that they concentrated as never before. At the end of it a beaming Konwitschny bent down and shook the leader's hand in congratulation.[10]

Goodall had no time to rehearse the *Walküre*, but he had the backing of a strong cast: Hans Hotter as Wotan, Martha Mödl as Brünnhilde, Ursula Böse as Fricka, Ramón Vinay as Siegmund, Amy Shuard as Sieglinde, Andreas Boehm as Hunding. "The stand-in steals the show," ran the headline in the *Evening Standard*, whose critic, the pseudonymous Adam Bell (actually David Cairns), said that "magnificent though Hotter was, the hero of the evening was ... that Cinderella of Covent Garden, Reginald Goodall. Mr Goodall, a small, blinking, bespectacled man too modest to take a solo curtain call, inspired the orchestra to playing of a beauty and mastery not previously heard this season." The *Times* critic was equally enthusiastic:

> There were some moments of poor ensemble, and some sections in which the music was in danger of going to sleep; but for long stretches [Goodall] guided the grandiose, lyrical music expansively and with a sympathy for its warm bloodstream that evoked the true Wagnerian magic. Wagnerites in the audience could themselves warm to a reading which gave the composer's imagination its head, and did not redirect it to serve private theories; conductor and orchestra were given an unusually warm reception before the start of the third act; the audience were welcoming the old, authentic Wagner back to Covent Garden, and would doubtless be even more pleased if Mr Goodall were to take over a complete second cycle one year. As his account of *Die Meistersinger* showed not long ago, Wagner is his métier.[11]

This time not even Webster and the Covent Garden directors could ignore the notices, let alone the audience's enthusiasm, and only three weeks after the *Walküre* it was agreed at a board meeting that Goodall should be asked to conduct *Tristan and Isolde* later in the season, provided Birgit Nilsson could be signed up to sing Isolde. (In the 1950s, changes to the repertory could be made at short notice.) Unfortunately she turned out to be unavailable.[12] Next, Goodall was offered two performances of *Parsifal*, but the amount of rehearsal-time available for a work he had never conducted before was inadequate by any standards and he turned it down. In the end he conducted yet another revival of *The Mastersingers* with a home-grown cast.

On the opening night the Walther, Ronald Dowd from Sadler's Wells, had tracheitis and by the first interval was in serious vocal difficulty. At the end of the second interval, which lasted almost an hour, David Webster came before the audience to announce that, as a result of the tenor's indisposition, the scene of the writing of the Prize Song would be omitted. Moreover, in the final scene, the Prize Song itself – which, of course, had not been written, though Webster failed to mention the fact – would be sung, not by Dowd, but by Edgar Evans, who up until then had been taking the small role of Kunz Vogelgesang. It was, Andrew Porter noted in his review of the evening, the first *Meistersinger* in which Vogelgesang had won Eva's hand.[13]

Goodall was convinced that Webster held him responsible for the disaster. He told friends that, after it, Webster never spoke to him again.[14] No doubt Goodall was exaggerating, but he had good reason to feel paranoid about Webster's intentions towards him. Shortly before *The Mastersingers*, Goodall had conducted a revival of Bartók's *Duke Bluebeard's Castle* at Sadler's Wells, and a few months later was to return there for a revival of *Tannhäuser*. He may not have known it, but Webster had played a part in securing both invitations to the Wells, as is made plain by an exchange of letters in November 1960 between Webster (by now Sir David) and the Earl of Drogheda, chairman of the Covent Garden board. Drogheda, nettled by criticism in the press that Meredith Davies, and not Goodall, had been given a revival of *Peter Grimes* to conduct, wrote to Webster:

> I am worried about the position of Goodall. I think that you are exposing us to criticism, and a little ridicule, by continuing to employ him and to show him as one of our three [assistant] conductors [the others were Downes and Bryan Balkwill] when at the same time he is never given any conducting to do. I do not believe that we should leave matters in their present state and I think you must make a definite move to dispense with his services.

Webster replied three days later:

> It has taken me several years to get Goodall into the Wells and I hope that they will be able to take him on to their staff. In any event we will dispense with his services at the end of this season.[15]

Sadler's Wells did not offer Goodall regular employment. Nor did Covent Garden sack him. Either Webster had no intention of getting rid of Goodall and was stringing his chairman along, or he had decided on reflection that such action would cause uproar not only in the press, but also among the company's leading singers. The Opera House had begun to create its own stars, some of whom had a high regard for Goodall, notably the Canadian tenor, Jon Vickers, who had been discovered by Webster in Toronto.

Vickers had got off to a difficult start when he arrived at Covent Garden in January 1957. Webster wanted him to make his company debut at short notice as Walther in the new production of *The Mastersingers* under Kubelik, but Vickers argued successfully that there was not enough time for him to learn the role thoroughly. However he agreed to study it with the German repertory coach, Norman Feasey. Vickers found Feasey's ideas about phrasing at odds with his own. Two days later he heard from a colleague that Feasey had told a staff meeting that although Vickers had a good voice, he had no idea how to use it and seemed to have no ability to learn. David Webster, said Feasey, should buy out his contract and send him back to Canada.

Vickers decided there was only one thing to do. He sat at his piano for eight hours a day and taught himself Walther's notes in a week. He then sought out Goodall, who was assisting Kubelik, and asked if he could go through the role with him. "Yes – now!" said Goodall. Vickers recalls:

> It was literally now. In those days Reggie did his coaching in the little retiring-room behind the Bedford box. It had a piano in it. We went straight up there and I sang the whole part. And he said, "Why aren't you singing the premiere?" I explained that I didn't want to make my Covent Garden debut in the role. "But you've got to do it," said Reggie. "I'm going to see Webster." And he stormed out of the room, leaving me standing there. He came back very disgruntled. "You're not doing it," he said. "I know," I replied, "I've already told Mr Webster I won't." "Well," said Reggie, "Webster told me he'd heard you weren't capable of learning it. I put him right – I told him you knew the whole thing."
> From that moment on, Reggie and I were great friends.[16]

Vickers worked on all his German roles with Goodall, starting with Siegmund in *Die Walküre*, which in 1958 he sang at Bayreuth: he remembers looking down into the Festspielhaus's orchestra pit and seeing Goodall there, sitting close to Knappertsbusch, who was conducting. Then came Parsifal, Florestan in *Fidelio* and, before he sang it under Karajan at Salzburg, Tristan – as well as Peter Grimes for his debut in the part at the Metropolitan, New York.

Vickers never sang the role of Walther on stage, though later in 1957 he took part in a performance of the quintet from Act 3 of *Meistersinger* for the BBC. The Eva was Joan Sutherland. Besides Eva, Goodall taught her Helmwige in *Walküre*, the Woodbird in *Siegfried*, and Brangäne for a concert performance of *Tristan* Act 2 conducted by Barbirolli. It looked at one point as though Sutherland might concentrate on German opera. The role of Sieglinde was mooted, and Goodall was keen to coach her for it, but she turned it down. The Italian repertoire beckoned. "I had all those extra notes at the top," says Dame Joan, "and it seemed a pity not to use them. Reggie was very disappointed, and I was sorry I had to disappoint him, because he had this love and enthusiasm for his work which glowed. It was the nearest I got to singing Brünnhilde."[17] Goodall always retained an affection for Sutherland, though he did not care for her chosen repertoire. Richard Nunn, a member of Covent Garden's music staff during the 1960s, once found him lurking in the shadows of the staff box during a performance of Donizetti's *La fille du régiment* with Sutherland. "Don't tell a soul I'm here," whispered Goodall, "but I rather like it – and I think she's terrific."[18]

Others besides Webster tried to find work for Goodall outside Covent Garden, not as part of some plot to get rid of him, but because they believed he should be given more opportunities to conduct. In December 1960, Bernard Keeffe, then head of opera planning, wrote to the BBC's new controller of music, William Glock:

> [Goodall] is a difficult conductor to cast here – his only interest is Wagner – and obviously comes second in our minds to Kempe, and in the future Solti. However I'm sure you know his worth, and it seems a pity that he could not have an occasional date with a BBC orchestra ...

Glock had been appointed to the BBC the previous year and was already sweeping aside many of the prejudices about performers and repertory that had paralysed its music department for the previous twenty years. Keeffe's letter was timely, for Glock was encouraging the performance of Bruckner's works, which were still regarded with suspicion in some quarters of the British musical establishment. Goodall was invited to conduct Bruckner's E-minor Mass at a Promenade Concert on 22 August 1961, with the BBC Singers and Choral Society and a wind band drawn from the BBC Symphony Orchestra.[19] It was the first time it had been heard at a Prom.

Goodall had not conducted any of Bruckner's church music since leaving St Alban's, Holborn, 25 years earlier; it was 15 years since he had last conducted a public concert. By way of a dry run, it was arranged for him to conduct the Mass with amateur forces at the Dartington Summer School, where Glock was director of music. *The Times* critic wrote that the Proms performance "started off with a beautifully delicate tonal radiance and plasticity as well as accuracy. It remained constantly expressive, but as the composer's chromaticism became more daring, so the singers and the accompanying wind band grew a little less single-minded in matters of intonation and ensemble, notably in the Benedictus."[20] The Mass was not broadcast: the BBC chose instead to relay a concert from the Edinburgh Festival conducted by Stokowski.

Later in the year Goodall conducted again for the BBC. The story of his neglect at Covent Garden had come to the ears of one of Glock's young Turks in the BBC's music department, the composer Alexander Goehr, who was fired with the romantic idea of rescuing Goodall from his "oppressors."²¹ It was the custom for the Covent Garden orchestra to give an annual studio concert for the BBC. Goehr was determined that in 1961 it should be Goodall's turn to conduct it. He went to see Goodall, who was reluctant to accept such a proposal; he seemed "bowed down". Goehr persevered, however. He approached Morris Smith, the Opera House's orchestral manager and a confidant of Webster's (they were members of the same masonic lodge), who made it clear that as far as Covent Garden was concerned a concert with Goodall was out of the question: it was too big a risk; almost any other conductor would be preferable. Goehr stood his ground, and Smith, realising that the concert would not take place unless Goodall participated, gave way.

With Goodall's co-operation, Goehr devised an unusual programme that was well-suited to the conductor's gifts: Dukas's Wagner-inspired overture, *Polyeucte*, Messiaen's early, brilliantly coloured *L'Ascension*, and Schumann's Fourth Symphony. Three, three-hour rehearsals were allotted to the concert, which was recorded on 18 December 1961 at Wembley Town Hall and broadcast three days later. Goodall was nervous, for he knew that the Covent Garden management was waiting for him to come unstuck. However a tape of the concert shows he did no such thing. The interpretations are arresting, while the playing is polished throughout.

Goodall's only conducting job at Covent Garden in 1961 was a revival in Russian of *Boris Godunov*, the opera that had first brought him to the house 25 years earlier, though on this occasion the composer's own orchestration was used, rather than Rimsky-Korsakov's. (Unfashionably, Goodall preferred Rimsky's glittering sonorities to Mussorgsky's stark original.) The title-role was sung by one of its most notable interpreters, the Bulgarian bass Boris Christoff, while the rest of the cast was drawn from the company itself: Josephine Veasey as Feodor, John Lanigan as Shuisky, Edgar Evans as Dmitri, Margreta Elkins as Marina, Michael Langdon as Varlaam, David Ward as Schelkalov. The Opera House's own resources at the time seemed infinite. With the help of his Russian-speaking assistant, David Lloyd-Jones, Goodall coached them for seven weeks, despite the fact that he was recovering from a cataract operation on both eyes. Peter Heyworth wrote of the first night:

> Reginald Goodall's conducting provided fresh evidence of his artistic distinction. He exactly caught Mussorgsky's elusive quality of phrase, the strange textures of his orchestral writing, and, above all, the epic dimensions of the score. Mr Christoff

generously made his appreciation of Mr Goodall's contribution to a fine evening very evident.[22]

The fourth and final performance of the revival took place on 10 June. Apart from a single performance of Rimsky-Korsakov's *Coq d'or* on 3 December 1962, it was the last time Goodall conducted at Covent Garden for 10 years. The period coincided almost exactly with Sir Georg Solti's term there as musical director. He and Goodall were poles apart, both in their personalities and their musical perceptions.

When Solti arrived at Covent Garden in September 1961, he had already established his Wagnerian credentials with a much-applauded recording of *Das Rheingold*, made in Vienna by Decca, that was to lead to the first-ever complete *Ring* on disc.[23] Not surprisingly he wanted to put his stamp on the Opera House with a new production of Wagner's tetralogy. His chosen producer was Hans Hotter, who was also to sing the role of Wotan. *Die Walküre* came first in 1961, *Siegfried* the following year. Goodall coached singers and attended rehearsals. Not everyone appreciated his efforts. Hotter, for one, found him impractical as a rehearsal conductor in the early stages of production: he thought Goodall was too intent on giving an interpretation, when all that was wanted was a clear outline of the music while producer and cast blocked out the moves.[24]

Before the next instalment of *The Ring* took place, Goodall was asked to prepare the singers and orchestra for a revival of *Meistersinger*, to be conducted by Rudolf Kempe. Joan Ingpen, who had succeeded Bernard Keeffe as head of opera planning, explained that Kempe was ill and would be arriving late for the rehearsals. "He wouldn't want me," said Goodall, "he doesn't like me." "But he has asked for you specifically," said Ingpen. Goodall, surprised, agreed to do the job. Kempe was so pleased with the results that he insisted on half his own rehearsal fee going to Goodall.[25] (Ingpen, who had been Solti's agent before going to Covent Garden, never told Goodall about the role she had played in his discharge from the army.)

Ironically, several critics compared Kempe's conducting of the opera unfavourably with Goodall's. One of them, Andrew Porter, was taken to task by Lord Drogheda, who, besides being chairman of the Covent Garden board, was also managing director of Porter's newspaper, the *Financial Times*. Porter was unrepentant. He wrote to Drogheda:

Dear Garrett,

Now that three separate critics have told you that Goodall is a more complete conductor of *Die Meistersinger* than Kempe [the other two were David Cairns and *The Observer's* Edmund Tracey], perhaps you'll see why so many people think it both <u>wasteful</u> and <u>wicked</u> that you make no proper use of him. Wasteful, because you bring in guest conductors for the works (*Wagner, Wozzeck, Peter Grimes*) in which he is supreme. Wicked, because this may well have undermined his confidence. The man who has conducted *Walküre, Meistersinger, Wozzeck, Grimes*, as Goodall has done, ought to be one of the <u>glories</u> of Covent Garden by now – like Sutherland, [Geraint] Evans, and co.

> Yours ever
> Andrew

Drogheda passed on the letter to Webster with a covering note[26]:

> 21st February 1963
>
> Dear David,
>
>   I do wish that you would be kind enough to help me to reply to a letter from Andrew Porter of which I attach a copy. The background to it is that I had complained to him about the way in which he is always comparing conductors like Solti and Kempe adversely with Goodall. I must say that I am at a loss what to reply to him but I am clear that he and other critics are going to go on whipping up feeling in this matter and, as you know, I have always thought that we were at fault in going on showing Goodall as a conductor and never using him as such.
>
> Yours ever,
> Garrett

Drogheda continued to be irritated by Goodall's position at Covent Garden, though it seems that by now he had accepted the fact that Goodall was not going to be sacked. Ten months later he wrote to Webster:

> 11th December 1963
>
> Dear David,
>
>   I see that Reginald Goodall is still shown as a Conductor in the Covent Garden programmes. It was agreed simply ages ago that his name should be removed, and that he should be shown as a member of the musical staff. Why is he still incorrectly described? Were instructions not transmitted to whomever is supposed to produce the programme? Or have you and Solti had second thoughts about the nature of Goodall's employment, in which case why was one not told?
>
> Yours
> Garrett

Webster was not afraid of "Droghedagrams," as the imperious chairman's missives had come to be known. He replied:

30th December 1963

Dear Garrett,

Georg and I discussed together the position of Goodall as conductor. We felt strongly that as a house we would gain nothing from taking his name from under this heading, and that it would cause him a lot of very unnecessary pain.

Yours, David

If Goodall had strong reservations about Kempe, he had few, if any, about Klemperer. Even at the end of Klemperer's career, when his powers had begun to wane, Goodall felt that "he always had something to offer." Goodall first assisted Klemperer in February 1961, when he came to Covent Garden to conduct and produce a new production of *Fidelio*. Up until then Klemperer's conducting had made little impact on Goodall, but the experience of working on *Fidelio* convinced him that Klemperer was a finer interpreter of Beethoven's music than Furtwängler. "Klemperer is more an architectural conductor," he told the critic Alan Blyth, "where Furtwängler was an instinctive one."[27] Impressed by Goodall's dedication and musical integrity, Klemperer insisted on having him as his assistant for his five subsequent visits to Covent Garden. The association did not end there. Klemperer had been advised by doctors that he should no longer conduct for the full three hours of a recording session. His producer at EMI, Walter Legge, agreed that an assistant conductor could spend the first half-hour or so of each session taking the Philharmonia Orchestra through the work to be recorded. Goodall first assisted Klemperer in this way in November 1961, on the slow movement of the Resurrection Symphony of Mahler, a composer he claimed not to understand. He knew the works that followed much better, for he had conducted most of them with the Wessex Philharmonic. They included piano concertos by Schumann and Liszt (both with Annie Fischer), and symphonies by Haydn, Mozart (Nos 40 and 41), Beethoven, Brahms, Dvořák (the *New World*), Schubert (the *Unfinished*) and Tchaikovsky (the Fourth and Fifth). He also rehearsed the Philharmonia for Klemperer's concert performances and recordings of *Le nozze di Figaro* and the first act of *Die Walküre*.[28]

Goodall regarded Klemperer as a "supreme musician – I had nothing but respect and devotion for him." On and off, he attended the sessions for nine years:

Klemperer would come early and sit at the back of the studio while I conducted. It made me very nervous. I'm told he shouted at some people, but he never interrupted me. He had his own way of letting me know if he thought I'd got something wrong. I remember a Bruckner symphony. The Eighth. I had taken a certain bit too slowly. When he conducted the passage himself, he turned and looked at me very hard, as though to say, 'This is how it should go, my boy.' I got the message. It was a lovely job – at least I thought it was.

At the end of the sessions, Goodall joined Klemperer to listen to the playbacks. Klemperer found him so shy that holding a conversation with him on any subject apart from music was impossible.[29] After his last visit to Covent Garden, for a revival of *Fidelio* in 1969, Klemperer gave Goodall a full score of the opera, which he inscribed: "To my dear colleague Reginald Goodall, the <u>excellent</u> conductor, with the very best wishes for a fulfilled life. Otto Klemperer. March 1969. London." Six months later, Klemperer told Peter Heyworth that he found Goodall "very good, very good, more than sympathetic. I cannot understand [why] a man like Webster and the whole committee – the directors of Covent Garden – don't take him as a good conductor."[30] After Klemperer died in 1973, the New Philharmonia Orchestra laid plans for a concert in his memory. The first choice for conductor was Pierre Boulez, but the orchestra's council decided that if for any reason he were not available, "a suitable concert under Reginald Goodall would probably provide a very fitting occasion as he was held in particular affection by Dr Klemperer."[31] In the event the concert was conducted by Rafael Kubelik.

Solti's *Ring* project, which was proving highly successful, continued in the autumn of 1963 with *Götterdämmerung*, and was rounded off in 1964 by *Das Rheingold* and two complete cycles. At the first stage-and-orchestra rehearsal of *Rheingold*, Solti asked Goodall to conduct, while he went to the back of the theatre to make notes and check the balance. On such occasions it is the assistant's responsibility to reproduce the conductor's chosen tempi as closely as possible. Goodall, however, took the music at a much broader pace than Solti, who shouted at him to go faster. Goodall failed to react. Solti shouted again. Still there was no reaction. Solti ran down to the orchestra-rail and, standing just behind Goodall, conducted at the tempo he wanted. Goodall was replaced.[32]

Looking back on the incident, Goodall said he should not have behaved as he did, but he had found it impossible to adapt to Solti's more dynamic view of the score: "Solti said to me, 'I don't think it's much use you rehearsing for me, because our tempos are so different' – and he was right."[33] None the less Goodall felt the humiliation keenly. Not only had he been berated publicly by the musical director, he had, he knew, also incurred the displeasure of Hans Hotter, an artist he held in high esteem.

According to George Hallam, the orchestra's sub-leader, Goodall "went right into his shell. People wouldn't see him for weeks. Whenever he came into Covent Garden, he would keep as near to the wall as possible and go straight to his room." For some years Hallam and Goodall had played sonatas together in their spare time, both in London and during the long provincial tours. Following the Solti incident, the sessions stopped abruptly and were never resumed. Hallam and Goodall had worked their way through the Brahms and Beethoven violin sonatas, and had then gone on to the music of Schoenberg, Webem and Berg. Hallam recalls:

> We used to play together in theatre dressing-rooms, in the Bedford box, wherever there was a piano. We would start to play a Brahms sonata, or perhaps the Schoenberg Violin Concerto, with Reggie taking the orchestral part – he was fascinated by 12-note music. At first he wouldn't say a word. Then something would trigger him off and the room would become full of excitement as he began to analyse the music, bar by bar, showing me how it was formed and how it should be interpreted. He showed me the movement of the harmonies and how the chords were related to one another. More than anything else he talked about the colour of the chords and what they meant. It was an incredible lesson in musicianship.[34]

Hallam formed a chamber ensemble from the Covent Garden orchestra to perform the works of the Second Viennese School and asked Goodall to conduct it at concerts at Park Lane House, but Goodall got cold feet and turned down the offer. Edward Downes conducted instead. Hallam regretted Goodall's lack of confidence: "One of the things I wanted to do most was Schoenberg's *Pierrot Lunaire* with Reggie conducting. He would have been marvellous, absolutely marvellous."

By the early 1960s, Goodall no longer coached in the Bedford box. He had his own room, high up under the theatre's roof and known to all who went there for coaching sessions as "Valhalla". At night the room was used by the cleaners. Stamina was needed to get there: having reached the heights of the amphitheatre bar, the visitor was faced with a further climb of fifty-one steps. The furnishings were spare: an upright piano, a cupboard for Goodall's scores, another for the cleaners' equipment, a few hard-backed chairs, two washbasins, a stone sink set at a curiously low height (for cleaning mops?), an Initial roller-towel dispenser, a convector heater (the room could be freezing in winter), a telephone and, in later years, a discarded bust of Andrew Mellon. A large, ill-fitting skylight let in the rain. Goodall considered the room excellent for his purposes: though cramped, it had a decent reverberant acoustic and was so far away from the main area of activity that few people knew whether he was in the house or not.

In the 1960s, Valhalla had only one drawback for Goodall. Before the era of quieter jets, one of the main flightpaths to Heathrow airport passed over the Opera House. As a result, coaching sessions were often drowned out by Boeing

707s, which appeared to be flying only a few feet above the skylight. Goodall was usually so absorbed by his work that he did not notice an offending aircraft until it was quite close. Then, to the delight of the singers present, he would spring to his feet, utter several oaths, snatch up the telephone, demand to be put through to Heathrow and castigate some clearly mystified official at the other end.[35]

The small but devoted band of regulars who trudged up to Valhalla for coaching with Goodall during the early 1960s included John Lanigan, John Dobson, Victor Godfrey, Amy Shuard, Otakar Kraus, Edgar Evans, Ronald Lewis, David Ward and Michael Langdon. Later in the decade they were joined by two future Bayreuth singers, the soprano Gwyneth Jones and the bass-baritone Donald McIntyre, who, like Jon Vickers before him, was to learn most of his German roles with Goodall. Despite the reversals in Goodall's fortunes, the sessions were by no means full of gloom and despondency. Langdon remembered "many laughs over operatic life in general ... [The] fact that he insisted on speaking in German for 90% of the time somehow made his comments on the inhabitants of the Opera House even funnier."[36] One of Goodall's most cherished comments was made, not in Valhalla, but in the staff box during a performance of a new opera. "God," said Goodall after a particularly thunderous moment, "that's the loudest noise I've heard in this house since Solti's *Figaro*." But whatever Goodall may have thought of Solti as an interpreter, he admired his drive and energy in running the musical side of the Opera House: "His was the most successful musical directorship of any of them. Bang! Bang! Bang! You knew when he was in the building all right. You need that discipline if you are to get results."

Apart from coaching singers and assisting Klemperer, Goodall played almost no part in the Opera House's affairs during the 1960s, though he remained on salary. His colleagues knew little about his home life, which he kept completely separate from the Opera House. In the late 1950s he and Eleanor had bought 4 Thistle Grove, the house in South Kensington they had rented before the war. Neighbours saw little of them, though occasionally Goodall was glimpsed in the street, shaking his fist at low-flying aircraft.[37] Eleanor lectured at a Roman Catholic teachers training college in Kensington Square. During a visit to Lourdes she had suffered a small stroke, but its effects had not proved long-lasting. On Sundays the Goodalls attended Mass, often at the Brompton Oratory. Goodall took with him scores of the music to be performed and, Beckmesser-like, complained loudly when things were not to his liking. He spent much of his spare time gardening, his greatest passion after music. He built a pond and stocked it with fish. Goodall filled the pages of his diary with comments about the garden's progress. There was little in the way of professional engagements to note down in it, apart from coaching sessions in Valhalla. Meanwhile Lord Drogheda continued to complain to Webster about Goodall:

27th February 1966

Dear David,

    Looking at the current Covent Garden programme on Friday night, I noticed that in the list of musical staff Reginald Goodall at the moment appears in solitary splendour as the one and only Conductor. This is really terribly nonsensical when he does not, in fact, conduct at all. I suppose you are still of [the] opinion that he must continue to be incorrectly described?

Yours ever,
Garrett

Edward Downes was now listed as assistant to the musical director; Bryan Balkwill had gone to Sadler's Wells. Webster still had not the heart to remove Goodall's name.

In 1966 the Goodalls decided to move to Barham, a village near Canterbury. Next to its church stands Barham Court, a fine old house with an eighteenth-century façade, which in the early 1950s had been split up into large flats. Goodall's college friend, Philip Blake, lived on the ground floor. In 1912, the architect Sir Edwin Lutyens had added a wing to the house to provide a summer drawing-room, which had since been converted into a small two-bedroom house called Stainton Lodge. When it came up for sale, Blake urged Goodall to look at it. Eleanor had retired from her teaching job and the Goodalls were thinking of moving to the country, since they had no particular reason to spend the whole week in London. Eleanor hoped that her husband might also retire, now that he had reached the age of 65. Goodall liked the look of the house immediately and decided to buy it even before he had been inside it ("Lutyens wasn't a tuppenny-ha'penny builder, you know"). It had its own two-acre garden, which would keep him well occupied, and there was a regular train service to London from Canterbury that would enable him to attend coaching sessions whenever necessary. Above all it was quiet. The Goodalls moved to Barham early in 1967. No sooner had they done so than Goodall received from Sadler's Wells a proposition that was to change his life.

CHAPTER 13

Triumph

I N MAY 1966 A Mr Christopher Foss of London NW11 wrote to Sadler's Wells Opera, asking if it would mount a production of *The Mastersingers* in 1968 to mark the centenary of the work's first performance. The managing director, Stephen Arlen, replied that the company had indeed considered putting on *The Mastersingers*, but that it was "chorally slightly out of our scope at the moment." Wagner's opera, he said, had been performed at Sadler's Wells before the war with a chorus of around 30 and an orchestra of 36. The most the current company could field was an orchestra of 56 and a chorus of 48. Arlen doubted if even that number of performers would be considered adequate in the mid-1960s.[1]

In fact the Sadler's Wells Opera consisted of two companies, known for administrative purposes as "S" and "W". Each one had an orchestra of 56 and a chorus of 48, as well as its own musical director. While one company played in London at Sadler's Wells Theatre, the other toured. Then they swapped over. It was a complicated arrangement – principal singers were shared by both companies – but Arlen accepted the necessity for it, because at the time Sadler's Wells bore the main responsibility for opera touring in Britain. The Carl Rosa company had collapsed and Covent Garden no longer visited the provinces. The Scottish and Welsh National Operas were in no position to plug the gaps: the former put on only five weeks of opera in 1966, the latter nine. Glyndebourne Touring Opera was not to start for another two years, the now defunct Kent Opera for three. The founding of Opera North was still eleven years away.

It was customary for the "S" company to play a four-week Christmas season at Stratford-upon-Avon, but there were indications that the Shakespeare Memorial Theatre would not be available to the company for much longer. Arlen knew that it would be virtually impossible to find an alternative venue during the Christmas period, since most other theatres of any size would be filled with pantomime. As a result, the "S" company would be kicking its heels for five to six weeks – a waste of both artistic and financial resources.

Arlen reasoned that everybody could be kept busy if the two companies were to combine at Sadler's Wells over Christmas and the New Year for a large-scale work not normally included in the repertory. Once more he considered the possibility of putting on *The Mastersingers*. In August 1966 he put the idea to the Sadler's Wells Trust's opera sub-committee. Jack Donaldson, the co-ordinating trustee who sat on both the Sadler's Wells and Royal Opera House boards, gave it his support.[2] A date for the production was fixed, January 1968. Covent Garden raised no objections: it had no immediate plan to revive the opera, though it might want to bring it back, either as a revival or a new production, in the following season.[3]

The choice of conductor was problematical. Stephen Arlen thought that neither of the company's two musical directors, Mario Bernardi and Bryan Balkwill, should be given the task in view of the exceptionally large amount of musical preparation entailed: it would leave insufficient time for their other commitments. Various alternatives were considered, among them Rudolf Kempe, Edward Downes, Sir Adrian Boult and Warwick Braithwaite, who had conducted the pre-war *Mastersingers* at Sadler's Wells and was once more a member of the company. For one reason or another none of them turned out to be a practical choice. The former music critic Edmund Tracey, now literary manager and a director of the Sadler's Wells Opera, put forward Goodall's name. Arlen was immediately attracted by the idea, not only on musical grounds, but also because it might offer opportunities to embarrass the Royal Opera House. Enthusiastic support for Goodall also came from Arlen's wife, the soprano Iris Kells, who as a former member of the Covent Garden company had known Goodall since the late 1940s.

The question was finally settled in January 1967 at a meeting of the opera sub-committee attended by Jack Donaldson, Arlen, Tracey and Leonard Hancock, a former colleague of Goodall's at Covent Garden and now head of music staff at Sadler's Wells. All agreed that Goodall should be invited to conduct. Only the chairman, the merchant banker Leopold de Rothschild, had reservations.[4] Goodall's first reaction to the invitation was that it had come "too late."[5] He was too old, he said; his conducting career was over. Also, he had found his two visits to Sadler's Wells in 1960 less than satisfactory. Though Andrew Porter had referred to his "rich handling" of *Duke Bluebeard's Castle*, Goodall had not felt at home with Bartók's score, while he had considered the orchestra too small to do *Tannhäuser* justice. (The *Times* critic wrote of the latter opera: "Because the dramatic pulse of the music, the true Wagnerian flow, is firmly guided, one is able to forget almost immediately the inevitable thinness of the string tone and the inadequacy of one or two of the voices – and even the rather namby-pamby scenery."[6])

Goodall was assured that the orchestra would be considerably larger for *The Mastersingers* than it had been for *Tannhäuser*. There would also be plenty of time for him to work with the principal singers. Goodall was impressed by Arlen's enthusiasm, but remained uncertain as to what he should do. He consulted friends at Covent Garden, among them the bass Victor Godfrey, who eventually persuaded him to accept the Sadler's Wells offer. As a result, Goodall agreed to conduct ten performances of *The Mastersingers* between January and March 1968, with approximately four weeks of stage rehearsals.[7] He was to be paid £75 a performance. Sir David Webster said he could have time-off from Covent Garden.

Glen Byam Shaw, the company's head of productions, was asked to direct, with the staff producer John Blatchley as his assistant. Arlen and Tracey thought the obvious candidate for the part of Walther von Stolzing was Alberto Remedios, a former shipyard welder from Liverpool. With his strong, lyrical voice and attractive stage-presence, he should not only sound right, but look the part as well. However some members of the music staff thought Remedios would never learn the long role; instead they favoured Ronald Dowd, the Walther in Goodall's unhappy *Mastersingers* at Covent Garden seven years earlier (others thought Braithwaite should be the conductor, rather than Goodall). But Byam Shaw threw his weight behind Remedios, and so did Goodall, who had first come across the tenor in the Sadler's Wells *Tannhäuser*, when he had sung the small part of the Minnesinger, Walter von der Vogelweide – "very loudly," Goodall recalled. (Donald McIntyre was a fellow Minnesinger in the production.) Later Goodall heard Remedios in *Boris Godunov* at Covent Garden: "He was doing the Pretender, Dmitri, with Downes conducting. He was having trouble with the Russian text, and they wanted to have him thrown out. But there was something about his voice I liked. I thought, I hear something there. When I said I was keen to have him as Walther, some of them at Sadler's Wells said, 'Oh, no, no – absolute disaster!' But of course he turned out to be marvellous."

Most of the other parts in *The Mastersingers* were also cast from the Sadler's Wells company, for example Margaret Curphey as Eva, Derek Hammond-Stroud as Beckmesser, Gregory Dempsey as David, Ann Robson as Magdelena. However the crucial role of Hans Sachs went to Norman Bailey, a British bass-baritone who at the time was a member of the Deutsche Oper am Rhein in Düsseldorf, though soon afterwards he was to join the Sadler's Wells Opera. He was the only member of the cast who had sung major Wagner roles on stage before. For Sadler's Wells he had to relearn Sachs in English. Goodall was put out when he discovered that Bailey could not start work as early as the rest of the cast. Bailey for his part was surprised by some of Goodall's tempi, which were generally much slower than he had been used to.[8] There were altercations, but the fact that Bailey had sung the role in German was important to Goodall. He felt he had someone to build on and depend on, whereas everybody else had to be taught from scratch. Goodall always addressed his Sachs as "Herr Bailey, dear." Goodall habitually called people he liked "dear": men, women and children.

The first night of *The Mastersingers* was fixed for 31 January 1968. Legend has it that Goodall spent at least a year working with the principal singers and orchestra, but the truth is otherwise. With the two Sadler's Wells companies in different parts of the country at any one moment, it would not have been possible anyway. One of the companies even went to Stratford for a short season running from Boxing Day until 6 January, which was cutting things fine as far as rehearsals for *The Mastersingers* were concerned. Much of the preliminary work was done on tour. The two orchestras had to be rehearsed separately by Leonard Hancock and Warwick Braithwaite, who supervised the early ensemble rehearsals as well. The two choruses were also rehearsed separately. Hancock, Braithwaite and the company's musical consultant, Tom Hammond, shared the job of teaching the cast their notes in readiness for Goodall's more detailed coaching, which began in mid-October. Goodall did not have a chance to rehearse with the orchestra until 20 and 22 December, when the "S" and "W" players joined forces for the first time. Three weeks passed before they met up again. The string section totalled fifty-two players, the most that could be squeezed into the Sadler's Wells pit; for the rest, it was decided that the woodwind and brass of "S" orchestra would play for Acts 1 and 2, and those of "W" for Act 3, a common practice in performances of Wagner's later operas, whose sheer length can prove exhausting for wind-players' lips. Goodall insisted on holding sectional rehearsals – for the strings and harp, or the woodwind and horns – but time was short and he had very few of them.

Richard Fisher, who assisted Goodall at rehearsals, remembers him as being calm and patient for the most part, though there were angry eruptions when it turned out that singers he particularly wanted to coach were not available. The Sadler's Wells staff soon learned to take seriously his threats to catch the next train back to Canterbury.[9] Early on, Goodall discovered that Alberto Remedios was working, not only on Walther for *The Mastersingers*, but also on the role of Mark for a revival of Tippett's *Midsummer Marriage* at Covent Garden. Leonard Hancock wrote Goodall a pacifying letter:

> [Stephen Arlen] agreed with you that this is totally unsatisfactory ... I have told our rehearsal planning office that Remedios is not to do more than one call per week on MIDSUMMER MARRIAGE and that this must not be on the same day as any rehearsal he may do with you ...
>
> As regards the other singers you asked for, I am afraid the Eva is unavailable because of commitments in Glasgow singing THE MAGIC FLUTE; we have no Pogner here at present as one of them is in Hamburg and the other God knows where; the David I think you will have twice; the Kothner once or twice and the Beckmesser twice. I hope this is enough to keep you busy and be assured that I will shove all available singers at you at every opportunity.[10]

Why, Goodall demanded to know, were so many of his singers out of London? It was explained to him that if Sadler's Wells did not tour, it would not get its grant from the Arts Council. He accepted the logic of the situation, though it did not prevent further outbursts.

Arlen made it clear that Goodall was to be made to feel wanted. Goodall responded with gratitude and devotion: Arlen was the first person in authority to have shown complete faith in him since Joan Cross more than twenty years earlier. A close bond of affection grew up between the two men, though in character they were very different. Arlen, who had been in the theatre all his working life, as actor, stage manager, director and administrator, was extrovert, ebullient, practical and hugely energetic. Ideas, said Edmund Tracey, "shot out of him like bullets from a machine-gun."[11] Some claimed Arlen had a strong streak of philistinism in him, but few denied his breadth of vision and instinctive feel for excellence. He was determined to harness Goodall's talents in a way that Covent Garden had signally failed to do.

Goodall's coaching sessions on *The Mastersingers* took place in Valhalla, his eyrie at Covent Garden. They continued throughout November and on into December. "In two and a half hours you might get through two pages of music," said Remedios. "Reggie would go over a phrase again and again until it was not just in your mind, but in your bloodstream."[12] Some singers were at first unnerved by the experience. Particular demands were made of Derek Hammond-Stroud, who was singing the role of Beckmesser. He became aware that Goodall identified himself closely with the frustration and anguish of the Nuremberg town clerk who is treated with ridicule by his fellow citizens. For Goodall, Beckmesser was a tragic, rather than a comic, character.[13]

Because of the immensity of the task, Glen Byam Shaw decided that he and John Blatchley should split the production between them. He himself would be responsible for Act 1 and Act 3, sc. 1, while Blatchley would do Act 2 and Act 3, sc. 2. Each sat in on the other's rehearsals and commented and criticised. Goodall hated Motley's toytown sets – he yearned for Wieland Wagner's near-abstractions – but he had a high regard for Byam Shaw, who before coming to Sadler's Wells had been director of the Shakespeare company at Stratford. Goodall attended all the rehearsals, but interfered very little. Only when he discovered that the six on-stage trumpeters in the final scene had been banished to the wings did he lose his temper. He was told there was no room for them on the stage; it was crammed to its limits with seventeen principals, twenty-five dancers and a chorus of more than eighty. Goodall issued an ultimatum. Either the trumpeters appeared on stage or he would withdraw from the production. Space was found for them.

The opera was to have been given complete, but timings for the acts at the first dress rehearsal made it clear that the performances would not be over until long after midnight. Last trains home would be missed and the company faced with huge overtime bills. In setting the starting time at 6 p.m., rather than earlier, the company had not taken into account Goodall's broad approach to the score. The management feared that Goodall might walk out when he heard that the opera would have to be cut by 25 minutes, but he accepted the situation without protest. He was a more practical man of the theatre than some were prepared to admit. However he did give Arlen one final, heart-stopping moment. On 30 January he said he did not want to conduct the premiere, due to take place the following day. He was tired, he said. He had prepared the performance and now his task was done. Everybody knew their work. There would be no problem about finding someone else to take his place. In the end Arlen talked him into conducting, though he was well aware that Goodall might change his mind again. Later that day Arlen gave a talk to an Arts Council arts administration course. One of the students, Nicholas Payne, asked him what *The Mastersingers* was going to be like. "A catastrophe," said Arlen, "or the greatest success we've ever had."

The next morning Arlen wrote Goodall a note, which was waiting for him when he arrived at the theatre for the performance:

My dear Reggie,

To wish you well tonight & to hope that our contribution has pleased you – we have tried to give you of our best in order that you could put the breath of life on to it. Your influence has been profound & has made a deep impression throughout the theatre. I hope you will honour us again & that tonight will be the start of a joyful collaboration in the future.

My thanks
Stephen

The applause that greeted Goodall when he took his curtain-call at the end of the opera was thunderous. He had not wanted to face the audience, but Arlen had told him that if he did not take a call, people would think he had not approved of the performance. Remedios held Goodall in a vice-like grip in case he tried to escape. Act 1 had been slow to catch fire, but Act 2 had transfixed the audience. Wilfred Stiff, who 40 years before had sung in Goodall's choir at St Alban's, Holborn, recalled coming out into the foyer: "Nobody could speak. Nobody spoke at all."[14] Nicholas Payne had a standing place in the upper circle, alongside a fellow arts-course student, Brian McMaster. At the second interval the two future opera-company administrators went round the corner for a coffee. Eventually Payne managed to speak. "God," he said. "I think that's the greatest conducting I've ever heard." Eleanor Goodall was also in the audience, tall and elegant in a black suit, with pearls and a cigarette-holder. She was heard to remark that she wished her husband would retire. After the final curtain-call she went backstage. Arlen and Tracey were also there. "My dear," Goodall said to his wife, "I don't think you know" – his mind went blank, though he recovered himself quickly – "Mr Sadler and Mr Wells."[15]

The press's verdict on the evening was unanimous. William Mann's review in *The Times* began:

> It is a delight and a relief to see *Die Meistersinger* back on a London stage after so long, and even more marvellous to hear it played with the nobility of style and splendour of tone, as well as the clarity of detail and flexibility of line, that Reginald Goodall draws from profound experience and love of Wagner's music. Mr Goodall, Wagnerites have known for years, is a great Wagner conductor in the tradition of Furtwängler, of Beecham at his most expansive. The tradition is not currently fashionable but last night we could all hear how magnificently valid it still is.

Ensemble had sometimes gone awry, said Mann, "but as a whole the performance was a triumph." In the *Sunday Telegraph* John Warrack invoked the name of another legendary interpreter of Wagner's operas:

> Unassuming, head in score, shying from the waves of applause that met him, [Goodall] lifted from the music an ennobling quality of a kind that I thought had passed from the Wagner scene with the death of Knappertsbusch.
>
> It was, indeed, impossible not to be reminded of that august figure at the start of the Prelude: its breadth and weight and sonority came from an older tradition than today's Wagner, with all its tense virtuosity, and in the hands of a conductor who did not know what he was about could have spread into inertia. It is not a matter of nostalgia, nor of the alleged "Wagner style" that once laid such a paralysing grip on Bayreuth: here, simply, is an understanding of how every detail in the teeming score relates to one of the grandest conceptions ever to possess the human imagination.[16]

There were quibbles about individual performances, but generally speaking the critics were generous in their praise of a cast that had learned to phrase the music with so fine a sense of line.

All ten performances were sold out. Goodall missed the third on 7 February: he felt unwell and Leonard Hancock conducted in his place. *The Times* published an interview with Goodall, in which he was asked if he had any ambitions left. He would like to conduct *Parsifal*, he said, and also *Götterdämmerung*, though it "would have to be in a complete *Ring* cycle, and I don't know if I'm not too old to do that now."[17] On 18 February, Lord Drogheda wrote to Joan Ingpen: "I am going tomorrow night to Sadler's Wells to hear Meistersinger. I long to know whether Goodall is as good as he was made out to be in last Thursday's Times. I should also like to know whether Solti saw the article in question." Solti went to the last performance of the run on 2 March. Refreshments were laid on for him in Arlen's office during the second interval.[18] He praised the production, the cast, even the programmes, but he did not mention the conducting.

Just two days later Goodall was rushed to hospital in Canterbury for a prostate operation. He had never heard of the condition and was much relieved when told that his case was not unique and that the Pope, Harold Macmillan and Laurence Olivier had all suffered from the same problem.[19] He returned to Barham on 12 March for a much needed rest.

Meanwhile Stephen Arlen was planning his biggest coup yet – the transfer of the company's operations from Rosebery Avenue to the capital's largest theatre, the London Coliseum in St Martin's Lane, where almost 40 years earlier Goodall had made his West End debut in a variety show. Arlen had long felt that Sadler's Wells Theatre was inadequate for an opera company that had more singers under contract than Covent Garden. Its stage was too small, the acoustics were poor, storage space was limited and it was too far from the centre of town to attract passing custom. There had been plans for the company to move to a new theatre-complex on the South Bank, but in July 1967 the Labour government had withdrawn its support from the project and Arlen had had to look for a theatre elsewhere. He heard that Cinerama wanted to relinquish its lease on the London Coliseum, and went to see the theatre's landlord, Prince Littler of the Stoll Corporation. Littler, an old friend, was sympathetic to the idea of Sadler's Wells being granted a lease. So was the Arts Council, though Arlen still had to find £130,000 to turn the theatre into an opera house. He managed to raise it, and by March 1968 it had become clear that the move could be made in time for the start of the new season in August. One of the first operas to be put on there would be a revival of *The Mastersingers*.

Arlen had been so encouraged by the opera's success at Sadler's Wells that within days of its opening he had already started to think about the company's next Wagner project. The larger stage and orchestra pit at the Coliseum offered endless possibilities. *Lohengrin* was considered first, then *Tannhäuser*, but the final choice fell on *The Valkyrie*, the second opera of Wagner's *Ring* cycle; it would be easier to cast than *Tannhäuser*. Before long the Sadler's Wells Trust's opera sub-committee was discussing the possibility of putting on the whole *Ring*, with Goodall conducting. It was "known to be his heart's desire," though there was one worry. Goodall was already sixty-six years old and had just had a prostate operation; by the time the project could be completed he would be rising seventy. Would he have the strength to carry it through? Bernard Williams, professor of philosophy at Cambridge and a Sadler's Wells trustee, said the risk was worth taking.[20] The chairman, Jack Donaldson (by now Lord Donaldson), warned that Covent Garden might consider *The Valkyrie*, let alone a complete *Ring*, an encroachment on its territory, but in fact it raised no objection, though it said "there should be further discussion about *The Ring* after *Valkyrie* was on."[21]

In May matters were taken a step further. Arlen told a meeting of the Covent Garden-Sadler's Wells co-ordinating committee, whose purpose was to ensure that clashes of repertoire were avoided, that he was planning to follow up *The Valkyrie* in January 1969 with *The Rhinegold* in February 1970. The two operas would be produced in such a way that they could be fitted into a complete cycle should it become possible to mount one, though for the time being such a possibility seemed remote. Covent Garden's previously co-operative attitude now changed: it expressed disquiet that Sadler's Wells should be venturing further into late Wagner.[22] Arlen sensed that Lord Drogheda and Sir David Webster, who were both at the meeting, would do all they could to thwart the Sadler's Wells *Ring*. He complained to Lord Donaldson that there had to be more give and take; the Opera House seemed to think it had priority in everything.[23]

Meanwhile Goodall had recovered from his operation. He told Arlen he would be happy to conduct the *Mastersingers* revival at the Coliseum, as well as the new *Valkyrie*. However he turned down an invitation to join the Sadler's Wells Opera; he thought it would be too much of an upheaval for him after more than 20 years at Covent Garden.[24] (Although the company had left Sadler's Wells Theatre, it retained its old name for the time being). There was only one irritation for Goodall. By now Remedios was a member of the Frankfurt Opera and could only manage four of the seven scheduled performances of *The Mastersingers*; Connell Byrne, an Australian from Mannheim, was to sing the other three.

The first season at the Coliseum opened inauspiciously on 21 August 1968 with a new production by Sir John Gielgud of *Don Giovanni*. It disappointed the critics and provoked a shoal of complaints from opponents of the company's move to the West End. However *The Mastersingers*, which followed four days later, did much to vindicate Arlen's gamble. This time, thanks to an earlier starting time, it was possible to perform the opera complete. Peter Heyworth wrote in *The Observer*:

> Splendid though *The Mastersingers* sounded in Rosebery Avenue, it was a quart in a pint bottle. Stage and orchestral pit were packed like the Black Hole of Calcutta, and, what was worse, at any rate for the audience, was the way in which the auditorium constricted the sound, so that it remained hard and congested. In such conditions Reginald Goodall achieved marvels, but to hear what is in so real a sense "his" *Mastersingers* in the Coliseum is to experience it with a new dimension of enjoyment. Here at last the sound has room to spread out and,

as it does so, the unforced grandeur and sheer generosity of Goodall's reading becomes even more overwhelming.

Desmond Shawe-Taylor in the *Sunday Times* found it "a noble, tender, distinguished, deeply musical interpretation." The cast had grown visibly and audibly into their parts, he said, though there were moments when Goodall's tempi "seemed to be hampering the singers, and paragraphs which sounded, to my ear, too slow for the character of the music." Shawe-Taylor produced figures which showed that Goodall's timings for the individual acts were much longer than Hans Richter's at the first Bayreuth performances of the opera in 1888 – by twelve minutes in Act 1, nine in Act 2, and eighteen in Act 3. Andrew Porter in the *Financial Times* noted that Goodall's performance was "broader – in Act 3, considerably broader – than the longest (by Knappertsbusch) ever recorded at Bayreuth. Occasionally it feels slow, in the Act 3 prelude for example, but nobly, naturally, so."[25]

Goodall himself was very conscious of his propensity towards measured tempi. The fourth performance at Sadler's Wells had been broadcast and the next day he had listened to a tape of it. Leonard Hancock asked him what he had thought of it. "It was too bloody slow," said Goodall. But far from speeding things up, he got slower still – much to the alarm of the management, which lived in constant dread of having to make overtime payments. The tenth performance at Sadler's Wells was thirteen minutes longer than the first. A similar phenomenon was noted at the Coliseum.[26] Goodall acknowledged the influence of both Knappertsbusch and Klemperer in the matter of tempo. When the writer and musician John Amis told Goodall that at Sadler's Wells he had heard more of the counterpoint in the overture than ever before, Goodall replied, "It's supposed to be heard, isn't it? It sets the tempo."[27] Goodall always maintained that Wagner was the last of the classical composers: in his music – unlike Richard Strauss's – there was no superfluity of notes. Even the smallest ones had to be heard. If they could not be articulated, then the basic tempo was too fast. Goodall thought it possible that another factor might also have contributed to his slow tempi. When he was younger, he said, he had always conducted choirs and orchestras from memory, but when he had come to opera, he had started to use a score. It was only fair to the singers: a memory lapse on the conductor's part could prove disastrous in opera. However he was not a conductor who could look down at a score and take in a page at a glance. He read a score slowly, even in performance, and it was possible that this affected the pace. Goodall believed that his conducting had lost some of its fire when he started to use scores.

The last performance of the *Mastersingers* revival at the Coliseum was on 18 September. Earlier in the day Arlen attended a meeting of the Covent

Garden-Sadler's Wells co-ordinating committee, along with Edmund Tracey and his administrative director, Edward Renton. Covent Garden fielded an unusually large team: Drogheda, Webster, Burnet Pavitt, who had been a member of the board since 1957, Joan Ingpen and Webster's deputy, John Tooley. Encouraged by the renewed success of *The Mastersingers*, Arlen spoke tentatively of completing the Sadler's Wells *Ring* with *Siegfried* in 1971 and *Götterdämmerung* in 1972. By now Covent Garden's disquiet had turned into open hostility. Its representatives argued that certain large-scale operas, for example *The Ring, Tristan* and, in the Italian repertoire, *Aida*, should be left to the Opera House. Operetta, on the other hand, was best suited to the Sadler's Wells company. Between the two extremes there was a pool of operas that could be performed at either house. In Covent Garden's view there would be considerable – and not unjustifiable – criticism if public funds were used to duplicate the repertory at a time of financial and economic stringency.

Arlen counter-attacked. As far as he was concerned there was no category of opera from which his company was excluded, though he thought it unlikely that it would want to attempt *Tristan, Turandot, Elektra* or any other large Strauss work. *The Ring* would be performed in English, without an international cast. It would complement, rather than compete with, Covent Garden's production, and attract a new audience that would eventually be drawn to the Opera House. What was more, the Sadler's Wells company would tour its production. *The Mastersingers*, said Arlen, had demonstrated not only the validity of this approach, but also its acceptability to the public. He rested his case. Covent Garden said that if Sadler's Wells went ahead, it might have to postpone a new *Ring* of its own for several years. The chairman of the meeting, Lord Donaldson, said the Arts Council's views should be sought, though personally he did not think the two *Ring*s would be incompatible.

Arlen had rather overplayed his hand in announcing dates for *Siegfried* and *Götterdämmerung* – it was uncertain if the Sadler's Wells company could cast them – but he remained as determined as ever to mount a complete *Ring* with Goodall, whom he considered "the most important single factor in the whole project."[28] The meeting with the Arts Council representatives was fixed for 22 October 1968. Arlen knew that the signs were unpropitious. When the Sadler's Wells Opera had performed a mile and a half away to the north of Covent Garden, it had posed little threat to the Opera House, which in any case tended to consider it beneath the salt; now that the company had set up shop only 650 yards away, it had begun to look more dangerous to Big Brother in Bow Street. Arlen also knew that Covent Garden was thinking about a new *Ring* of its own, to be conducted by Colin Davis, who was due to succeed Solti as musical director at the end of the 1970–71 season. As for the Arts Council, its chairman, Lord Goodman, was known not to like Wagner, while the chairman of its music panel, Lord Harewood, was reckoned to be less than enthusiastic about Goodall.

The meeting to decide the fate of the Sadler's Wells *Ring* was held in Sir David Webster's office at the Opera House. The Covent Garden and Sadler's Wells representatives, ranged on either side of a long table, repeated their respective positions. Speaking first for the Arts Council, Lord Harewood said it was one thing for both houses to put on performances of *Bohème* or *Butterfly* on the same evening and play to capacity houses; no real damage would be done, though there might be adverse press comment. But trying to justify a *Ring* at Sadler's Wells at a time when a new production was in the offing at Covent Garden was a different matter altogether.

Lord Goodman said it was unreasonable to base the case for a Sadler's Wells *Ring* on the need to provide an outlet for Goodall's talent, though his claims should, of course, be considered. Nor was the fact that the performances would be in English sufficient justification for having two *Ring* cycles in London at public expense. The argument that *The Ring* could be toured would appeal in principle to the Arts Council, but had limited force if the production could not be taken to more than four places. Therefore, said Lord Goodman, it would be sensible for Sadler's Wells to exercise a measure of self-denial, even of self-sacrifice, particularly at such an early stage in its career at the Coliseum. It should not try to compete with Covent Garden, nor should it act provocatively.

The meeting appeared to be over. Lord Drogheda picked up his papers and put them in his briefcase. Edmund Tracey, who was acting as one of the Sadler's Wells representatives, was puzzled. "Am I to understand," he asked Lord Goodman, "that we are not to do *The Valkyrie* next season?" Goodman replied that he understood correctly. But with great respect, said Tracey, Sadler's Wells had already engaged not only a conductor for it, but also a designer, two producers, a translator and a number of singers. What was to happen to them all? Goodman appeared to have been taken by surprise. Well in that case, he said, after a moment's pause, Sadler's Wells had no alternative but to go ahead with *The Valkyrie*. However it was to be treated as an experiment. If it were to provoke a public demand for a further instalment of *The Ring* in English, then it might be appropriate to reconsider the general policy.[29]

Plans for *The Valkyrie*, by now re-scheduled for August 1969, were indeed quite far advanced. Goodall had agreed to conduct, Ralph Koltai had been signed up as designer, Glen Byam Shaw and John Blatchley were to share the production, Alberto Remedios was to be the Siegmund and Norman Bailey the Wotan, and Andrew Porter had been commissioned to do the new translation (*The Mastersingers* had been sung in a revision of Frederick Jameson's old version).

There was also a Brünnhilde, Rita Hunter, a former member of the company. Like Remedios she came from Merseyside, where they had shared the same singing teacher, Edwin Francis. Because of her generously proportioned figure, Hunter had proved difficult to cast, and in 1966 Sadler's Wells had not renewed her contract. But Arlen had not forgotten her voice, with its strong, clear top. He invited her to start looking at the role of Brünnhilde in April 1968, though at this point there was no question of her rejoining the company. Andrew Porter was asked to start his translation with Act 2.[30] Three weeks later he wrote a verse-letter to Edmund Tracey, in the style of Wagner's alliterative *Ring* libretto:

> Soon I will send you
> the central scene –
> Brŷnhilde bringing
> the doom of death.
> Read it with rigour
> and right what is wrong.
> Hunter can have it;
> lusting to learn,
> she asked for it early
> and earns her reward.
> Give it to Goodall,
> conductor most great,
> lest he should loathe it
> and long to amend.
> Hand it to Hancock,
> I'd hear what he thinks ...

for it is just possible – though I hope not – that you mightn't approve the manner. The principle is direct clear intelligible statement, even where the German syntax may be tortuous; for if the English is hard to understand (or to sing) there's no point in doing it in English. On the other hand there are places where, it seems to me, the words, particularly proper names, must fall to the notes to which Wagner set them (e.g. "Sieglinde sieht/Siegmund/dort nicht"), and in these places a moment of, well, somewhat unnatural English is the lesser evil. The main difference from [previous translators like] Jameson, Newman and co. (apart from an absence of prithee, wight, nathless, bethink you Volsung, etc) is an insistence on phrasing the words to the musical phrases.[31]

Goodall began work with Rita Hunter in October 1968:

After she'd been coming to me for a time she said, it's expensive for me coming up for all these rehearsals [she lived at Northolt in Middlesex]. Do you think they could pay my fare? I said, I'll see what I can do about it. I went to Stephen Arlen and he said, Do you think she can do it? I said, I think she can do it beautifully. All right, he said, I'll give her a salary. It was small, it wasn't much. But from that she went on.[32]

As Hunter makes clear in her memoirs, *Wait till the Sun Shines, Nellie*, her relationship with Goodall was not always an easy one. He could be very demanding of singers. There were disputes about missed coaching sessions.[33]

In January 1969 Stephen Arlen had to postpone *The Valkyrie* once more. Norman Bailey, the Wotan, had been asked to sing Hans Sachs at the Bayreuth Festival that summer. Unfortunately, the dates of the festival clashed with those of *The Valkyrie*. Arlen felt that in view of Bayreuth's importance to Bailey's career he had no alternative but to release him. *The Valkyrie* was rescheduled again, for January 1970. To help fill the gap at the Coliseum, Goodall agreed to conduct four performances of *The Mastersingers* in September, by which time Bailey would have returned from Germany.[34]

Only two weeks after Arlen's announcement, Bailey made an unexpected appearance as Sachs in London, not at the Coliseum, but at Covent Garden in a new production of *Meistersinger* conducted by Solti. The German baritone, Hubert Hofmann, had been due to sing the role, but had fallen ill and Bailey took his place on the first night. Before it started David Webster told the audience that Covent Garden had searched all over Europe for a substitute Sachs; then, finally, it had managed to find one just down the road. It was a patronising speech and instead of raising the intended laugh, it earned jeers from the gallery. The next day, the *Evening Standard's* diarist noted tartly: "It might have saved time and money if Covent Garden had thought of Mr Bailey in the first place. Perhaps they did not know he had been chosen to sing Hans Sachs at this year's Bayreuth Festival." Desmond Shawe-Taylor wrote of Bailey's Covent Garden Sachs that it was "the outstanding success of the performance."[35] Comparisons were made with Goodall's conducting of the work, though not necessarily to Solti's detriment. William Mann wrote in *The Times*:

> Georg Solti's reading on Friday night abounded in nervous vitality, bustling expectancy, highly coloured detail (especially delightful in David's catalogue of the approved Modes). In the Sadler's Wells performances Reginald Goodall's motto is the Hound of Heaven's "deliberate speed, majestic instancy;" his interpretation was a ravishing dream of a long-dead golden age – and therewith, inevitably, one sometimes wished it did not all the time sound so sleepy. Solti's Nurembergers are wide-awake and full of energy; what the music lacks in his reading is magical serenity, at the end of Act 1, in Eva's visit to Sachs in Act 2, and then the night-scented sleep-music associated with the Night Watchman.[36]

This may have been the occasion when Solti, coming up from the pit to take a curtain-call, remarked in exasperation to Norman Feasey and the staff producer Ande Anderson, "Well that's another good review for Reggie Goodall!"[37]

The delay in putting on *The Valkyrie* at the Coliseum gave Goodall time for other projects. On 17 February 1969 he conducted a Bruckner symphony for the first time, the Eighth, in a broadcast performance with the BBC Symphony Orchestra. Peter Heyworth was at the BBC's Maida Vale studios to hear it:

> In the first movement the orchestra had difficulty in following Goodall's elusive beat, so that there were a number of ragged entries. But as the performance got under way it gained in assurance and conviction, and by the time it had been brought to a triumphant conclusion (for once even that dicey finale sounded really conclusive), I realised that I had been present at a memorable occasion, for I have heard few more searching performances of a Bruckner symphony.[38]

Goodall repeated the work at the Proms on 3 September. John Warrack echoed many listeners' feelings when he wrote in the *Sunday Telegraph* four days later:

> Where, except with Klemperer, can one now hear Bruckner playing of this sublime innocence and grandeur, of this directness of detail and blithe Schubertian openness combined with a vision of where it all fits in the huge design? Goodall can draw from the chorus of Wagner tubas in the Adagio that peculiar sombre dignity of sound which eludes more vigorous maestri ... If there were some slips of ensemble and, even with him, a slight faltering in momentum at one point in that structurally very difficult finale, the dignity and freshness of the whole conception overrode any such reservations.

When *The Mastersingers* was revived at the Coliseum a week later, there was a new Nightwatchman, the Welsh bass Gwynne Howell. He had been scheduled to sing the role the previous year in what would have been his first professional stage appearance, but Goodall had thought him too inexperienced and had had him replaced before the first night. Before taking up singing professionally, Howell had been senior planning officer for Manchester city corporation. He had heard that Goodall was a powerful figure and imagined someone akin to the city bosses he had come across in the north. He was taken aback when he attended his first production rehearsal. Goodall appeared to have been dressed by Oxfam – his trousers were hitched a good three inches above his shoes – and he seemed to be curiously indecisive. "Did you like that, Reggie?" Norman Bailey asked him about a certain phrase. "I'm not sure, dear," replied Goodall, looking perplexed. As the rehearsal continued, Howell realised that his first impressions were wrong. Goodall was exerting an unmistakable authority over the proceedings: "Everybody was taller than Reggie, yet many of them seemed to turn to jelly when he spoke to them." Howell was so unnerved by the occasion that he sang the Nightwatchman's second verse before the first. Now, a year later, he was being given another chance to sing the role. His reviews were excellent, and before the second performance he was called up to the conductor's room, where Goodall told him enigmatically, "My wife thinks you're the best Nightwatchman we've had – but she's not a musician." Howell, who went on to sing Gurnemanz, King Marke, the Wanderer and Hunding for Goodall, wondered whether he had been paid a compliment or not.[39]

The months leading up to the first night of *The Valkyrie* on 29 January 1970 were fraught with difficult moments. Once again singers were often not available when Goodall wanted them. Alberto Remedios was still in Frankfurt and not due back in London until 15 December; Leonard Hancock and Tom Hammond both flew to Germany to work with him. Hugh Beresford, who was to sing Siegmund at some of the later performances, was in Düsseldorf. Clifford Grant, the Hunding, spent part of October 1969 in America (Tom Hammond assured Goodall that Grant was "very well advanced and knows this role from memory, which is something to be thankful for"[40]). Norman Bailey was away in Amsterdam in November, while the Fricka, Ann Howard, was tied up with rehearsals and performances of *The Rake's Progress*. The eight Valkyries – Margaret Curphey, Donna Faye Carr, Patricia Purcell, Katherine Pring, Janice Chapman, Ann Robson, Anna Cooper and Gillian Knight – had to be rehearsed in groups, both in London and on tour. It was mid-December before they could work together. As in the case of *The Mastersingers*, the actual rehearsal situation hardly squares with the myth of limitless preparation, though on this occasion Goodall did get more sectional rehearsals with the orchestra: strings, trumpets and trombones, timpani, woodwinds, horns and Wagner tubas. As he told Richard Fisher, "You have no idea what hard work it is to get *The Ring* off the ground when nobody knows it."

There were further problems when production rehearsals began. Remedios was commuting between Germany and London, a fact kept hidden from Goodall, until the afternoon when Remedios, who was feeling tired, admitted that he had been singing in *Rigoletto* the previous night in Frankfurt. Goodall hurled his score to the ground in fury. *Rigoletto*! The choice of opera could not have been worse. Glen Byam Shaw and Richard Fisher calmed Goodall down and the rehearsal started again. It went well. "Alberto, dear," said Goodall when it was over, "when you sing like that I can forgive you anything."

David Cairns's review in the *New Statesman* gives an idea of the impact the performances had on critics and public alike:

> If there is any justice and any sanity in our musical life, the production of *The Valkyrie* now enthralling large audiences at the Coliseum will be the first step – a giant step – towards a complete *Ring* cycle in English. To those who object that

it is unnecessary for Sadler's Wells to duplicate with a local cast what Covent Garden already do with an international one (as the opera committee of the Arts Council are known to have objected when the plan was put up to them a year or two ago), the answer is, first, that the box office does better business with Wagner than with almost anything else in the company's repertoire, and secondly that Wagner at the Royal Opera House and Wagner at the Coliseum are two separate and complementary experiences, both of them thoroughly 'necessary.' Indeed, the word seems cold and cautious after last Friday's tremendous performance. Life without having seen it is hardly imaginable. What made it tremendous was, above all, the fact of its being given in English, and the sudden sharpening of focus and intensifying of reality that followed from that.

The orchestral playing had not been immaculate, said Cairns, but Goodall's mastery was more assured than ever before:

> Some reports of the first night of this *Valkyrie* spoke of longueurs, and splendours spoiled by inordinately slow tempi. The third performance, the one I heard, lasted some minutes longer than Knappertsbusch's monumental reading as measured by the Bayreuth time-keeper in 1951. But, as always, relative, not absolute, tempo is the thing in Wagner. And Goodall's understanding of this truth is unexcelled today. In his hands the score simply flows – though with none of the lack of variety of pace and mood the metaphor may suggest.

Remedios, said Cairns, was not only equal to the heroics of Siegmund's music, but could draw "a lyrical line rare among Wagner tenors." Norman Bailey and Rita Hunter were a Wotan and Brünnhilde "of splendid achievement and greater promise."[41]

The Arts Council-Covent Garden case against a Sadler's Wells *Ring* collapsed, and both bodies withdrew their objections. *The Valkyrie's* success was discussed on 18 February at a meeting of Covent Garden's opera sub-committee. Georg Solti, John Tooley and Joan Ingpen were among those present. The general conclusion was that the "development of a race of indigenous Wagner singers (albeit English and not German-singing) could come in useful for Covent Garden in cases of emergency." Goodall is not mentioned in the minutes of the meeting.

Webster was not present. He had had a fall that winter while walking in Covent Garden market and was not well. He was sixty-six years old and due to retire from the Opera House at the end of the season. According to his biographer, Webster

> ... considered it extremely bad luck that Goodall's altogether unlooked-for success – unlooked-for by him, at any rate – made his non-use at Covent Garden a central failure. It irked him that others had solved a problem he couldn't, and whatever had gone wrong through the years it was now too late to put right at Covent Garden.[42]

Webster wrote to Lord Drogheda:

> I am afraid that I am still dubious about Goodall for miscellaneous works in the
> repertory but maybe we should have paid greater attention to his Wagner. We
> are incidentally using him for Parsifal next season.[43]

Rudolf Kempe had been first choice for the revival of the opera, but he said
he would not return to the house except for a new production.[44] Goodall was
invited to conduct instead:

> I said I didn't want to do it. So they said to Solti [Goodall always pronounced
> the name "Salty"], you must talk to Goodall. And he sent for me. So I said, "Mr
> Solti, you've been here ten years and you're going now, and now you ask me to do
> one of the most important works in the repertory. That's why I don't want to do
> it." He said, "No, Goodall, I was warned against you when I came here." Can you
> imagine that? "But I know you're a fine musician. I'd like you to do it." It must
> have been what's-his-name, Webster. I don't know what they warned Solti about.
> I'm not a fixer. I don't try to get things. Anyway I agreed to do *Parsifal*.[45]

On 30 June 1970 a farewell gala was given for Webster at the Royal Opera
House. Goodall conducted the prelude to Act 3 of *Meistersinger* which was
greeted with affectionate and pointedly long applause. Just over eleven months
later Webster was dead.

CHAPTER 14

Resounding Ring

I T WAS decided that the next instalment of the Sadler's Wells *Ring*, in January 1971, would be the final opera, *Götterdämmerung* or *Twilight of the Gods*. Casting it was no longer a problem. With his performance as Sieg-mund in *The Valkyrie*, Alberto Remedios had shown that the role of Siegfried was well within his grasp, while Rita Hunter had already proved herself as Brünn-hilde. Goodall maintained that the company needed more experience in Wag-ner before attempting *The Rhinegold*, which would now be done in 1972: with its single span of music embracing four long scenes it was, he said, the hardest of all the *Ring* operas to pull off – and certainly the hardest to conduct. *Siegfried* would be left until last, in order that Remedios might be given as much time as possible to master the long and demanding title-role.

There were plenty of pessimists both inside and outside the company who doubted that *The Ring* would ever be completed. Sadler's Wells Opera faced a financial crisis and there was even talk of closure. Although *The Masters-ingers* and *The Valkyrie* had both been box-office successes, some of the other works in the company's repertoire had not fared so well, either financially or artistically. When only one of the Sadler's Wells companies was in residence, the orchestra and chorus often sounded under-nourished in the Coliseum's huge spaces, while productions designed for Sadler's Wells Theatre could look lost on its stage. Some voices that had seemed big enough in Rosebery Avenue turned out to be too small for St Martin's Lane. Eventually it was decided that from the 1970–71 season the "S" and "W" companies would be merged. The new single company would play in London from August until the end of March. Then, for ten weeks only, it would split into two separate ensembles, which would go out on tour simultaneously. During this period the Coliseum would be let out to visiting companies. The arrange-ment, which was to prove successful, had particular advantages for Goodall. The whole company would be in London during the months leading up to *Götterdämmerung* and singers would be more readily available than they had been in the past. It would also be easier to secure the number of orchestral rehearsals he wanted.

It was a busy time for Goodall. In April and May 1970 he did preliminary work on *Götterdämmerung* with Remedios, Hunter and Norman Bailey, who was to sing Gunther. He also coached Donald McIntyre in the roles of Klingsor and the Dutchman for that summer's Bayreuth Festival. In July he started rehearsals for another revival of *The Mastersingers* at the Coliseum, and on 6 August conducted the BBC Symphony Orchestra in Bruckner's Seventh Symphony at the Proms. The programme also included the *Siegfried Idyll* and Beethoven's concert aria, *Ah! perfido*, with Heather Harper as soloist. Hans Keller, who had become a loyal champion of Goodall's in the BBC music division, wrote to him about the performance of the Bruckner:

10 August 1970

One of the most outstanding interpretations I have ever heard: many thanks! Incidentally, even people who do not normally take to Bruckner found themselves deeply involved – which just shows how much depends on (1) feeling it all spontaneously, (2) thinking it all clearly, (3) making (a) music without vanity and (b), therefore, sense.

I am going against my principle of never criticising tempi as such (tempo being a function of structure, and hence of phrasing) by asking whether the scherzo might not, perhaps, be a little faster and yet retain your shapings, which, of course, were wonderfully well-defined and firm. It is, after all, "very quick" – the only fast movement, in fact. Do you really think (as I suspect you do) that it would lose strength and articulation?

It was a deeply important evening, anyway.

Goodall wrote back saying that he thought Keller was quite right about the scherzo.

There were four performances of *The Mastersingers*. The final one, on 19 September, was the last Goodall ever gave of the opera. In all he had conducted it thirty-two times – fourteen for Covent Garden, eighteen for Sadler's Wells. Coaching on *Götterdämmerung* began in earnest as soon as *The Mastersingers* was over. The first night, arranged for 29 January 1971, was still four months away, but Goodall felt he had not a moment to lose. Even an opera house with a cast and orchestra long experienced in Wagner regards a new production of *Götterdämmerung* as a major challenge. At the Coliseum only two members of the cast had performed their roles before: Norman Bailey, who had sung Gunther at Bayreuth the previous year, and Anne Evans, who had sung Wellgunde, the second Rhinemaiden, for the Geneva Opera. Yet the performances made an even greater impact than had those of *The Valkyrie*. In the *Sunday Times*, Desmond Shawe-Taylor wrote that "on every page of the vast score there was abundant evidence of intensive coaching and rehearsal." The orchestra

... played very finely for [Goodall], more securely than at the premiere of "Die Walküre," although there were a few fluffs and slips, even a false entry in Siegfried's Funeral March; after all, the Sadler's Wells Orchestra isn't the Vienna

Philharmonic, and it takes a long while to master more than five hours of music. But they played as though they loved and understood the meaning of every phrase; they gave their all; and the climaxes, neither too hectic nor too frequent, were climaxes indeed.

Though his regard for Goodall remained as strong as ever, Arlen's relationship with Charles Mackerras, the company's musical director since the beginning of 1970, was far from smooth; there were constant clashes over policy.[1] It looked at one point as though Mackerras might resign. During the *Götterdämmerung* rehearsals Arlen told Glen Byam Shaw and John Blatchley that, if that were to happen, he was not sure what course of action he should take. He could try to persuade Mackerras to stay on; he could invite Alexander Gibson of Scottish Opera to replace him – or he could ask Goodall to become musical director. The idea, said Arlen, was not so far-fetched. Whatever impression Goodall might have given at Covent Garden, at the Coliseum he was a figure of authority: people showed him respect. He was temperamental and unpredictable, but he achieved results. And though he might give the impression of being vague, he actually missed very little of what was going on, for he was Machiavellian, even ruthless, when it came to achieving his own ends in musical matters. Arlen would not expect Goodall to be musical director in a conventional sense; he would not have to deal with paperwork or conduct *Rigoletto*. He would conduct the Wagner repertory and anything else that interested him. He would coach singers and train the orchestra. He would be an influence for good, the keeper of the company's standards. It was clear to Byam Shaw and Blatchley that Arlen was serious about the idea, though nothing came of it. Mackerras decided not to resign.[2]

After *Götterdämmerung* had finished, *The Valkyrie* was revived at the Coliseum before being taken on tour. Goodall had warned Sadler's Wells some months earlier that he would not conduct it; he did not care for the reduced orchestral forces used for the tour performances. In any case, he was involved in rehearsals for the revival of *Parsifal* he was due to conduct at Covent Garden. Mackerras and Charles Groves shared the *Valkyrie* performances in his place. Goodall held *Parsifal* in special reverence. "Musically," he said, "it's the quintessence of a lifetime. The distillation of creative genius. I can't even tell you in which way, because I'm not a musicologist. But I sense the depth of it."[3] Prospects for the revival were good: Goodall had a first-class orchestra at his disposal, there was a reasonable amount of rehearsal-time, and the cast included a number of artists he knew well: Jon Vickers as Parsifal, Amy Shuard as Kundry, Norman Bailey as Amfortas, Donald McIntyre as Klingsor. The Gurnemanz was Franz Crass, while the Flowermaidens were led by the 26-year-old Kiri Te Kanawa, making her Covent Garden debut. More than one critic picked her out for special mention. Fifteen years later Goodall was asked if he had a particular memory of her. There was a long pause. "I remember ticking her off for being late for rehearsal," he replied. "She said she had been parking her car, if you please."

Unfortunately both Crass and McIntyre fell ill before the opening. McIntyre recovered in time for the third of the six performances, but Crass never appeared at all. At the first night, on 21 April 1971, his place was taken by the celebrated German bass Gottlob Frick, who at 65 had agreed to come out of semi-retirement in order to save the performance. So great was his success that he considered singing on the second night as well, but then thought better of it. Ernst Wiemann from Hamburg appeared instead, followed by Peter Meven from Düsseldorf at the third and fourth performances, the Belgian Louis Hendrikx at the fifth, and Meven again at the sixth. Goodall convinced himself that he was the victim of a conspiracy organised by the head of opera planning, Joan Ingpen.[4] The notion was absurd, though Goodall was correct in his belief that Ingpen did not rate him highly as a conductor.

Parsifal was always a dangerous opera for Goodall. If he was in a depressed state while working on it, he was inclined to identify too closely with Amfortas's suffering, with the result that his conducting, particularly in Act 1, could become dangerously prolix. Critical opinion was divided on the first night. For Peter Heyworth the performance "was – for the most part – a disappointment ... the music rarely developed that inner momentum that is an unfailing hallmark of [Goodall's] best performances." Desmond Shawe-Taylor, on the other hand, thought that "his entire performance, notwithstanding some orchestral roughnesses that will doubtless disappear with repetition, was profoundly beautiful and perceptive." Martin Cooper of the *Daily Telegraph* wrote that the "eloquence and intensity of the orchestral playing was a most remarkable feature throughout the evening ... but not all the very slow tempi justified themselves and they made some insurmountable difficulties for the singers."[5] Covent Garden's view of the revival is reflected in the minutes of an opera sub-committee meeting:

> This production had been so plagued by illness that the very fact that it had gone ahead was an achievement in itself. Vickers and Frick had given marvellous performances. Goodall had drawn some remarkably beautiful playing from the orchestra and the performance as a whole had been distinctive; but it was arguable that there had at times been a certain lack of dramatic impulse.[6]

Norman Bailey thought the performances got better as they went on.[7] The fifth one was recorded by the BBC. Vickers gave Goodall an engraved silver pocketwatch to mark their collaboration. "Dear Reggie," he wrote in an accompanying note, "Please accept this little gift with my sincerest thanks for all your kindnesses to me through the years; and with my great admiration for your artistic integrity and devotion. Sincerely, Jon."

On 10 July 1971 Eleanor Goodall fell heavily in the kitchen at Barham while preparing lunch. Goodall, who was at the far end of the garden, failed to hear her shouts for help and more than an hour passed before he returned to the house to find her lying on the floor and in great pain. She had broken her hip. An ambulance was summoned and she was taken to hospital in Canterbury. When she returned home nineteen days later she was still in a very weak state; not only was she suffering from the after-effects of her accident, she also had heart trouble. The Goodalls' doctor was worried. Eleanor had had a stroke some ten years before; she was now 70 and there was a danger she might have another one. He arranged for her to go into a nursing home near Dover, where she could be looked after properly. She was to remain there for some months.

Goodall was filled with irrational guilt that he had not discovered his wife earlier. He brooded on plans for the next stage of *The Ring*. *Götterdämmerung* was to be revived on 5 February 1972, followed by the first night of the new *Rhinegold* on 1 March. There were to be five performances of the first opera and six of the second. Goodall had agreed to conduct all of them. He started to coach the singers in late September and worked on until 20 December, when production rehearsals began. In November he broke off briefly to conduct another performance of Bruckner's Seventh Symphony, this time at the Royal Festival Hall with Janet Baker singing Wagner's *Wesendonck-Lieder* in the first half of the programme. "The orchestral playing throughout was firm, responsive, and eloquent," wrote the critic Noel Goodwin. "How Mr Goodall achieves it with such a basic simplicity of platform gesture is his own mysterious secret."[8]

Early in January 1972 Goodall learned that Stephen Arlen was seriously ill with cancer of the oesophagus. Deeply depressed, he wrote to Richard Fisher, by now head of opera planning, to say that he wanted to be relieved of all his commitments after *Götterdämmerung* and *Rhinegold*. He no longer had any wish to conduct *Siegfried*, let alone the complete *Ring*. Fisher wrote back on 12 January, begging him "not to ask us to accept such a serious decision at this particular time when Stephen is ill and we are all trying so hard to take the right decisions about everything in his absence." Exactly a week later Arlen died at the age of 58. He had been ill for only five weeks. Goodall felt that what with Eleanor's illness, and now Arlen's death, his world had collapsed. He worked on for another fortnight, but then withdrew from the *Götterdämmerung* revival on the day before it opened, and also from the new *Rhinegold*.

His assistant, John Barker, conducted *Götterdämmerung*. It was put out that Goodall was ill. The first night of *Rhinegold* was conducted by Charles Mackerras, who cancelled all his other commitments at the Coliseum and mastered the score in three weeks. He got a good press. Bryan Magee wrote in *Music and Musicians*:

> In the orchestra pit we missed Reginald Goodall, on whose unique Wagnerian gifts this whole *Ring* project is founded (as my colleague Ronald Crichton has so penetratingly put it, he conducts Wagner as if communicating by private line with Erda), but Charles Mackerras, standing in, showed himself again an efficient Wagnerian. He was good at providing the get-up-and-go that this work in particular needs, though there were still occasional pools of sag in the surface tension. The orchestra, on unprecedentedly fine form nowadays, played for him with brilliance and warmth.[9]

On 6 February, Glen Byam Shaw wrote to Goodall, urging him not to give up altogether. He ended his letter:

> I can truly say that all of us who have worked with you have a true and absolute belief in you. You must complete your Ring. You must. For Wagner and for Stephen. In the meantime we will battle on.

John Blatchley, *The Ring*'s co-producer, wrote a week later:

> Get well my dear friend – come back to us soon – come back for "Siegfried" and YOUR "Ring." When you return I promise you we will have 23 trumpeters – 9 Night Watchmen – 336 Nibelungs, 84 "Rainbow" harps – a stage full of anvils and your own two devoted and loyal friends to try and make it all work.

In his reply Goodall thanked Blatchley for his good wishes, but made no reference to the future. For the next two months the Coliseum heard nothing from him. He spent most of his time at Barham, reading scores and working in his garden. Eleanor could still not walk properly and had returned to hospital in Canterbury. Goodall wondered if he should not cut his ties with London finally and devote himself to looking after her, but the hospital advised that it would be better if she were cared for by its geriatric unit. In April, Goodall wrote to Hazel Vivienne, the Sadler's Wells chorus master, saying that he was feeling much better and that he was about to start coaching at Covent Garden again.[10]

By early May there were clear signs that he wanted to resume work on the Coliseum *Ring*. When he had withdrawn from the *Götterdämmerung* revival in February, he had also abandoned a plan to record its two final scenes for the Unicorn company, with Hunter and Remedios heading the cast. Now he was talking of resurrecting it.[11] On 16 May he telephoned Richard Fisher at the Coliseum, demanding to know why he had not been sent the dates for *Siegfried* and the first complete *Ring* cycle. He managed to suggest that Sadler's Wells was most remiss in not providing him with the information. Goodall was definitely back in business. Later that day Fisher wrote to him:

> It is a long time since Wotan summoned one of his Ravens and it was nice to feel that one was on call again. I am sorry that you have not had an official letter from us about SIEGFRIED ... We had no intention of being discourteous in any way: quite the contrary since we regard you as such an old friend as to be practically a member of the company.

The *Siegfried* was to open on 8 February 1973, followed by two complete cycles between 31 July and 25 August.

Though Goodall had recovered, Eleanor was still far from well. She was now in a nursing home again, but returned to Barham for weekends. At the beginning of August the Goodalls celebrated their fortieth wedding anniversary with champagne in the garden. It was a hot day and they dozed off. Goodall told Alberto Remedios that when they woke up they were surprised to find that it was ten o'clock at night and dark. Remedios asked how big the bottle had been. "A magnum, dear," said Goodall. "It's very good for you, champagne. A tonic."

The three-months' rest had given him a new zest for work. He even accepted with equanimity the arrival of Lord Harewood as Stephen Arlen's successor at the Coliseum. The appointment could easily have strengthened Goodall's resolve not to continue with *The Ring*, for when Harewood had been head of opera planning at Covent Garden during the 1950s, he had shown little enthusiasm for Goodall as a conductor; he had thought him incompetent. Goodall had no reason to suppose that Harewood had changed his opinion in the meantime. Unlike Siegfried and Gunther in *Götterdämmerung*, Goodall and Harewood were never to swear an oath of blood-brotherhood, but they got on well enough. If the going ever got rough between them, Edmund Tracey was on hand to calm Goodall down over tea at the Waldorf or the Charing Cross Hotel. As time passed Harewood modified his view of Goodall. "It's quite simple," he said in 1983. "Reggie has no talent. Genius, yes, but no talent."[12] Three years later he wrote of Goodall's working methods:

> Here was no magician waving a wand so that everything came suddenly right on the night, rather an analyst with the knowledge and the patience to take everything apart, the time and the will to put it together again, and the soul of a poet, so that the finished product shone with the composer's light and illuminated the score as seldom before.[13]

Goodall spent a good deal of time in London during the months leading up to the first night of *Siegfried*, though weekends were spent at Barham with Eleanor. Maisie Aldridge, his friend from the Wessex days, had found him a quiet bed-sittingroom in Addison Gardens, Holland Park, with a view of trees and flowerbeds and the back of St John the Baptist's church, Holland Road; by coincidence Goodall's old mentor, Healey Willan, had been its organist before emigrating to Canada. Previously, when he had stayed in London, Goodall had lodged in a house that backed on to the building site of the new Kensington Hilton Hotel. Goodall found the noise from it intolerable and complained to the contractors frequently. He once stormed on to the site and poked a workman in the back with his umbrella. The man, who was cutting through a large piece of steel with an oxy-acetylene torch, turned round and set the umbrella on fire.[14]

Aldridge, who lived nearby, had lost touch with Goodall for many years, but had met him again in the street after seeing him walk past her window. He came to rely on her a good deal when he was in London. She did his shopping, cooked his supper (left to his own devices, Goodall lived on a diet of potato-crisps at lunchtime and cream cakes for tea), gave him lifts (he never learned to drive), took his messages (he refused to have a telephone in London, which exasperated both his friends and the opera houses) and offered encouragement. She was at all times concerned for his health and watched over him accordingly.

Once again Goodall had a heavy programme ahead of him. *Siegfried* was to be followed by a revival of *Rhinegold*. In addition, the *Götterdämmerung* excerpts were to be recorded at last on 30 and 31 December 1972. Rita Hunter spent November and most of December at the Metropolitan Opera in New York, where she understudied Birgit Nilsson as Brünnhilde in both *Die Walküre* and *Siegfried*, and sang the role herself in a single performance of *Walküre*. She got back to London on 23 December. Goodall was anxious to get down to work with her on *Siegfried*. Hunter, whose mother was ill, felt he was putting unnecessary pressure on her. Goodall said it was essential for her to do more work on the *Siegfried* duet. The situation became uncomfortable. On 19 January, to Goodall's annoyance, Hunter flew to Munich for the weekend to sing the *Walküre* Brünnhilde in place of Birgit Nilsson, whose father had died. As she came off the stage after a successful performance, Hunter learned that she too had been bereaved. Her mother had died.

Accounts of what happened next between Goodall and Hunter differ. Hunter says in her memoirs that as soon as she landed in London on the Monday morning she was told that "Reggie was wanting me to go to a rehearsal that afternoon ... I can't even write what I called him" – yet the whole of that day was devoted to rehearsals of Acts 1 and 2 of *Siegfried*, in which Brünnhilde does not appear. Goodall knew nothing of Hunter's loss until the following afternoon, when he arrived for a rehearsal of Act 3 to discover that the cover, Judith Turner, was singing Brünnhilde, because Hunter had gone to Liverpool for her mother's funeral. He was told that the theatre hoped to see her back on Friday afternoon.[15] Hunter maintains that Goodall harassed her to resume work and that when she did get back to London he sulked: "Reggie Goodall never forgave me for that week off, and I never forgave him."[16] Goodall was deeply hurt by Hunter's attack, which was published four years before he died. He thought it poor reward for putting her on the map: "She didn't come to me as someone who had absolutely swept the boards of places. She was an unknown person. And then she talks about me in that way." He admitted he had been "furious with her – I wasn't very nice about it either," but he remained adamant that it was not the funeral, but Hunter's long absence in America that had annoyed him.[17]

Despite the atmosphere of ill-feeling at rehearsal, the first night of *Siegfried* went off successfully. Once again the reviews were good, though Peter Heyworth complained that the forging scene had failed to convey "the music's exuberant sense of physical action, its elation at an heroic task triumphantly accomplished." Lord Harewood said in a letter to *The Times* that he had never heard anyone sing the young Siegfried as beautifully as Remedios had. Elisabeth Furtwängler, the conductor's widow, wrote to the paper agreeing with him.[18] Goodall's verdict, delivered to Edmund Tracey at the end of the performance, was succinct: "Wasn't our boy wonderful?"[19] But as the run continued, Goodall grew increasingly despondent. The disputes of the rehearsal-period had begun to take their toll. Matters were not helped when Hunter fell ill and missed two of the performances; Judith Turner took her place. Once more Goodall wondered if he really wanted to continue. He started to complain that his eyes were giving him trouble and that he was having difficulty reading the score. The company knew from past experience that this indicated a loss of confidence in himself and it came as no surprise when he withdrew from both the first and second nights of the *Rhinegold* revival. John Barker stood in for him.

Yet again Goodall's participation in the complete cycles of *The Ring* seemed to be in jeopardy. However he was persuaded to conduct the third and final *Rhinegold* (his first-ever) on 30 March. It went so well that his confidence was restored and the next day he started to jot down in his diary ideas about casting for the cycles: "[Anne] Evans Norn. Who Rhinemaidens – S[arah] Walker?" He even asked for, and got, an increase in his conducting fee, which was put up from £150 to £250; it was probably the only time in his life that he made such a request. Two weeks later he started work with the first group of singers – Katherine Pring as Waltraute, Clifford Grant as Fafner and Hagen, Rita Hunter, Remedios, Norman Welsby as Donner and Gunther. When he heard Anne Evans sing Helmwige's first "Ho-jo-to-ho!" from *The Valkyrie*, he remarked, "You'll sing Brünnhilde one day, dear." She thought it unlikely. The Wanderer in *Siegfried* was being sung by Norman Bailey for the first time. Don Garrard had performed the role the previous February, because Bailey had been singing Kurwenal in Tristan at Covent Garden. Goodall had taken Bailey's "defection" as a personal affront. When Bailey appeared for his first coaching session on the Wanderer, Goodall was abusive. Bailey was taken aback: "It was all very difficult. I told Reggie I thought it would be better if I went outside until he calmed down. But it was the only really bad experience I had with him."[20]

Not since the first night of *Peter Grimes* in 1945 had a Sadler's Wells production generated so much public interest. Both cycles were sold out within a short time of the box office opening. EMI, with financial backing from the Peter Moores Foundation, recorded *Siegfried* live during the cycles, though a plan for the BBC to film the same opera for television collapsed when the stage management demanded extra money for it. One of the many foreign critics who came to London for The *Ring* was John Rockwell, who reviewed it for the *New York Times*:

> It is easy to be cynical, especially from afar. Well-known conductors have spoken disparagingly about Mr Goodall's skills, and certainly nobody loves a Grand Old Man as much as the British. And when the Grand Old Man happens to be British himself, and to have been unduly neglected for years, objectivity might easily be overcome by nostalgic local chauvinism.
>
> Yet to these American ears, Mr Goodall's conducting of the "Ring" was indeed impressive. Much of what passes for Wagner conducting these days sounds thin, brisk and trivial. Mr Goodall knows the secret of weighty, long, flexible, Wagnerian phrasing. At times his reading lacked precision and intensity (most notably in the first act of "Siegfried"). But mostly it breathed a conviction sorely lacking these days: Motifs could expand and deploy themselves unhastened, and page after page that sometimes seems like padding sounded inspired instead ...
>
> To call the Goodall "Ring" perfect in all details would of course be wrong, and one has even noticed a slight debunking counter-current in the London press of late. Naturally, there were weaknesses. Some of the singers weren't quite up to par. The production looks modishly modern, yet lacks a firm point of view. Yet the achievement remains a considerable one – certainly far more impressive than what Bayreuth offered this summer – and one of which Britons can be legitimately proud.[21]

Lord Harewood told Goodall that he had never enjoyed a *Ring* as much: "it was an absolutely overwhelming experience, and one for which I will be eternally grateful."[22] Though Goodall affected to be indifferent to the general acclamation, he was in fact pleased by it, for in spite of his natural modesty, he had, deep down, a touching streak of vanity in him. He even began to enjoy his curtain-calls, though he always refused to take one on his own. Audiences rose to their feet as he tottered on to the stage, blinking into the lights and peering at his cast as though he had never seen any of them before.

As soon as the cycles were over Goodall returned to Barham and his garden. From time to time he went to London to have tea with Edmund Tracey or to work on Wagner roles with Donald McIntyre at Covent Garden. He also had a series of meetings with Colin Davis, Solti's successor at the Opera House, to discuss *The Ring* with him. Davis was to conduct *Das Rheingold* and *Die Walküre* for the first time the following year and was anxious to have Goodall's advice. The two operas marked the start of a new production of *The Ring* at Covent Garden, to be directed by Götz Friedrich.

Towards the end of 1973 Lord Harewood wrote to Goodall to tell him that the next *Ring* cycles at the Coliseum, scheduled for January 1975, would have to be postponed for a year, because it had proved impossible to find room for all the rehearsals he had asked for. The decision, Lord Harewood told him, had only been taken after "a good deal of heart-searching, including consultation with Charles Mackerras.²³ Goodall, as suspicious as ever of anything remotely resembling a plot against him, was outraged. If he had been musical director, he said, "or someone in equal official authority," he would have been given all the rehearsals he wanted. In the circumstances he thought it best "if I don't undertake the conducting of another 'Ring' cycle for the ENO."²⁴. (It had just been announced that the company was to be renamed the English National Opera.)

However he did agree to conduct a Wagner concert in October 1974 with the ENO orchestra at the Snape Maltings, the hall that Benjamin Britten had built for the Aldeburgh Festival. It was an emotional occasion for Goodall. He had never been invited to Aldeburgh before and he saw the concert as an act of reconciliation with Britten, though the composer was in Germany at the time and could not attend it. The programme consisted of the *Mastersingers* prelude, Siegfried's Death and Funeral March from *Götterdämmerung*, and Act 1 of *The Valkyrie*, with Alberto Remedios as Siegmund, Margaret Curphey as Sieglinde, and Gwynne Howell as Hunding.

Britten had had a heart operation and was very unwell. In a Christmas card he sent to Goodall, he said how delighted he was that the concert had been a success. Goodall replied:

12 January 1975

My Dear Ben,

Thank you for your card and greetings.

I'm glad you were pleased with the reports of the concert – we all considered it a great honour to be asked to Snape and to play in your magnificent hall.

Why is it creative artists always get things right – the accoustics [sic] at Snape and Bayreuth are superb.

Ben, dear, I didn't know or realize until I read the fine article about you in the Times how ill you had been and what you had been through.²⁵

But I thought you looked so well and relaxed in the photograph – and that you have started to compose again is wonderful news – though the loss of your conducting is a great blow.

Do you remember how you used to deprecate your conducting – and it was always so marvellous, not only in your own works, but those of other composers also.

Love and best wishes to you and Peter
Reggie

The news that Goodall no longer wished to conduct *The Ring* at the Coliseum came as a particular disappointment to Peter Moores, vice-chairman of the Littlewoods organisation and the driving force behind the plan to record it. His foundation had put £13,500 into *Siegfried* and was prepared to bear the total recording costs of the other three operas. Moores went to see Goodall at Covent Garden and pleaded with him to continue. "No dear," Goodall replied, "it's too much for me." Moores told him it would be a tragedy if the recording project were to collapse, because *Siegfried* had been a great success and everybody was waiting for the next instalment. Goodall perked up. "Oh, how nice of you to say so," he said. "Well if you want it, I'll do it."[26] Goodall even told the Coliseum that he would conduct a complete cycle in 1976 after all, though later he changed his mind yet again.[27] However Goodall did record *The Rhinegold* live at the Coliseum in March 1975 and followed it up with *The Valkyrie* in December of that year.

A month before *The Rhinegold* Goodall went to an investiture at Buckingham Palace. He had been made a CBE in the new year's honours list, though when he had received the letter of notification from 10 Downing Street the previous November, he had thrown it on to his piano unopened, thinking it was an income-tax demand. He was embarrassed when, some time later, he got a telephone call asking why he had not replied. The CBE was not the only honour he received at that time. The universities of Newcastle-upon-Tyne and Leeds both conferred honorary doctorates of music on him, and the *Evening Standard* gave him its newly-instituted award for outstanding achievement in opera: the writer Bernard Levin said that he and his fellow judges, who included Dame Eva Turner and the critic William Mann, would be in danger of making themselves look ridiculous if they gave it to anyone else.[28]

Plans were made to record *Götterdämmerung* at three performances laid on specially for the purpose in December 1976 and January 1977. But if Moores and EMI thought the complete English *Ring* was within their grasp at last, they were soon to be disillusioned. First, there were financial differences with Rita Hunter, and there was talk of Margaret Curphey singing the role of Brünnhilde instead of her.[29] Then the ENO chorus turned down the fee it had been offered by EMI. The Hunter problem was resolved. That of the chorus was not, and at the last moment EMI cancelled the recording. Goodall was so disappointed that he refused to conduct the first night and Nicholas Braithwaite, who had been assisting him, replaced him. The audience was told that Goodall had fallen ill that morning.

Fortunately there was one more opportunity to record *Götterdämmerung*, for Goodall had agreed to conduct two final cycles of *The Ring* for the company during the summer of 1977. By recording the dress rehearsal and the two performances EMI got the takes it needed. The project had cost the Peter Moores Foundation a total of £119,000. Moores thought it money well spent. In *The Times*, William Mann described the result as

> ... an historic enterprise, an integral recording of Wagner's *Ring des Nibelung*en in intelligible English, decently sung, stylishly played (give or take some fluffs, inevitable in live performance), conducted with an immense sense of the music's majesty by a musician who understands Wagner as profoundly, down to the tiniest detail, as any mortal can, yet who can direct the music with an eloquence that sounds quite spontaneous.

Reviewing the *Götterdämmerung* in *The Gramophone*, Alan Blyth found Hunter's Brünnhilde "unflinching and untiring in delivery, intelligent and sensitive in execution." Remedios was "as fresh vocally in his death throes as in the love duet." The ENO orchestra was not the Vienna or Berlin Philharmonic, said Blyth, but anyone investing in the complete recording was "in for a life-enhancing experience."[30]

The ENO *Ring* was by no means Goodall's sole preoccupation during the mid-Seventies. In May 1974 he conducted another Bruckner symphony, the Ninth, with the BBC Symphony Orchestra at the Maida Vale studios[31], while in September of the same year he assisted Colin Davis with the rehearsals for *Rheingold* and *Walküre* at Covent Garden. It was the first time Goodall had worked on *The Ring* at the Opera House for some years. Many critics complained about Davis's funereal tempi, which, said Rodney Milnes in *The Spectator*, made Goodall sound like Jack Brabham (a well-known racing driver of the day)[32]; they lacked the underlying forward impulse inherent in Goodall's conducting. Davis was not the only conductor who thought that slowness was the key to Goodall's success, though he soon learned his mistake. The following year Davis added *Siegfried* to the first two operas and conducted two "cycles" of them (*Götterdämmerung* was not unveiled until 1976). Goodall agreed to conduct a third one. Desmond Shawe-Taylor wrote of his *Rheingold* and *Walküre*:

> At Covent Garden ... we could again admire the easy lyrical approach, the fine balance and transparency of tone, and the sense of abundant space and time – the

latter no less evident despite the fact that he had this year lopped five minutes or more from the playing-time of "Das Rheingold" and of each act of "Die Walküre." But there was also, as it seemed to me, something disconcertingly light-weight and low-voltage in the general impact, especially in that of "Das Rheingold."[33]

Goodall himself was unhappy about the two evenings. He had tried to put his own stamp on the performances, but had failed to do so. He felt he had been given too little time to rehearse *Siegfried* and pulled out of it on the day of the performance. Colin Davis took his place.

The six performances Goodall gave of *Fidelio* in March and April 1976 were scarcely more successful. James King and Jon Vickers shared the role of Florestan, and Marita Napier and Hildegard Behrens, making her house debut, that of Leonore. Six weeks before the opening performance Goodall wrote to John Tooley, who had succeeded David Webster as Covent Garden's administrator:

17 February 1976

With the present arrangements for "Fidelio" we have a cast change every two performances – which makes it impossible, so far as I'm concerned, to obtain an adequate interpretation.

The "Florestans" are switched in and out of "Fidelio", to avoid changes in other operas – if no cast change is necessitated in Grimes, Figaro, or Cav & Pag, to name only three operas, these incessant changes in Fidelio seem very pointed.

The critic Stephen Walsh wrote of the first night that Goodall "conducted the piece as slowly as Klemperer can ever have done, and by no means always with compensating weight and authority."[34]

The one opera he still longed to conduct was *Tristan und Isolde*. Jon Vickers had tried for years to persuade Covent Garden to mount a new production of it for Goodall, but, though promises were made, it had never materialised. At the beginning of 1974 John Tooley told Goodall that "our determination to arrange some performances for you at Covent Garden remains. Unhappily, these could not take place before the 1976/77 season, and it might even be 1977/78."[35] Goodall was sceptical about his chances. None the less he lived in hope. He asked the artists' agent Robert Slotover if he could arrange for him to try out *Tristan* "in a small German house."

Slotover explained that it would not be easy – *Tristan* tended to be done only by the larger companies – but he managed to find a sympathetic musical director in Lübeck, who was happy to invite Goodall to conduct a performance there in May 1975. Knowing he would get very little rehearsal, and wanting to familiarise himself with the production, Goodall went to Lübeck to hear a performance under another conductor. He was disappointed by it. "There wasn't an ounce of poetry in the whole thing," he told Slotover on his return to London. Had it been any other opera, Goodall would almost certainly have called off the plan at this point, but so great was his desire to conduct *Tristan* that three weeks later he returned to Lübeck to rehearse the orchestra. The visit turned out badly. Not only did the players claim they could not follow his beat, they seemed unwilling to accept his ideas about phrasing. Suddenly Goodall realised that the German repertory system involved greater compromises than he was prepared to make, and both he and the Lübeck management agreed that there was no point in him attempting to conduct an actual performance.[36]

For more than two years there had been talk at the Coliseum of a new Goodall/Byam Shaw production of *Tristan*, but nobody seemed to show much enthusiasm for it, apart from Edmund Tracey and Brian McMaster, who had succeeded Richard Fisher as head of opera planning. In 1976 McMaster was appointed administrator of the Welsh National Opera, which had firm plans for a new production of *Tristan* to open in September 1979. It was to be conducted by the company's musical director, Richard Armstrong. McMaster asked Armstrong how he would feel if Goodall were asked to conduct the opera instead of him. Armstrong reacted favourably to the idea, "firstly," he says, "because I was a great admirer of Reggie's – I knew I would learn a lot from him. And secondly, because at that time we were trying to develop the orchestra. Having Reggie to coach the players in Wagner style seemed to me important. "[37]

McMaster made his offer to Goodall over lunch at the Strand Palace Hotel. Goodall accepted it. Afterwards they walked back to the Opera House. Just before they reached the stage door, Goodall exclaimed in childlike wonder, "I'm going to do *Tristan*," and executed a little dance in the street.

CHAPTER 15

Tristan

S OME MONTHS AFTER Brian McMaster made his offer to Goodall, Lord Harewood at last decided that the ENO would also mount a production of *Tristan*, with Glen Byam Shaw and John Blatchley as joint-producers and a cast headed by Alberto Remedios and Rita Hunter. Goodall agreed to conduct, despite the fact that it was scheduled to open in January 1980, only a month after the last performance of the Welsh production. He now had to coach two casts, and rehearse two orchestras, for an opera he had never conducted before. To complicate matters, Cardiff's production was to be sung in the original German, the Coliseum's in a new English translation by Andrew Porter. It was a formidable prospect for a man who had already passed his seventy-sixth birthday.

For the Isolde in Wales Goodall chose a soprano who had sung for him at the Coliseum in both *The Mastersingers* and *The Ring*, Margaret Curphey. The Tristan was to be John Mitchinson, a tenor with a fine heroic voice who was better known in the concert hall than the opera house; he had worked with Goodall once before, in 1969, when he had sung the part of Siegmund in a BBC broadcast of Act 1 of *Die Walküre*. Like their London counterparts, both Curphey and Mitchinson were new to their roles.

Goodall set about reading and re-reading all the literature about the opera he could lay his hands on. He analysed the harmonies and, in his own words, "took the score to pieces ... I looked at every orchestral line ... first clarinet, second clarinet, fourth horn, and played it on the piano quite a lot myself to get the sound of it into shape. Then I started with the singers."[1] Goodall was not afraid to admit that he found the opera's underlying philosophy hard to understand:

> I really don't know what *Tristan*'s about. Its basic idea is "unbegreifbar" [beyond one's grasp]. I mean, they take this death drink in Act I; but what are they going to come together about? You'd have thought they would fling themselves into each other's arms for those last few moments on earth, but they just stand and wait. Wagner was very much influenced by Schopenhauer, that life is cruel and death is the only ultimate solution. Tristan dies, but does Isolde die? When she sings "höchste Lust" ("highest love") at the end, she joins him – but where, in what way? Not physically, it's more a mental thing, but I don't know exactly. It's hopeless to demand a completely logical plot. Anyway, Wagner didn't like everything to be specific; he preferred to leave something to the imagination. Like Elsa in *Lohengrin*, we shouldn't ask too many questions. We must just take it as it

comes; the music says everything. What it says may be different to every person, but to put it into words ... well, one hopes people will sense something. Perhaps that's the wonder of music, that it speaks to you and you can't put it into words.[2]

By May 1978 Goodall was already complaining to Jeremy Caulton, McMaster's successor as head of opera planning at the ENO, that he had not seen enough of either Hunter or Remedios. He also told Caulton that he would like to do some work with Linda Esther Gray, the Scottish soprano who was to understudy the role of Isolde's companion, Brangäne, in the ENO production. Earlier in the year he had heard her sing Micaëla in *Carmen* at the Coliseum and had been impressed.[3]

On 6 June Goodall had a tempestuous encounter with Rita Hunter, who had gone to his room at Covent Garden for a coaching session. Hunter says he accused her of not knowing the role and that she replied that the reason she was there was to learn it with him.[4] Recriminations bounced back and forth. Two days later Hunter wrote to Goodall to say that she had withdrawn from the *Tristan*. She and Goodall never worked together again. The question of her replacement as Isolde had to wait. The ENO's season had finished a week earlier and the company was on holiday.

Goodall returned to Barham. Some time earlier he had brought Eleanor to a nursing home in the village, so that he could push her up to Stainton Lodge in a wheelchair at weekends. By now, however, she had grown more infirm than ever and her mind had begun to wander. On 30 July, three days before their forty-sixth wedding anniversary, she died at the age of seventy-seven. After a Requiem Mass at the Roman Catholic church of St Thomas in Canterbury she was buried at Barham. Goodall smothered his sense of loss in work.

As soon as the holidays were over, Harewood, Tracey and Caulton addressed themselves to the Isolde problem. Various suggestions were made, but nothing came of them and the production was rescheduled for August 1981, to allow time to find a new soprano. Goodall started to coach Linda Esther Gray as Brangäne and soon came to the conclusion that he had a potential Isolde on his hands. In September 1978 he told the ENO management that he wanted to work with her on Isolde as a long-term project.[5] By January 1979, Gray, a pupil of Dame Eva Turner's, had made such strides that Goodall had no difficulty in convincing Lord Harewood that she should sing the role in the Coliseum's production.[6] He also schemed to have her as Isolde in Wales.

Margaret Curphey had had an operation for an arthritic hip and it had begun to look doubtful if she would be fit enough for the first night in Cardiff. Goodall said he was not prepared to take any risks and insisted on her being replaced. When he told McMaster and Armstrong that he wanted Linda Esther Gray for the part, they expressed doubts about the wisdom of having someone who was only 30 years old and still relatively inexperienced; her only Wagner role to date had been Eva in the Scottish Opera's *Meistersinger*, which was nothing like as demanding as Isolde. They were in any case reluctant to drop Curphey as long as there was a chance that she might make a complete recovery; the opening was still six months away.

On the morning of 5 April, McMaster and Armstrong attended a WNO press conference in London, at which it was announced that the Isolde would be Curphey. In the afternoon they went to the New Gallery, Regent Street, where, to keep Goodall happy, they had agreed to hear Gray sing some of the role at a specially arranged audition. As soon as she began the *Liebestod* from Act 3, they realised that Goodall's enthusiasm about Gray was not misplaced. Not only was her singing very beautiful; she appeared to have a remarkable understanding of the role.[7] Eventually a compromise was reached: Gray would sing the first five performances and Curphey would take over from her in November[8] (though, as it turned out, she was not well enough to do so; Anna Green sang in her place). The Coliseum was not amused to learn that its Isolde was to perform the role in Cardiff first.

The WNO *Tristan* was a particularly happy experience for Goodall. He was nervous about having to face a new company, but McMaster and Armstrong worked hard to put him at his ease. He had a first-rate assistant in Anthony Negus and he was on excellent terms with the leader of the orchestra, John Stein. He asked for – and got – eight double basses, and was given all the orchestral rehearsals he needed, though they were no more in number than Armstrong himself would have had for a new production. Much of the work was done in the sectional rehearsals. "In the full orchestral rehearsals," said Armstrong, "he didn't talk to the players very much. He just let them get on with it. It was in the sectionals that he really educated them in terms of phrasing, interpretation and weighting of notes."[9] Goodall was keen that the players should understand what was happening on stage. He explained to the harpist, for example, that the precise moment of Tristan's death was indicated by her chord of C, G flat and B flat. She was to dampen it immediately his arm fell lifeless. It was not to continue reverberating.

Goodall enjoyed an excellent working relationship with both John Mitchinson and Gwynne Howell, who was singing King Marke. Above all he had Linda Esther Gray as his Isolde. She was his discovery, as Alberto Remedios had been before her, and a close musical rapport grew up between them. "For months we lived within the text and the harmonies," Gray has said. "Reggie would play the chords and then discuss what they meant, what they told him. Everything came out of the harmonies. He was always discovering new layers of meaning. It was like doing *Lieder* with him, except that there were pages and pages of it."[10]

Goodall asked McMaster for Peter Hall as producer, but Hall had to turn the offer down because of his "rather alarming" commitments at the National Theatre.[11] Next, McMaster approached the Swedish film director Ingmar Bergman and then the German theatre director Rudolf Noelte. Both had other engagements. Finally the choice fell on Peter Brenner, son of the celebrated Austrian director, Walter Felsenstein. His production was straightforward. Goodall had only one major disagreement with him. Brenner felt that the audience would be bored by the length of Act 2 and wanted the traditional cut to be made in the love duet. Goodall told him that "if they're bored, it will be our fault, not Wagner's. He's not written too much music." Goodall had his way.

If Goodall's epic approach to *The Ring* at the Coliseum reflected the influence of Hans Knappertsbusch, much of his *Tristan* had an intensity and drive that owed a good deal more to Furtwängler. Goodall never heard Furtwängler conduct *Tristan* in the theatre, but in 1952 had attended the sessions at the Kingsway Hall for his acclaimed recording of the opera with Kirsten Flagstad; they had made a deep impression on him. When the Welsh production opened at the New Theatre, Cardiff, on 8 September 1979 the critics were taken aback by what Max Loppert of the *Financial Times* called the "massive vigour" of Goodall's conducting: "surging forward on a high tide of rhythmic energy, much of the first act came near to engulfing the senses."[12]

In *The Spectator*, Rodney Milnes wrote that

> ... the first act comes as a complete surprise: fast but never driven; intensely, almost operatically dramatic yet never facile, the tension under control from first bar to last. The overflowing eroticism of the second act makes Carlos Kleiber, the ranking *Tristan* conductor of the day, sound positively mimsy by comparison, and in the third we were on more familiar, Parsifal-pain-like territory, the long, aching arcs of Tristan's love-death delirium drawn out with well-nigh intolerable realism.[13]

There was widespread enthusiasm for the Isolde. William Mann commented:

> Wagner's music, the most divine that he ever wrote for singing voices, was exquisitely delivered by Linda Esther Gray as Isolde, at 31 far too young to sing the part, if her glorious, well-built soprano is to survive for the two or three decades, at least, which it deserves. Yet I am thankful to have seen and heard her now in the role, so generous and rich was the sound, so vivid the declamation, so vivid her acting within the statuesque, *plastique*, style prescribed by the producer Peter Brenner.[14]

In the love scene, said Mann, Gray and Mitchinson "sang gloriously for all they were worth".

After the initial performances in Cardiff, Goodall conducted *Tristan* on tour, in Birmingham, Bristol and Liverpool, as well as at the Dominion Theatre, London. There was also a concert performance at the Snape Maltings on 24 November.

1. Goodall and his brother Billie, *c.* 1906

2. Goodall as a choirboy, Lincoln Cathedral, *c.* 1912

3. George J. Bennett, Goodall's choirmaster at Lincoln

4. Albert Goodall, 1924

5. Goodall with the choirboys of St Alban's, Holborn, 1934

6. St Alban's, Holborn: annual dinner for choirmen and servers, with Father Eves standing centre rear, Eleanor Goodall on his left, and Goodall centre front

7. Goodall with Maisie Aldridge in the 1930s

8. Goodall rehearsing one of his amateur orchestras in the 1930s

9. Rehearsing *Peter Grimes* in early 1945

10. The Sadler's Wells Opera tour of occupied Germany, 1945

11. Benjamin Britten plays during rehearsals for *Peter Grimes*, 1945, with, from right, Goodall, Eric Crozier and the designer, Kenneth Green

12 & 13. *The Rape of Lucretia*, Glyndebourne, 1946: with Owen Brannigan (left) and Edmund Donlevy; below, with Britten and Rudolf Bing

14. Goodall with ballet mistress Peggy van Praagh during rehearsals for *Khadra*, Sadler's Wells Opera-Ballet, 1946

15. Goodall and Karl Rankl (right) auditioning a player for the new Covent Garden orchestra, 1946

16. Goodall photographed by Angus McBean in the mid 1940s

17. Rehearsing the Wiesbaden Opera orchestra for *Peter Grimes*, 1954

18. With Carlos Kleiber, 1986

19. Erich Kleiber

20. At a recording session with
    Otto Klemperer

21. Franz Konwitschny

22. Goodall en route to Bulawayo, 1953, with Edith Coates
    (left) and Adele Leigh

23 & 24. Goodall in Bulawayo, 1953

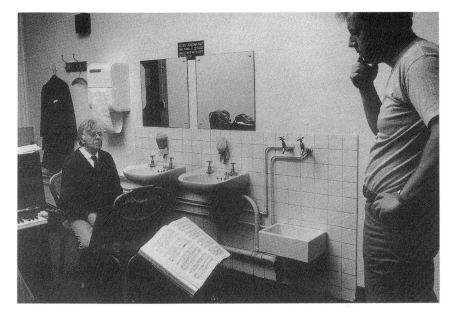

25. Coaching session with Gwynne Howell in "Valhalla"

26. Goodall at the London Coliseum, 1969

27. Goodall and his wife Eleanor, 1965

28. Barham Court; Goodall's house is on the right

29. Norman Bailey as Hans Sachs in *The Mastersingers*, Sadler's Wells, 1968

30. Curtain call: Rita Hunter, Goodall and Alberto Remedios,
    1973 *Ring* cycle at the Coliseum

31. With Linda Esther Gray at a *Tristan* recording session, 1981

32. Rehearsing *The Valkyrie* with Anne Evans and Anthony Negus, WNO, 1984

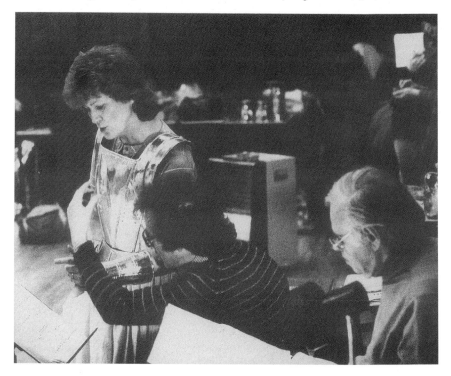

33. Honorary doctorate at Oxford, with Sir Claus Moser, 1986

34. Goodall's last conducting engagement: rehearsing *Parsifal* for the 1987 Proms with
Gwynne Howell (standing) and Warren Ellsworth

35. Farewell: Goodall leaves the Royal Albert Hall after the *Parsifal* Prom, with Lionel
 Friend immediately behind him

Britten had died in 1976, but Peter Pears (by now Sir Peter) was there and invited Goodall to the composer's old home, the Red House, where the Britten-Pears Library had been set up. Afterwards Goodall told Maisie Aldridge that he had been touched by Pears's generosity and moved by his visit to the house where Britten had lived and worked. Earlier in the year Goodall had presented the library with its most valued, and valuable, possession.

In the early 1970s, Britten's assistant, Rosamund Strode, had asked the composer what had happened to the composition sketch of *Peter Grimes*. He said he thought it might be in the Library of Congress in Washington, along with the full score of the opera. In 1978 Strode started to write to known owners of Britten manuscripts, asking them if their scores could be microfilmed for the Britten-Pears Library. Eric Crozier happened to mention to her that Britten had given the *Grimes* composition sketch to Goodall after the first performance in 1945. Strode wrote at once to Goodall, care of the Coliseum. A month passed before she received a telephone call from him in January 1979. He sounded diffident. He still had the manuscript, he said, and would be delighted to lend it for filming. "In fact," he continued, "I really think the library ought to keep it. It would be far better for you to have it than me."

Strode was dumbfounded. She informed the trustees, two of whom, Isador Caplan and Donald Mitchell, took Goodall to lunch at the Garrick Club on 6 February. They expressed their gratitude for the gift, but asked Goodall if he realised that he could make a good deal of money if he were to sell the manuscript on the open market. Goodall said he had no wish to sell it to anyone; he wanted to donate it to the Britten-Pears Library, of whose existence he had not been aware until he had received Rosamund Strode's letter. Nor was there was any question of the gift being deferred until after his death – the library was to have it immediately. Goodall added that the manuscript was not in a very good state. When Caplan and Mitchell collected it from the Royal Opera House later that afternoon, they discovered that he had not been exaggerating. It was "in a shocking condition".[15] Goodall, who had not looked at the manuscript for some time, had kept it along with other unneeded scores in a cupboard at Barham that was badly affected by damp. Pages were stained and discoloured. On its arrival at the Red House the score was microfilmed in its original state and two years later restored by the Stationery Office bindery at the British Library.[16] Donald Mitchell was to describe it as the crown of the Britten-Pears collection.[17]

Goodall was euphoric about the success of the Welsh *Tristan*. He gave interviews to the press and even agreed to take part in *Desert Island Discs*, a popular radio programme in which a "castaway" chooses eight records and chats about his or her life. The presenter, Roy Plomley, failed to prise much information out of him and as a result the musical extracts lasted longer than usual. They were:

1. Alleluia, from the Mass for the Third Sunday after Easter (Monks of the Abbey of St Pierre de Solesmes/Gajard).
2. Bach, Prelude and Fugue in C, BWV 846 (Sviatoslav Richter). Goodall asked for a piano, rather than a harpsichord, version.
3. Bach, Kyrie Eleison from the Mass in B minor (BBC Chorus/NPO/ Klemperer).
4. Bach, Sarabande from Cello Suite No.1 in G (Pablo Casals).
5. Beethoven, final pages of Symphony No. 9 (Bruno Kittel Choir/Berlin Philharmonic/Furtwängler).
6. Wagner, "Ihn selbst am Kreuze" from *Parsifal*, Act 3 (Weber/Windgassen/ Bayreuth chorus and orchestra/Knappertsbusch).
7. Tchaikovsky, first movement of Symphony No. 6 in B minor (Berlin Philharmonic/Furtwängler). Goodall said he particularly admired "the yearning, the pathos" that Furtwängler got into the music.
8. Debussy, *Prélude à l'après-midi d'un faune* (Berlin Philharmonic/Karajan).

For a book Goodall chose Milton's *Paradise Lost* and for a luxury item "an English garden". Asked which record he would take if he could only have one, he picked the Bach prelude and fugue. The experience, Goodall told Plomley before the microphone had been turned off, "wasn't as bad as I thought it would be." The programme (which Goodall had never heard of) was broadcast on 5 January 1980. The next day he went into St Thomas's Hospital in London for an operation to repair a detached retina in his left eye, which had been troubling him since early October. Afterwards he went to recuperate for a week at Enton Hall, a natural health clinic near Godalming in Surrey. He did not appreciate the strict dietary arrangements. Brian McMaster sent some chocolates. Goodall wrote to him on 18 January:

> Thank you very much indeed for the sumptuous box of chocolates.
> Here I am in this place – for breakfast they brought me a sour grapefruit! and for tea (my favourite meal) a thin dish of China tea – nothing else, and when I asked for some chocolate they almost evicted me! and then your lovely box of chocolates arrived, and saved my life.

Goodall's self-confidence and enjoyment of life during this period owed much to a friendship he had formed with Joyce Farrell, an impoverished divorcee, thirty years his junior, who lived with her two teenage sons in the main house at Barham Court. Like Goodall, she was both lonely and something of an eccentric. They became companions. She cooked his Sunday lunch and drove him to Dover in her battered old Mini for meals at his favourite hotel, the White Cliffs, where in the past he had often stayed with Eleanor. Joyce Farrell's taste in music tended towards Shirley Bassey and the Beatles, but it did not bother Goodall. What mattered to him was that she was funny and unpretentious. He helped her out financially, took her to the ballet at Covent Garden and proposed marriage to her more than once.

In October 1980 Goodall returned to Cardiff, where he gave two further performances of *Tristan*, to houses that were less than half full. On 15 November he conducted the work in Coventry, where the theatre was packed. The next day he went to Swansea for a week, to start recording *Tristan* for Decca with the WNO cast (see Discography, page 211). Sessions took place at the Brangwyn Hall, or Brangäne Hall as Goodall preferred to call it. To ensure that the overall shape of his conception was retained, the opera was recorded in long takes lasting up to forty minutes. The recording was completed at a second set of sessions in January 1981.

The ENO *Tristan*, which opened at the London Coliseum on 8 August 1981, came as something of an anti-climax. Musically the performance was on a high level, but the production and designs received a good deal of criticism. Goodall was depressed throughout the rehearsal period. Though surrounded by familiar singers – Linda Esther Gray and Gwynne Howell from the WNO production, Alberto Remedios as Tristan, Norman Bailey as Kurwenal – he found it a considerable strain having to start all over again on the opera, and in a different language. Although he approved of *The Ring* being performed in English, he was never convinced that Tristan worked in translation:

> It's a linguistically much more difficult work than *The Ring*. I very much wanted the English National Opera to have it sung in German. So much of *The Ring* consists of people giving each other information, whereas in *Tristan* they're expressing the state of their souls ... Wagner fully supported opera in the vernacular and he didn't hesitate to alter the note values in *Tannhäuser* for a French translation. But, in *Tristan*, even the Germans don't understand parts of the text. I think that, in Act II, what Wagner really wanted was to express not the reality of love, but the *idea* of love. In fact Cosima noted in her diaries that Wagner once said of *Tristan*, "How little words contributed to the drama ... it's characters one wants, not speeches". But, basically, the decision to do *Tristan* in English was an English National Opera policy decision. The musical decision might be that you do it in German.[18]

For Goodall the *Klang*, or sound, of the Tristan text was inextricably bound up with the *Klang* of the music.

Goodall felt great respect for Glen Byam Shaw – "he had maturity and he knew the theatre. Distinguished, that's what he was" – but he was not convinced he was the right producer for *Tristan*; it was, Goodall asserted, too esoteric, too philosophical, too German for him. Byam Shaw had retired from the ENO the previous June aged 78 and had returned as a guest for *Tristan*. It was agreed that he would produce Act 2, while John Blatchley would tackle Acts 1 and 3. The arrangement had worked in the past, but Byam Shaw was now tired and found it hard to get to grips with the opera. Further difficulties arose when it was found that Hayden Griffin's semi-abstract set did not fit the stage. There were also snags with the lighting and, as a result, Blatchley found himself having to waste valuable hours sorting out technical problems when he should have been spending time with the cast. Goodall took one look at the set and disliked it. One of the few bright spots for him came on 13 July, his eightieth birthday, when Lord Harewood produced a large cake with a lot of candles on it.

Blatchley began to notice tell-tale danger signs in Goodall's behaviour: he would dash off after rehearsal without bothering to say goodbye; sometimes he missed a rehearsal altogether. "Reggie just switched off," said Linda Esther Gray. Blatchley felt let down by him: "We were like a rowing eight without the cox," he said later. A week before the first night Edmund Tracey received an urgent message, asking him to go the auditorium, where he found Goodall stretched out on a row of seats in the stalls. Goodall said he was withdrawing from the production; he was exhausted and could not go on any longer.[19] The first dress rehearsal was conducted by his trusted assistant, Lionel Friend. Tracey debated what steps should be taken to lure Goodall back. He could not be rung up, because he did not have a telephone in London. Nor was there any point in sending him a message via Maisie Aldridge; he would only ignore it. Tracey persuaded Lord Harewood to turn up unannounced at Goodall's bed-sitting-room in Holland Park. Goodall was surprised – and flattered – to find the managing director, and the Queen's first cousin to boot, on his doorstep. Harewood told Goodall that he was vital to the production; the singers in particular depended on him. The cajolery worked and Goodall returned to the Coliseum, but his depression did not lift during the run of performances, and he made it clear that he would not conduct a revival of the production under any circumstances.

After Goodall had conducted his sixth and last *Tristan* on 5 September, Lord Harewood wrote to ask if he would consider "doing it in a German production, if we can borrow one ... and provide you with a proper frame in which to put forward the music. I think it is tough on Alberto not to do it again when he has taken the trouble to learn it in English, and the same probably goes for Linda and Norman Bailey, each of whom of course knew it before in German."[20] The idea appealed to Goodall, who asked if it might be possible to have Götz Friedrich as producer. He rated Friedrich's first *Ring* production at Covent Garden second only to Wieland Wagner's at Bayreuth. Harewood promised to look into the matter.

The chorus of praise that greeted the release of the WNO *Tristan* recording did much to restore Goodall's morale. "I have heard Reginald Goodall conduct 'Tristan and Isolde' three times in the theatre," wrote Alan Blyth. "All those performances were memorable in one way or another, but they are surpassed by his recording of the work ... which fully deserves the over-used epithet great. Here, directing the team with which he worked so hard and lovingly in Wales, he has achieved the most searing interpretation of the opera on disc since Furtwängler's a generation ago."[21]

To the WNO's delight, Goodall accepted an invitation to attend the recording's North American launch in November 1981, along with Brian McMaster, Linda Esther Gray and John Mitchinson. It took place in Chicago, headquarters of Standard Oil (Indiana), whose British subsidiary, Amoco, had sponsored the recording. The visit lasted for four days. Goodall had not been to America for fifty-six years. His brother Billie had hoped to come up from California to meet him, but was unable to do so because of ill health. The American musical press flew in from New York and there was a press conference and a heavy schedule of radio interviews. At first Goodall's replies to questions were monosyllabic. Then he became more confident – and more forthcoming. Local journalists in particular were fascinated to hear Goodall's views on his old boss, Georg Solti, by now well entrenched as musical director of the Chicago Symphony Orchestra. Goodall seemed tireless. Amoco laid on a stretch limousine for him and he thoroughly enjoyed the superstar treatment he was receiving for the first time in his career.[22] Reviews of the recording were good: "A Superb 'Tristan' By Way of Wales" ran the headline in the *New York Times*.[23] No sooner was Goodall back in Britain than the Royal College of Music conferred a fellowship on him, an honour that caused him amusement in view of his somewhat chequered relationship with the establishment in the past.

By now Goodall's fame had spread to the Continent and he received numerous invitations to conduct there – *Parsifal* at the Geneva Opera, *Tristan* in Bonn, a recording of Wagner's *Wesendonck-Lieder* for a Dutch company with Elly Ameling as soloist. He refused them all, feeling they had come too late in his life. At home, Peter Pears asked him to conduct Bruckner's Eighth Symphony at the Aldeburgh Festival ("I do not know whether we could get your favourite Welsh Opera Orchestra, but we could have a try ...").[24] That too was turned down. On the other hand he did accept two separate offers to conduct Beethoven's Ninth Symphony, at the Leeds and Edinburgh festivals, though to the annoyance of both organisations he later changed his mind and decided not to do them.

Goodall's next operatic project after the ENO *Tristan* was a new production of *Parsifal* in German for the Welsh National Opera, with Donald McIntyre as

Gurnemanz, the American tenor Warren Ellsworth in the title-role, and Linda Esther Gray as Kundry. It was to open in February 1983. Goodall looked forward to it keenly, and spent most of 1982 coaching the singers. In mid-November, however, he received the distressing news that Joyce Farrell had died of cancer. He travelled up to Newcastle-upon-Tyne for her funeral. "Your mother was one of the most wonderful women I have ever met," he told her son, Nicholas. "She understood the stars."[25]

Production rehearsals for *Parsifal* started in Cardiff on Monday 4 January 1983. Four days later Goodall returned to Barham for the weekend. No sooner was he there than he began to suffer severe abdominal pains. He caught a train to London, where Maisie Aldridge arranged for him to see a doctor. A strangulated hernia was diagnosed and Goodall was rushed to St Stephen's Hospital, Fulham, for an operation. He was told that he must not conduct again for two months. The *Parsifal* seemed to be jinxed. The producer should have been the German theatre and film director Rudolf Noelte, but he had withdrawn at a late stage. Mike Ashman replaced him, while Anthony Negus took over the music rehearsals.

Goodall was in hospital for eight days. Maisie Aldridge arranged for him to convalesce at a Roman Catholic nursing home at Bognor Regis on the Sussex coast, but Goodall, at his most stubborn, insisted on returning to Addison Gardens instead. While climbing the stairs to his bed-sitting-room, which was on the second floor, he collapsed. Only then did he admit that he was not as strong as he made out. Grumbling loudly, he was packed off to Bognor by hired car. A nurse who lived in the next-door flat volunteered to accompany him, to make sure that he arrived safely. Worried by his claim that he would be returning to London as soon as her back was turned, she removed his house-keys from his coat pocket and handed them over to the nursing home staff when they reached their destination. After a fortnight in Bognor, Goodall went to Barham. Five days later – and only one month after the operation – he returned to Cardiff. But the rehearsals exhausted him and, with the first night only eight days away, he withdrew from the production for the second time. Anthony Negus conducted all the performances in his place.

Back at Barham once more, Goodall recovered quickly. He arranged to have the house painted and started to tidy up the garden. "Warm day," he noted in his diary on 6 March. "Bone meal on clematis." Already he was thinking about his next project. For some time the WNO had been planning a complete *Ring* in English, with the first instalment, *The Rhinegold*, to open in October 1983. The producer was to be the Swede, Göran Järvefelt, and the conductor, Richard Armstrong. To Brian McMaster, Goodall made no secret of the fact that he was annoyed that he had not been asked to conduct. He said he was particularly anxious to tackle *The Valkyrie* again: he had not done justice to it at the Coliseum, especially its first act, which, he felt, had lacked rhythmic energy and excitement. McMaster was careful to change the subject whenever it surfaced, but was suddenly presented with an unexpected opportunity to grant Goodall at least part of his wish.

Covent Garden had invited Armstrong to conduct a new production of Verdi's *Forza del destino* in the spring of 1984. It represented an important step forward in his career, but unfortunately it clashed with the WNO's *Valkyrie*. Armstrong was torn, but in the end decided that his loyalty lay with the Welsh *Ring*. McMaster pointed out to him, however, that he could always conduct *The Valkyrie* later, when the WNO mounted the complete cycle. If Goodall did the initial performances of *Valkyrie*, then Armstrong could go to Covent Garden for *Forza* with a clear conscience. Armstrong accepted the logic of McMaster's argument, while Goodall jumped at the offer to conduct *Valkyrie*. (To Armstrong's chagrin Covent Garden later abandoned its plan for *Forza* and replaced it with a borrowed production of Giordano's *Andrea Chénier*, which was much less to his taste.)

The *Valkyrie* cast included Warren Ellsworth as Siegmund and Kathryn Harries as Sieglinde. Anne Evans was to sing her first Brünnhilde; Goodall's prediction that one day she would sing the role had turned out to be correct. Coaching sessions began in June and continued on and off for seven months. Goodall enjoyed them for both musical and personal reasons. He had admired Ellsworth's wild impetuosity as Parsifal and came to regard him as the son he had never had; with Evans he established a friendship that was to last until his death. The year brought other pleasures. In July his nephew David Tetley, son of his half-sister Agnes, took to him to Lincoln, where he explored his childhood haunts. Meanwhile he was in constant touch with the English National Opera, which had not only secured the services of Götz Friedrich for *Tristan* in 1985, but was also planning a new production of *Parsifal* for 1986. Goodall agreed to conduct both productions.

The ENO considered Laurence Dale a possible candidate for the role of Parsifal. Edmund Tracey tried to persuade Goodall to go and hear him in Monteverdi's *Orfeo* at the Coliseum. "No dear," said Goodall, "I won't go to that. Monteverdi's too pure for me – I like my music to be more corrupt." Later, though he did not admit it to Tracey, he did attend a performance of *Orfeo*. He was spotted sitting at the back of the stalls by Anne Evans, who happened to be in the audience. Fearing, perhaps, that she might think he had undergone some kind of musical conversion, he explained hastily, "They want me to hear a singer." "But what do you think of the opera?" she asked. "Huh!" he said with an impious grin. "Bring on von Karajan and the Berlin

Philharmonic! Bring on eight double basses! That's what I say." Dale worked with Goodall, but did not sing Parsifal. His successful career was to take him into a different repertory.

Goodall's conducting of *The Valkyrie*, which opened in Cardiff on 18 February 1984, demonstrated that he had indeed rethought his approach to the opera. Max Loppert wrote in the *Financial Times*:

> Musically, it was an evening of miracles. Goodall may be the greatest living Wagner conductor – after Saturday can there be any shred of doubt remaining? – but that does not mean his Wagner performances are fixed in form, content, and dimension; incredible to witness and to relate, he is still a developing Wagnerian.
>
> Returning to the pit at an age (just short of 79) when he might have been feared lost to it forever, he gave a display of powers not just undiminished but positively and palpably increased, of new resources of energy, command, and control. For while the reading of the opera had all the qualities admired in past Goodall *Valkyries* – the inexorable drawing of each act on an unbroken thread of musical and dramatic logic, the ability to move the action towards climaxes of overwhelming grandeur without ever appearing to strain up to them, the suffusion of every strand of sound with a glow of lyricism – they were here matched by an urgency of momentum that has seldom been counted one of them.
>
> By the clock, I am informed, this was a notably "fast" Goodall *Valkyrie*. It did not feel fast; what the whole performance communicated was a sense of Wagnerian power, unforced and unconstrained, beyond all previous experience. The introduction to Act 2 and its final half-hour achieved indescribable grandeur; in the rapturous outpourings earlier and at the finale, one could almost feel the small auditorium swelling (but never splitting) in the effort of accommodating such a flow of glorious sound.[26]

Few who were present in the New Theatre would quarrel with that verdict, though Loppert was wrong about Goodall's age. He was approaching, not his seventy-ninth birthday, but his eighty-third. Goodall conducted the last of his eight performances of *The Valkyrie* in Birmingham on 7 April. Anne Evans remembers him being in a foul temper that night. He went out and conducted the introduction to Act 2 with a daemonic ferocity she had never heard in the music before. It was the last time he ever conducted a *Ring* opera.

After an Easter break spent at the White Cliffs Hotel at Dover, Goodall started rehearsals for a recording of the Welsh *Parsifal* for EMI, which had been planned for the previous year, but had had to be postponed because of his hernia operation. There was one newcomer to the cast. Linda Esther Gray had decided that the role of Kundry, with its formidably wide tessitura, was not for her and Bayreuth's Kundry, the German mezzo-soprano Waltraud Meier, took her place. Sessions were held at the Brangwyn Hall, Swansea, in June. Goodall was not entirely happy with his part in the recording and felt the results might have been better if he had had a chance to conduct the production in the theatre first. He also complained that he had had to start work on the recording too soon after the *Valkyrie* performances and that he was tired as a result. None the less the reviews were favourable.

Goodall was due to return to Wales in early August to re-rehearse *Parsifal* for a concert performance at the 1984 Edinburgh Festival. He never got there. On 31 July he was taken as an emergency case to Canterbury's Chaucer Hospital, where he had his appendix removed. On 16 September, while he was still convalescing, the BBC televised a documentary about him, *The Quest for Reginald Goodall*, which had been made earlier in the year. In the course of the programme he was interviewed at length by its director, Humphrey Burton. At first Goodall was nervous and his replies tended to be elliptical and enigmatic. Sentences trailed away into silence. What was *Parsifal* about? "That I don't know. I have my own ... but I can't put it into words." Friends and colleagues were also interviewed. It was suggested to Joan Cross that, in an international house, it might have been difficult for David Webster to provide Goodall with the rehearsal time he needed. "Rubbish!" she replied scornfully. Goodall said that he had had long experience of opera; he would not ask for twenty rehearsals if he thought ten would do. Peter Pears told Burton that Goodall's *Grimes* "was far and away the greatest I've ever seen or taken part in." Greater than the composer's own? asked Burton. "Yes," said Pears. There were precious glimpses of Goodall rehearsing Act 3 of *The Valkyrie* with the WNO orchestra. "I'm eighty-three, but I haven't got the end of *Walküre* right yet," he said, "but that may be because I'm stupid."

Those who assumed that he had retired from opera for good were to be proved wrong, for once again he demonstrated remarkable powers of recovery. At the beginning of October he started to coach the cast for the ENO's second attempt at *Tristan*, which was to open on 26 January 1985. As promised, Götz Friedrich was the director, though for reasons of economy the sets had to come from a production he had mounted eleven years earlier for the Netherlands Opera. Critics complained that they looked dated. As in 1981 the Tristan was to be Alberto Remedios and the Isolde Linda Esther Gray, but Gray was going through an uneasy vocal patch, and Bayreuth's Isolde, the American soprano Johanna Meier, took over from her. Meier had sung the role with Goodall in Bristol and Oxford during the WNO's revival of the opera in 1980. Now she had just six weeks to re-learn it in English.

Goodall spent Christmas at the Chaucer Hotel in Canterbury, but was back at the Coliseum to resume rehearsals on Boxing Day afternoon. Five days later it was announced in the 1985 new year's honours list that he had been awarded a knighthood for services to music. He was inundated with messages of congratulation. There was a letter from Keith Falkner, by now also knighted, who in 1930 had performed in variety with him at the Coliseum. Another letter recalled Goodall's first conducting engagement at Covent Garden in 1947:

> Dear Reggie,
>
> Many many congratulations. I have been waiting for it to happen for some time. Who would have thought of us when we worked on 'Manon' all those years past as two of many many K.B.E.s.
>
> Much love with delight
> Fred (Ashton)

Goodall loved the note he received from his Welsh Tristan, John Mitchinson. "My goodness," it read in part, "the butler will now have to polish the Rolls Royce night <u>and</u> morning … Put your fees up immediately." Goodall told EMI that he did not want the word "Sir" to appear on the *Parsifal* records. During a coaching session in "Valhalla", his room at Covent Garden, Goodall asked Lionel Friend if he knew what had made him accept the knighthood. Friend said he had no idea. "To do down people like Feasey," said Goodall. "They've been doing me down since 1936 when I first came here." Norman Feasey, his old adversary at Covent Garden, did indeed raise an eyebrow about the honour, though he was among the first to offer Goodall congratulations. Maisie Aldridge went with Goodall to the investiture. Afterwards he told friends that the music, provided by a military ensemble, had not been up to much. What had been played? "Oh, you know, *Chu Chin Chow*. Jiggy things like that." Not that Goodall was against popular music on principle. He once told Alberto Remedios that he liked musicals. His favourite one, he said, was *Southern Pacific* (sic).

It is not hard to detect an air of disappointment in the reviews for the second Coliseum *Tristan*. The *Guardian's* Tom Sutcliffe, who eleven months before had admired the fluency, assurance and urgency of Goodall's WNO *Valkyrie*, felt that in *Tristan* "the music stubbornly refused to glow".[27] For Peter Heyworth in *The Observer*

> … there were passages in the first act (notably in Isolde's narration) where the music seemed to fall into a trough. In spite of some deeply poetic passages, a similar lack of tension also made itself felt intermittently in Act II. Only in the last act, which opened with an enthralling account of the prelude, did Goodall strike his best form. But at no point did I feel that he succeeded in drawing from the ENO orchestra that passionate sense of commitment which makes his performances with the Welsh National Opera so exciting."[28]

Goodall himself was disappointed by the results, though he was enthusiastic about Götz Friedrich's production and much taken by Linda Finnie's Brangäne and John Tomlinson's King Marke. It was not so surprising if Goodall's powers were beginning to wane. Among other long-living conductors, Beecham had made his last appearance in the opera house at the age of seventy-nine, Klemperer at eighty-three; by coincidence the last opera either of them conducted was *Fidelio*. Goodall was by now only five months off his eighty-fourth birthday and conducting an opera that was almost twice as long as Beethoven's. After his sixth, and last, performance of *Tristan* on 22 February 1985, he retired to the White Cliffs for a brief rest and then went to Barham, where he pruned the roses. Two days later he was back in London to discuss the ENO's forthcoming production of *Parsifal* with Lord Harewood. It was to open on 15 March 1986, with Warren Ellsworth in the title-role and Gwynne Howell as Gurnemanz.

The producer was to be the East German, Joachim Herz, who was worried at first that Goodall might want to interfere with his production. Lord Harewood assured him that Goodall had "always been a <u>collaborator</u> and not a dictator".[29] Harewood's assessment was correct. Although Goodall could be obtuse on occasion, his general approach to production was far from being conservative, as the following exchange with an American interviewer makes clear:

> Bruce Duffie: It seems now that we've gone away from the naturalistic, realistic productions of Wagner (and of other operas). Are we pulling the operas out of shape with these [new] kinds of productions?
>
> Reginald Goodall: I don't think so – I think we're making them deeper. We're getting to the aesthetic. The inner meaning ... is much more important now.
>
> BD: Are we making them deeper, or are we finding more depth in them?
>
> RG: We're finding more depth in them. The producers are searching for more depth, and I'm all for these new approaches, even [when] they're wrong in a way ...
>
> BD: How much authority can the conductor have? Can you say, "This is wrong, we shouldn't do it ... ?"
>
> RG: Well, if you engage a producer who's supposed to have a name, and you start altering his conception, aren't you spoiling it? What if the producer came to me and said I must take the opera at a certain tempo ... I think you must get the right producer and let him work.[30]

Goodall did not care for naturalistic productions in Wagner: he liked Ralph Koltai's space-age sets for the ENO *Ring*, and once told Glen Byam Shaw that if Fricka had been given her rams in *The Valkyrie*, he would have had no alternative but to retire to his garden.[31]

Herz's mind was finally set at rest when he met Goodall for a preliminary discussion. But not everything went smoothly. It proved difficult to find a singer for the role of Kundry, while Andrew Porter fell behind with the translation, which had been commissioned specially. Goodall began to get agitated. He announced that he wanted to perform the opera in German[32], but was told firmly that it would be against company policy to do so.

By the time he started to coach the cast in May he had recovered his good temper. Even the fact that he still did not have a Kundry did not worry him unduly. He began to bombard Anne Evans with telephone calls. She was not convinced that the role was right for her, but eventually she gave in to the combined pleas of Goodall and the ENO's new managing director, Peter Jonas. Lord Harewood had left the company at the end of the 1984–85 season. At a farewell gala for him Goodall conducted the "Wahn" monologue from *The Mastersingers*, with Gwynne Howell as Hans Sachs.

As the production rehearsals approached, Goodall's confidence faltered. He was beginning to tire easily. He was also afflicted by a deterioration in his hearing, which meant that he could no longer take such an active part in production rehearsals as he once had with Glen Byam Shaw on *The Ring*. He took to wearing hearing-aids, but soon abandoned them, because, he said, they made the music sound "tinny". Wolf Münzner's designs depressed him – some scenes, said one reviewer, were "swagged with what look like the intestines of Amfortas, or possibly what just passed through them.[33] Meanwhile there were worries about Goodall's health. In January he fainted during a rehearsal, though he quickly recovered. It was not the first time it had happened. But he soldiered on. He had told Edmund Tracey that the production was to be his swansong[34] and he was determined not to miss it.

The first night brought a new drama. Warren Ellsworth fell ill with influenza and Siegfried Jerusalem, who was singing Erik in *Der fliegende Holländer* at Covent Garden, was called in to perform the role of Parsifal in German. "He did a splendid job in entering a new production cold, and sang magnificently, particularly in the third act," wrote Paul Griffiths in *The Times*.[35] Critical reaction to Goodall's conducting was mixed, Tom Sutcliffe thought that "the old sense of Goodall's organic coherence came and went, like a radio whose battery is running down." Michael Kennedy, on the other hand, attending a later performance for the *Telegraph*, wrote of "the beautiful orchestral playing under Sir Reginald Goodall's extraordinarily magnetic and imposing direction. Textures are translucent, the melodic line and pulse are sustained however slow the tempo (and the tempi are not, as it happens, all that slow) and there is unfailingly sympathetic concern for a favourable balance between stage and pit."[36]

Goodall's performance of *Parsifal* on 4 April 1986 marked the last occasion on which he conducted a complete opera. Earlier in the day he had been upset by the news that Peter Pears had died at the age of seventy-five. Goodall felt that after Britten's death Pears had gone out of his way to make him feel welcome at

Aldeburgh, and in doing so had finally buried old feuds. Goodall had not seen Pears since the previous June, when, on the fortieth anniversary of the premiere of *Peter Grimes*, the singer had unveiled a commemorative plaque at the Old Mill at Snape, where Britten had completed the opera. Other survivors from that historic first night had also been present: Joan Cross, Roderick Jones, the first Balstrode, and the chorus master, Alan Melville.

No sooner was *Parsifal* over than Goodall was back in "Valhalla", coaching Warren Ellsworth in new repertory. The Opera House rarely, if ever, asked him to coach singers for its productions, though it continued to pay him an annual salary. In January 1986, his fortieth year as a member of the company, it had been increased to £10,760 and from then on was treated as an ex-gratia pension. It was not much, but it was double what he had been paid by the house ten years earlier. Fortunately Goodall, a generous man with money, had a good head for figures and juggled his savings astutely, investing in unit trusts, government stocks and building societies.

In April, Goodall was invited to the Coliseum for the unveiling in the foyer of a bust of him by the sculptor Michael Black. He looked at the head disapprovingly. "It's smiling," he said. (If anything, it's scowling.) On 21 May he conducted the student orchestra of the Royal Academy of Music in the Prelude and *Liebestod* from *Tristan* at a gala concert at the Barbican in aid of Academy funds. The soprano soloist was Jane Eaglen. He enjoyed working with the students and told them he hoped to conduct them again one day. At the end of the concert an attractive young woman came to Goodall's room and engaged him in conversation. She was softly spoken and he found it hard to hear what she was saying ("she was very nice, very polite"). He was sure he had seen her somewhere before, though he could not place her. Only when her husband joined her did he realise who she was – the Academy's president, Princess Diana.

A week later Goodall heard Harrison Birtwistle's new opera, *The Mask of Orpheus*, at the Coliseum. He was fascinated by it – "a marvellous piece, not a trace of showbiz", he told his old friend Felix Aprahamian, who was also in the audience. On 8 June he was at the Snape Maltings to conduct a concert performance of *Parsifal* Act 3, with ENO forces. It was dedicated to Joan Cross, the company's one-time director, who later in the year was to celebrate her eighty-fifth birthday. The performance reached a level of intensity that Goodall had achieved only sporadically during the run at the Coliseum. From a physical point of view, he found it a relief not having to conduct the whole opera.

On 25 June he attended a ceremony at the Sheldonian Theatre, Oxford, where the honorary degree of doctor of music was conferred on him. Of all the awards that came his way this was the one of which he was most proud. His only sorrow was that Eleanor was not alive to witness the ceremony. Oxford had been her university. Now it had honoured him. He thought it an unusual distinction for someone who regarded himself as being uneducated.

Not all was well with Goodall, however. He was having more blackouts. One attack occurred when he was alone in his garden. He did not know how much time had elapsed before he came round. In early July he was dining at the White Cliffs Hotel with Maisie Aldridge, when, without warning, he fell from his chair on to the floor, where he lay unconscious for ten minutes. Ambulance men arrived and gave him oxygen. They offered to take him to hospital, but he refused to go with them. He spent the night at the hotel, and the next day appeared to have recovered. He consulted his doctor, who referred him to the cardiac unit at Canterbury. On 2 September he went into Guy's Hospital, London, where he had a pacemaker inserted to improve his circulation and thus prevent further black-outs. Admonished by a friend for not taking medical advice sooner, he replied, "I don't like doctors and I don't like medicine." But he had to admit that he was feeling better than he had done for months.

Although he did little coaching now, he spent a good deal of time in London attending other people's performances. He was at Covent Garden for *Siegfried* and *Götterdämmerung* when Richard Armstrong and the WNO performed a complete *Ring* cycle there in late September; the following week he went to Westminster Cathedral to hear Jennifer Bate give the British premiere of Messiaen's vast organ work, *Livre du Saint Sacrement*. He heard Lionel Friend conduct *The Rape of Lucretia* for the ENO and attended lectures of the Wagner Society, which had made him its president in succession to Dame Eva Turner. When he wasn't out, he spent the evenings with Maisie Aldridge. During the day he would go to "Valhalla" at Covent Garden to study scores. He had not been able to play the piano for some time because of arthritis in his hands, but he was still able to pick out chords. In November he was distressed to find that the telephone had been removed from the room. "That's how they treat musicians in this place," he told a friend. "I asked a cleaning lady about it and she said they had given it to a girl who sits in an office and does nothing." When news of the telephone's disappearance reached Sir John Tooley's ears, it was returned immediately.

On 21 December, Goodall took part in a gala at the Coliseum for Lord Goodman, who was retiring as chairman of the ENO board. He conducted the Prelude and *Liebestod* from *Tristan*, again with Jane Eaglen. "You thought I was dead, didn't you?" he remarked to the orchestra, when he arrived for the first rehearsal. There was applause and laughter. But Goodall was disappointed by his performance: "I felt it had lost something. I used to get, not excitement, but a feeling of smouldering power into the music, in the prelude mostly and towards the end of the *Liebestod*. Something used to sweep me into the orchestra. I didn't get it this time."

Following the death of Klemperer, the two conductors Goodall most admired were Karajan – "You can say what you like, but he's a great conductor" – and Carlos Kleiber, whom he considered a finer conductor than his father, Erich. But in many other conductors of international repute he missed a sense of individuality; listening to their performances, he said, he found it hard to tell them apart – and they travelled about far too much. What he liked about Richard Armstrong at the WNO and Mark Elder at the ENO was that they concentrated on their own companies. The same went for Simon Rattle and the City of Birmingham Symphony Orchestra: "He stays with his orchestra. He stays in that one place. He's more for the *Sacre du printemps* than he is for *Parsifal* or *Götterdämmerung*. He's too young for that yet. But he does what he can do and he does it damn well." Goodall hoped that Armstrong would be chosen as Colin Davis's successor at Covent Garden.

"Carlos Kleiber's got *Geist*," said Goodall, who frequently attended Kleiber's rehearsals and performances in London. (*Geist* embraces both intelligence and spirituality.) Kleiber wrote to Goodall to tell him how much he admired his recording of *The Ring* at the Coliseum. When Kleiber came to Covent Garden in January 1987 to conduct a new production of *Otello*, he asked where Goodall was. He wanted to see him. Goodall's account of their meeting tells as much about his feeling of isolation at the Opera House as it does about his pleasure over Kleiber's recognition of his work:

> Carlos Kleiber must meet Goodall! That set them all by the ears, you know. They were furious. He had asked particularly for me. So the woman from the office had to phone up: "Where would I find Goodall?" Kleiber came rushing up with his arms open. "Ah Herr Goodall," he said. "Your *Ring* is so … " And I said, "No, no, I don't think so … " But he seemed to think it was. He wanted to know why I wasn't working on *Otello*. I suppose I could have worked on it if I'd asked to, but I wouldn't like to have got in through the back door.

Goodall felt, not without reason, that the junior members of the Covent Garden music staff considered him an old dodderer who had nothing useful to contribute to the house. "I don't know why they're like that," he said. "In Wales I'm great friends with all the music staff. At the Coliseum, too".

On 9 August 1987, Goodall gave another concert performance of *Parsifal* Act 3 with the ENO company, this time at the Proms. It was the final conducting engagement of his career. His energy at the morning rehearsal in the Albert Hall was prodigious. He gave more cues to singers than he had for many years. Though he sat on a chair for much of the rehearsal, he leapt up for climactic moments, for example the *sforzando* at Gurnemanz's "Höchstes Heil!" and the trombone entry during the transition into the last scene. His left hand was used rarely, though he held it aloft as the brass thundered out the Grail theme, while his right hand vibrated in sympathy with the timpani. He was happy and relaxed. By the evening the chair had gone and he stood throughout the eighty-minute performance.

On this occasion the critics were unanimous in their response to Goodall's conducting. David Cairns wrote in the *Sunday Times*:

> Goodall showed once again that as a Wagner conductor he has no equal. His control of the musical architecture is absolute. The huge span of the score was shaped as if in a single phrase. At the same time the music seemed to move spontaneously, by its own inner force, and with a glowing beauty of sound, an inevitability of rise and fall and a kind of natural momentousness of expression that will remain the ideal. Admirable work by the soloists – Gwynne Howell, Warren Ellsworth, Neil Howlett – and the ENO orchestra, playing like men and women inspired.[37]

Far from being exhausted by the concert, Goodall insisted on going on to a celebratory party at the home of Lionel Friend. As he left the Albert Hall he was cheered by the large crowd that had gathered at the artists entrance. For once he looked pleased about his reception.

CHAPTER 16

The Final Years

A LTHOUGH GOODALL had conducted for the last time, his career was not quite over. He spent late September and early October 1987 working with Anne Evans on the role of the *Siegfried* Brünnhilde, which she was to sing in German for the first time, in Turin. On the night of 15 October the south of England was battered by gales. Window panes at Barham were smashed, the electricity supply was cut off, and eighteen trees in Goodall's garden were uprooted. He spent more than £2,000 on clearing away the old trees and planting new ones. He did not begrudge the money. He said that although it was unlikely he would live to see the saplings grow, it was his duty to repair the landscape for those who came after him.

Meanwhile the new season at Covent Garden had opened. Bernard Haitink had succeeded Colin Davis as musical director and Goodall hoped for a change in the Opera House's fortunes. He felt it had lost direction: the most worthwhile operatic work in Britain, he said, was being done, not at Covent Garden, but at the Coliseum and in Wales:

> There's an awful lot of baloney at Covent Garden now. I don't know if poor Hainix [Haitink] can cope with it. He's a man I admire and respect, but he'll have to be strong. And he must spend a lot of time there. If he sends for me, I'll tell him what I think. Otherwise I'll keep out of it.

Goodall always referred to Haitink as "Hainix". It seems he misheard the name when he first encountered it and from then on could think of it only as Hainix.

Haitink did send for Goodall, to ask him if he would coach the Flowermaidens for the new production of *Parsifal* he was to conduct in the New Year. Goodall was excited by the invitation – he felt wanted – and he started work with the singers at the end of October. Haitink was pleased with the results and wrote Goodall a letter of thanks, in which he expressed the hope that he would also help with the new production of *Das Rheingold* later in the year. Goodall was gratified: "Everyone seemed to think the Flowermaidens were very good. Warren Ellsworth [who sang Parsifal at one of the performances] said he could tell I'd coached them!"

Goodall had grown very unsteady on his feet. One evening in January 1988, as he was crossing St Martin's Lane, he was dealt a glancing blow by a car and he fell into the gutter. His trousers were torn and he was badly shaken, but he continued on his way to the Coliseum, where he attended a performance of *Hansel and Gretel*. He had a similar accident in Addison Gardens. Crossing the road with Goodall was a frightening experience at the best of times. He held the view that pedestrians took precedence over cars and would fight his way through swirling traffic, cursing the drivers as he went. Once he was seen to whack the bonnet of a passing car with a walking stick. Fortunately for Goodall the speeding motorist did not stop.[1] That particular incident had occurred when his eyesight had been reasonably good. Now the retina in his left eye had become detached again and he could only see properly with the right one. He found it hard to judge distances. A specialist at St Thomas's Hospital advised him that an operation would do little, if anything, to improve matters. Goodall was distressed that his sight should be giving trouble at the very moment when Covent Garden wanted to use his talents again. Nevertheless he started to coach the Rhinemaidens, though within days he was forced to give up.

At the beginning of April 1988 Goodall felt exhausted. He was urged to consult a doctor, but he said he had decided not to bother the medical profession any more: "I'm just, you know, passing out. Maisie [Aldridge] thinks I'm nineteen. I say, Maisie, I'm eighty-six. And most people are dead when they're eighty-six." Eventually he did see a doctor, who diagnosed shingles. It was to prove a very painful attack. Goodall spent much of the following two months at the Kingston nursing home near Barham. In June, however, he felt well enough to return to London for a gala for Sir John Tooley, who was retiring from Covent Garden at the end of the season. He asked Anne Evans to accompany him. Goodall had been asked to conduct the *Meistersinger* quintet at the gala, but had had to turn it down. Colin Davis conducted instead. "They say Wagner was a rotter," said Goodall, "but a rotter couldn't write music like that." He thoroughly enjoyed being at the Opera House again, but was disappointed by most of the programme. For him, the two star-turns were Jennifer Penney's dancing in an extract from the ballet *Manon*, and Joan Sutherland's singing of the mad scene from *Lucia di Lammermoor*. He stayed the night at Evans's home and the next day was driven back to Barham. He was tired, but happy, and slept for most of the journey on the back seat of the car. He woke up just before Canterbury and insisted on going to the Chaucer Hotel for lunch. The dining-room was practically empty. A waitress told him that nowadays it was rarely busy at lunchtime. "All these damned tourists," Goodall said crossly. "They just want to drink Coca-Cola in snack bars."

On the evening of 25 August Goodall fell in his bathroom at Barham and found he could not pull himself up again. He slept on the floor. It was cold, but he had the sense to cover himself with towels. He was discovered the next day by a neighbour, Mary Parsons, who had come in to give him some lunch.

Though unhurt, Goodall was forced to the conclusion that he could no longer cope with the problems of living on his own. He moved to the Saxon Lodge nursing home at Bridge, a village not far from Barham. The following month he put his house on the market. He gave up his bed-sitting-room in Holland Park and in November asked Anne Evans to clear out "Valhalla". It was a melancholy task. The most precious item she found there was his vocal score of *Peter Grimes*, autographed by the composer. In it Goodall had noted some of Britten's own wishes on points of interpretation. He asked for the score to be sent to the Britten-Pears library at Aldeburgh.

From then on he rarely visited London, though he often took a taxi into Canterbury to shop or get his hair cut. He was not Saxon Lodge's most compliant resident. He could be cantankerous, particularly when its owner, Mrs Richards, tried to get him to take exercise to prevent his joints seizing up. Whenever he thought he had behaved rudely, and was in danger of being thrown out, he bought her a bunch of red roses as a peace offering. As time passed he came to regard Bridge as home. He developed a grand passion for one of Mrs Richards's assistants, who not surprisingly turned down his proposals of marriage; she was eighteen years old. On good days, usually when friends came to visit him, Goodall was cheerful and eager for gossip about the musical world. On bad days he longed for death. He said he had outgrown his usefulness and wanted to have his pacemaker removed; it was only prolonging his life unnecessarily.

Early in 1989 he heard that Anne Evans was to sing the role of Brünnhilde at Bayreuth that year. She was to join two of his other protégés in the cast, John Tomlinson as Wotan and Linda Finnie as Fricka. Goodall was jubilant about the hat-trick. Jeremy Isaacs, Covent Garden's new general director, offered to send him to Bayreuth to attend one of the cycles. Goodall accepted with alacrity, and arrangements for the visit were put in hand, but at the last minute he decided he could not face the journey.

In February of 1989 he had been taken to the Chaucer Hospital for another hernia operation; in October he suffered a mild stroke. Anne Evans hastened to Bridge. Goodall seemed cheerful enough, though one side of his mouth drooped slightly. The doctor arrived to check him over:

RG: Have I had it?
Doctor: No, you haven't.
RG: Oh, damn! Well how long have I got?
Doctor: Well how long is a piece of string?

Goodall laughed. Eventually his mouth regained its original shape.

In April 1990 Maisie Aldridge arranged for him to spend a few days in London. He stayed in a nursing home and went with her to a performance of

Meistersinger at Covent Garden. He slept through most of it. He felt unwell and soon returned to Mrs Richards and Saxon Lodge, where he took to his bed. He spent much of the time listening to tapes of the Bayreuth *Ring* on a pair of headphones he had been given. One afternoon Mrs Richards ran to his room after hearing clapping and what she took to be cries for help; she thought he must have fallen out of bed. What he was actually shouting was "Bravo! Bloody bravo!" He had been listening to *Siegfried*. The tapes took Goodall's mind off his physical troubles. Cancer of the prostate had been diagnosed. Mrs Richards contacted Goodall's nephew, David Tetley, who came down from Yorkshire immediately with his wife, Sally. By 4 May Goodall was clearly sinking and Anne Evans went to Bridge with Maisie Aldridge to see him. By now he was blind, but he was serene. He told Evans, "I'd like to have one more go at *The Ring*, dear. I never got bits of it right. It's the work of a lifetime." That night, while listening to *Götterdämmerung*, he drifted into a coma and never came out of it. He died at lunchtime the following day. Sally Tetley and Mrs Richards were with him. On 14 May, after a simple funeral service at the Roman Catholic church in Canterbury, he was buried next to Eleanor at Barham.

Notes

Introduction and Acknowledgments

1   *Opera*, July 1990.
2   Goodall is referring here to Boulez's essay, "Approaches to Parsifal" ("Chemins vers Parsifal"), first published in the 1970 Bayreuth programme book for *Parsifal* and reprinted in *Orientations*: *Collected Writings* by Pierre Boulez (Faber, 1986).
3   *Classics*, September 1992.

Chapter 1: Lincoln

1   St Peter-at-Arches was declared redundant and in 1933 dismantled. Some of its exterior stonework and most of its furnishings were saved and three years later incorporated into a new church of similar design at St Giles, a rapidly expanding suburb of Lincoln.
2   The Spread Eagle stood on what is now the site of the Waterside shopping centre.
3   Interview with the author, 1988.
4   *Boy on a Hill* by Reg Woodward (Woodward, 1984).
5   *Boy on a Hill*, op. cit.
6   *Family Enterprise: The story of some North Country organ builders* by Laurence Elvin (Elvin, 1986). It has an invaluable chapter on Bennett.
7   *Boy on a Hill*, op. cit.
8   Later, in 1921, Wakeford was found guilty under the Clergy Discipline Act of sharing a hotel bedroom in Peterborough with a young unmarried woman. An account of this bizarre case can be found in *Dangerous Precincts* by John Treherne (Jonathan Cape, 1987).
9   From Woolley's unpublished memoirs, 1895–1920, deposited in the Lincolnshire Archives (MF 2/19).
10   *Lincolnshire Chronicle*, 2 December 1911.
11   *Lincolnshire Chronicle*, 29 November 1913.
12   Magistrates hearings reported in *Lincolnshire Chronicle*, 7 and 10 April 1911.
13   Trial reported in *Lincolnshire Chronicle*, 19 and 23 June 1911.

Chapter 2: Exile

1   St Luke vestry records, now deposited at the Mills Memorial Library, McMaster University, Hamilton.
2   St Alban's, whose corner-stone was laid in 1887, was designed to supersede Toronto's original cathedral, St James', which was considered neither large nor imposing enough to justify its status. By 1935, however, it had become clear that funds to build a nave would never be forthcoming, and the following year the episcopal seat returned to St James's. St Alban's now serves as chapel for an Anglican boys' school, Royal St George's College.
3   *Healey Willan: Life and Music* by F. R. C. Clarke (Toronto University Press, 1983).
4   *In the Fullness of Time: A History of the Church of Saint Mary Magdalene, Toronto* by David Greig (St Mary Magdalene, 1990).
5   Canon Robert W. Cowan of Lethbridge, Alberta, interview with the author, 1990.
6   Canon Cowan, op. cit.
7   Dr Alan T. Prince of Manotic, Ontario, interview with the author, 1990.

8   William Goodall, who became an American citizen in 1937, spent most of his working life in public service. Under a WPA scheme during the Depression he established recreational camps for young people in 13 mid-Western States. While working for the Red Cross in World War II, he drew on this experience to set up and direct recreational centres for military personnel, first in St Louis and then in Italy. His activities after the war included a stint in West Germany for the cultural affairs office of the US State Department. In 1953 he was appointed director of the Audubon Society of the West, a post he retained until he retired. He died in 1987 at Pomona, California, his home for 40 years. He married twice.

Chapter 3: Sacred and Profane

1   *St Alban's Monthly Paper*, November 1928.
2   *Sunday Times*, 29 March 1925.
3   *Interpretation in Song* (Macmillan, 1912).
4   Plunket Greene borrowed the phrase from Dr W. A. Aikin's *The Voice: an introduction to practical phonology* (Longmans, 1910).
5   *Am I Too Loud?* by Gerald Moore (Hamish Hamilton, 1962). In 1931, at the Salle Chopin in Paris, Warlich and Moore gave what was billed as the first public performance in France of Brahms's *Vier ernste Gesänge*, a claim Moore found "hard to believe, even allowing for the French indifference to Brahms."
6   *Monthly Musical Record*, December 1934. Westrup was later professor of music at Birmingham and then Oxford.

Chapter 4: High Holborn

1   St *Alban's Monthly Paper*, December 1930.
2   *Sunday Times; The Observer*, 24 November 1929.
3   *Conversations with Klemperer*, edited by Peter Heyworth (Gollancz, 1973).
4   In 1988 Goodall gave many of his scores, including this one, to the Royal College of Music library.
5   *Daily Telegraph*, 22 January 1932.
6   *The Times*, 23 January 1932.
7   Ralph Nicholson, interview with the author, 1987.
8   Interview with the author, 1987.
9   *The Times*, 23 November 1934.
10   *Daily Telegraph*, 22 November 1934.
11   *Monthly Musical Record*, December 1934. Another quotation from the *MMR* editorial appears at the end of Chapter 3.
12   Interview with the author, 1987.
13   Wilfred Stiff, interview with the author, 1986.
14   Felix Aprahamian, interview with the author, 1987. A detailed description of the instrument can be found in the January 1928 issue of *The Organ*.
15   From Frank de Jonge's introduction to *Father Eves of St Alban's, Holborn* by Maud A. Morgan (SPCK, 1956). Father de Jonge, a curate at St Alban's in the Thirties, was later vicar of St Mary the Virgin, Somers Town.
16   *St Alban's Monthly Paper*, May 1936.

Chapter 5: Young Britten

1   Letter from Britten to E. Benbow of the BBC music department, 24 January 1934 (BBC Written Archives).
2   Letter from Britten to Leslie Woodgate, 18 February 1934 (BBC Written Archives). The St Mark's choirmaster was Maurice Vinden.

3   It is possible that Arthur Benjamin recommended Goodall to Britten. He had taught both of them piano at the Royal College. Benjamin gave Goodall a good deal of support during the early part of his career.

4   Letter to the author, 16 October 1987.

5   Wilfred Stiff was one of the very few boys who did not come from the parish. He lived in Crouch End. After the second world war he became manager of the Liverpool Philharmonic Orchestra and later chairman of the concert artists' agency, Ibbs and Tillett.

6   Diary entry for 17 December 1934. Earlier in the evening Britten was at the Wigmore Hall to hear Henri Temianka (violin) and Betty Humby (piano) give the first performance of three movements from his Suite Op.6. He then rushed to Notting Hill Gate for *A Boy Was Born*, which had been placed after the interval.

7   *The Observer*, 23 December 1934.

8   *Daily Telegraph*, 18 December 1934.

9   Britten's diary, 29 December 1935 (Britten-Pears Library).

10   *Musical Times*, February 1936.

11   Britten's diary, 6 December 1935. (Britten-Pears Library).

12   Britten's diary, 24 January 1936. (Britten-Pears Library).

13   During the rehearsal period for the *Te Deum*, Britten and Auden discussed the possibility of working on a song cycle. The outcome was *Our Hunting Fathers*, Britten's first work to employ a large orchestra. He conducted its premiere at the Norfolk and Norwich Festival in September 1936.

14   *Sunday Referee*, 2 February 1936.

15   *The Observer*, 2 February 1936. To end the concert, Lemare conducted the combined Carlyle Singers and St Alban's choir in a performance of Bax's *Mater ora Filium* for unaccompanied double chorus.

16   *Musical Times*, March 1936. The reviewer was the magazine's assistant editor, William McNaught, who later became editor.

Chapter 6: Amateur Nights

1   *Daily Telegraph*, 22 April 1930; *The Stage*, 24 April. The show opened on Easter Monday, 21 April.

2   Interview with the author, 1988.

3   Interview with the author, 1986.

4   Letter dated 23 April 1933 (Royal College of Music archives).

5   Philip Blake, a fellow conducting student; interview with the author, 1986.

6   *The Times*, 20 April 1934.

7   Charles Robinson, interview with the author, 1987. Robinson, Goodall's first cousin, was a member of the choir.

8   Richard Temple Savage, interview with the author, 1987.

9   *Daily Telegraph*, 14 December 1934; *The Times*, 15 December.

10   Letter dated 21 August 1934. Boyd Neel gave the first British performance of the Riisager concerto at the 1938 ISCM festival, with Herbert Barr as soloist.

11   "Migrant Conductors: The English musicians for whom there is no place at home," *Daily Telegraph*, 10 December, 1938.

12   *The Times*, 6 May 1935; *Daily Telegraph*, 4 May 1935.

13   Ruth Dyson, interview with the author, 1989.

14   Cressida Ridley, daughter of Sir Maurice Bonham Carter; conversation with the author, 1988.

15   Sir John Stephenson, conversation with the author, 1988.

16   *Daily Telegraph*, 24 May 1939.

17   Robert Bossert, interview with the author, 1988.

18   Norman Feasey, interview with the author, 1986.
19   *Sunday Times*, 28 March 1937.
20   Allen had left the Royal College by then, but remained an influential figure in British musical life. His successor, Sir George Dyson, also encouraged Goodall and gave him a certain amount of part-time teaching work at the college.
21   *Daily Telegraph*, 3 April 1938.
22   Interview with the author, 1986.
23   Quoted in *The British Press and Jews under Nazi Rule* by Andrew Sharf (Oxford University Press, 1964).
24   The president of the series, known as the London Theatre Concerts, was Beecham, who conducted one of the events. Betty Humby became his second wife in 1943. After the war William Glock co-founded the summer school of music at Bryanston; in 1959 he was appointed the BBC's music controller. The exact nature of Humby's dispute with Goodall is not known.
25   Letter from Maisie Aldridge to her mother, 7 May 1939. Cruft, son of the double bass player Eugene Cruft, played the oboe in the LPO. In the Sixties he became the Arts Council's music director.
26   Letters dated 21 May and 19 July 1939.
27   Wagner's treatise, *Über das Dirigieren* (*On Conducting*), was published in 1869. Though Goodall read German easily, his copy of it (now in the Royal College of Music library) is in Edward Dannreuther's English translation, published in London in 1919.

Chapter 7: Bournemouth at War

1   *Bournemouth Daily Echo*, 5 January 1940. The initials K. L. stood for Kenneth Lark, the pseudonym Whitlock used for his light music compositions.
2   Austin's comment is quoted in *Conductors' Gallery* by Donald Brook (Rockcliff, 1945).
3   Reports of council meetings and readers' letters protesting about the sackings, *Bournemouth Daily Echo*, 4–27 April 1940.
4   Until the discovery in the 1990s of a review and programme for the Wessex concert, it was thought the premiere of the work had taken place almost a year later, on 4 October 1941, when it was given in a string quartet version by the Blech Quartet at the Wigmore Hall.
5   *Bournemouth Daily Echo*, 20 May 1940.
6   Interview with the author, 1987.
7   Robert Bossert, interview with the author, 1987.
8   Letter to Maisie Aldridge, 17 January 1940.
9   Whitlock's diary, 20 June 1941. Several entries refer to Whitlock's unsuccessful attempts to interest MI5 in Goodall (Percy Whitlock Trust).
10   *Daily Express*, 8 August 1941.
11   *Picture Post*, 21 June 1941; *Time and Tide*, 28 June.
12   Letter to Maisie Aldridge from R. Gill, assistant chief constable of Hampshire, 23 July 1942; also letter to Fistoulari from Maisie Aldridge, 7 August 1942.
13   *The Times*, 7 September 1940.
14   *The Times*, 15 March 1941.
15   Interview with the author, 1987.
16   Interview with the author, 1986.
17   Interview with the author, 1987.
18   Letter to Maisie Aldridge, 13 October, 1940.
19   Interview with the author, 1987.
20   Council-meeting reports and letters, *Bournemouth Daily Echo*, 3–21 March 1942.
21   Goodall's comment is quoted in a letter to Maisie Aldridge from the critic Clinton Gray-Fisk, 13 June 1942.

22 *New English Weekly*, 14 May 1942.
23 The original "Pony" Moore was an American "black" minstrel, George Washington Moore, who died in 1909. His soubriquet originated when, as a youth, he drove forty ponies at the head of a circus procession.
24 *Congleton Chronicle*, 12 February 1943.

Chapter 8: Private's Progress

 1 Most orchestral concerts in London at this time were given at the Royal Albert Hall and the Phoenix and Cambridge theatres. The Orpheum, later renamed the Odeon, opened in 1930 and closed in 1974. A block of flats now stands on its site at 850 Finchley Road. *Musical Opinion* (March 1942) called the Orpheum a "handsome and commodious place, with very good acoustics." It held more people than Queen's Hall.
 2 After the war Morris, Walton, Alexandra, Brain, Hirsch, Emms and Max Gilbert, all RAF players at Uxbridge, became leading members of the Philharmonia Orchestra.
 3 *Letters from a Life: Selected Letters and Diaries of Benjamin Britten*, Vol.2, edited by Donald Mitchell and Philip Reed (Faber, 1991).
 4 Concert reviewed in the *South Wales Evening Post*, 28 June 1943.
 5 Joan Ingpen, interview with the author, 1992.
 6 The correspondence is preserved at the BBC Written Archives Centre.

Chapter 9: Enter Grimes

 1 *The Times*, 18 May 1945.
 2 *Birmingham Post*, 1 May 1945.
 3 *Eastern Daily Press*, 10 February 1942.
 4 "Peter Grimes: An Unpublished Article of 1946" (*Opera*, June 1965).
 5 *Manchester Guardian*, 24 February 1945.
 6 *Sheffield Telegraph*, 10 March 1945.
 7 *Manchester Guardian*, 1 April 1946 and 12 November 1945; *Sheffield Telegraph*, 8 September 1945.
 8 *Bristol Evening Post*, 1 December 1944.
 9 "George Crabbe: the Poet and the Man" by E.M. Forster, *The Listener*, 29 May 1941; reprinted in *Benjamin Britten: Peter Grimes* compiled by Philip Brett (Cambridge University Press, 1983).
10 Interview with Joan Cross, *The Times*, 1 June 1985.
11 "Peter Grimes: An Unpublished Article of 1946," op. cit.
12 Letter to Elizabeth Mayer, 19 July 1944, included in *Letters from a Life: Selected Letters and Diaries of Benjamin Britten*, Vol. 2, op. cit.
13 The story, recorded in the journals of Coates's husband, Harry Powell Lloyd, has been authenticated by other members of the company at that time.
14 "Peter Grimes: An Unpublished Article of 1946," op. cit.
15 *A Life in the Theatre* by Tyrone Guthrie (Hamish Hamilton, 1960).
16 Minutes of meeting of Sadler's Wells governors, 10 May 1945.
17 Letter to the author from Elizabeth Abercrombie.
18 Letter to Dyson confirming Covent Garden's acceptance of the Sadler's Wells board's decision, dated 14 June 1945 (Covent Garden archives).
19 Interview with Cross in *Remembering Britten* by Alan Blyth (Hutchinson, 1981).
20 From a report sent "by wireless" to the *New York Times*, 8 June 1945.
21 Janet Kersley, interview with the author, 1990.
22 Interview in *The Times*, 1 June 1985.
23 Interview with the author, 1987.

24 Letter written by Guthrie, quoted in *Tyrone Guthrie* by James Forsyth (Hamish Hamilton, 1976).
25 Goodall addressed his letter, dated 1 June 1945, to the BBC's director of music. He seems not to have realised that Hely-Hutchinson had succeeded Arthur Bliss in the post.
26 Report to the director of music, 8 June 1945 (BBC Written Archives).
27 Memos, 8 and 11 June 1945 (BBC Written Archives).
28 Letter to Tyrone Guthrie, 19 July 1945.
29 Memo, 17 July 1945 (BBC Written Archives).
30 Letter, 1 August 1945.
31 The postcard expressing Walton's views was accompanied by a letter, dated 29 June 1945, to Evelyn Donald of the British Council's music department: "You may suppress this if you think it's too drastic! I'm inclined to think it should be passed on." Much of the information in this chapter about the projected *Grimes* recording comes from memoranda, letters, etc, preserved in British Council file BW2/181 at the National Archives, Kew.
32 Letter included in *Letters from a Life: Selected Letters and Diaries of Benjamin Britten*, Vol. 2, op. cit.
33 Letter from the company secretary, Sheila Fergusson, to the general manager of Sadler's Wells Theatre, George Chamberlain, 2 August 1945 (Sadler's Wells Archive, Finsbury Library).
34 Letter from Sheila Fergusson to George Chamberlain (Sadler's Wells Archive, Finsbury Library).
35 Peter Pears, quoted in *Britten* by Christopher Headington (Eyre Methuen, 1981).
36 Letter to George Chamberlain, 18 August 1945 (Sadler's Wells Archive, Finsbury Library).
37 Internal British Council memo from Evelyn Donald to Brian Kennedy-Cooke, 2 August 1945.
38 Interview with the author, 1987.

Chapter 10: From Berlin to Lucretia

1 Letter to George Chamberlain, 21 August 1945 (Sadler's Wells archive, Finsbury Library).
2 Letter to the Sadler's Wells governors, August 1945 (Sadler's Wells archive, Finsbury Library):
3 Dyson wrote to Cross and Pears on 31 July 1945. News about Pears's reply is given in Dyson's letter to Chamberlain, 21 August 1945, op. cit.
4 Letter to Chamberlain, 21 August 1945 (Finsbury Library).
5 Romayne Grigorova, interview with the author, 1988.
6 Interview with the author, 1988.
7 From Powell Lloyd's manuscript of a projected biography of Edith Coates; the account of the incident in Lloyd's journal actually names Goodall (Powell Lloyd archive, Cambridge University Library music department).
8 *British Zone Review*, 29 September 1945.
9 Powell Lloyd's journal, 4 October 1945 (Powell Lloyd archive, Cambridge University Library music department).
10 Cast-lists for the ballets are given in *The Sadler's Wells Theatre Ballet* by Hugh Fisher (A. & C. Black, 1956).
11 Leo Kersley's obituary of Goodall, *Dancing Times*, June 1990.
12 *Evening Standard*, 8 February 1946.
13 *The Times*, 8 February 1946.
14 Letter from Alan Melville to the author, August 1990.
15 *The Times*, 24 January 1946. The performance was on 22 January.
16 *The Spectator*, 1 February 1946.

17   BBC internal memo, 4 January 1946. J. R. Denny was an assistant in the music department (BBC Written Archives).

18   Letter from Rudolf Bing to Audrey Christie, 9 November 1945 (Glyndebourne archives).

19   Letter from Bing to Audrey Christie, 15 January 1946 (Glyndebourne archives).

20   Kenneth Essex, interview with the author, 1991.

21   Letter from Beecham's wife, Betty Humby, to Audrey Christie, 3 November 1945 (Glyndebourne archives); the letter is reproduced in *John Christie of Glyndebourne* by Wilfrid Blunt (Geoffrey Bles, 1968).

22   Letter from Bing to Britten and Crozier, 1 May 1946 (Glyndebourne Archives).

23   Interview with the author, 1987.

24   Interview with the author, 1991.

25   Eric Crozier, interview with the author, 1986.

26   Letter from Bing to Audrey Christie, 25 February 1946 (Glyndebourne archives).

27   Moran Caplat, interview with the author, 1991.

28   Victor Hely-Hutchinson put the problem to Britten in a letter dated 2 May 1946. He offered to broadcast Act 1 only. Presumably the composer rejected the idea (BBC Written Archives).

29   CDs of excerpts from this performance invariably claim, incorrectly, that the conductor is Britten.

30   *Britten* by Christopher Headington (Eyre Methuen, 1981).

31   Information contained in a letter to Christie from Britten and Crozier, 19 October 1946 (Glyndebourne archives).

32   Letter to Christie from Britten and Crozier, 19 October 1946 (Glyndebourne archives).

33   Information about Goodall's behaviour at rehearsals from interviews with Eric Crozier and Nancy Evans (Mrs Crozier), 1986, and Denis Dowling, 1991.

34   Eric Crozier, interview with the author, 1986.

35   Denis Dowling, interview with the author, 1991.

36   Memo from J. D. Bicknell of HMV's artists department to B. Mittel, assistant to the company's managing director, 27 June 1946 (EMI archives).

37   Draft minutes of music committee meeting, 23 April 1947 (British Council file BW2/387 at the National Archives, Kew).

38   *Gramophone Record*, April 1948; *The Gramophone*, March 1948.

39   Letter from Eric Crozier to Goodall, 4 June 1947.

40   Goodall himself was the source of this information.

Chapter 11: Covent Garden

1   Letter to Goodall from James Robertson, who had succeeded Clive Carey as director of the Sadler's Wells Opera; 6 September 1946.

2   *Time and Tide*, 25 January 1947.

3   *Notes on a Programme for Covent Garden*, an unsigned document dated April 1945 (Covent Garden archives).

4   *Time and Tide*, 8 February 1947; *The Times*, 31 January 1947; *New Statesman and Nation*, 15 March 1947.

5   Speech to the annual conference of the Incorporated Society of Musicians, Brighton, 5 January 1949.

6   Letter dated 15 May 1948 (Covent Garden archives).

7   Lord Harewood, interview with the author, 1991.

8   *Opera on Record*, edited by Alan Blyth (Hutchinson, 1979).

9   Minutes of meetings of the Covent Garden Opera Trust, 22 December 1947; 14 January, 16 March, 3 June, 20 July 1948.

10   *New Statesman and Nation*, 14 April 1948. The production of *Traviata* opened on 6 April.

11   Letter in Covent Garden archives.

12   Review of *Grimes* by Ernest Bradbury, *Yorkshire Post*, 9 April 1949.

13   Letter to Webster from Covent Garden's stage manager, Cliff Clifford, 9 April 1949 (Covent Garden archives).

14   Richard Temple Savage, interview with the author, 1987. Goodall also conducted *The Mastersingers* in Liverpool on 17 March, when the Eva was Irmgard Seefried. In Leeds the opera was conducted by Peter Gellhorn.

15   Minutes of Covent Garden Opera Trust meeting, 21 June 1949.

16   *The Times*, 1 October 1949.

17   Interview with the author, 1987.

18   Webster confirmed the plan in a letter to Rankl dated 2 March 1950.

19   *New Statesman and Nation*, 16 December 1950.

20   *The Spectator*, 22 December 1950.

21   Letter from Webster to Rankl, 14 November 1950 (Covent Garden archives).

22   Emanuel Young, interview with the author, 1986.

23   Goodall's verdict is recorded in a letter from Webster to Kleiber dated 17 August 1951 (Covent Garden archives).

24   Anecdote told to the author by Ande Anderson, 1991.

25   Interview with the author, 1986. Feasey died in 1989, one year before Goodall. Although the *Traviata* story has been retold in several guises, Feasey's version is authentic. The incident occurred during a provincial tour, almost certainly in 1949.

26   The Bürgerreuth inn, later an Italian restaurant. The Festspielhaus is not, as Goodall's card suggests, some way out in the country, but sits on a hill on the northern edge of the town, with rolling fields to one side of it.

27   Quoted in *The Quiet Showman* by Montague Haltrecht (Collins, 1975). Other memories of Goodall at Bayreuth from Sir Edward Downes, John Denison, etc.

28   *Sunday Times*, 19 August 1951. Unlike Goodall, Newman was not impressed by the performance of the Ninth Symphony: "Furtwängler conducted, and, as is his way, made it a 'conductor's piece' rather than a composer's work. All the familiar Furtwängler effects were there, the eccentricities of tempo, the exaggerated dynamics ... For me the whole thing was too much Furtwängler and too little Beethoven" (*Sunday Times*, 5 August 1951).

29   Letter from Hans Knappertsbusch to Wieland Wagner, 13 April 1953, quoted in Oswald Georg Bauer's "Vierzig Jahre Neubayreuth," published in the programme books for the 1991 Bayreuth *Ring*.

30   Interview with Barry Millington, *The Arts This Week*, BBC Radio 3, 4 February 1970.

31   *The Quiet Showman*, op. cit. Wieland Wagner's offer was made in 1953.

32   Letter to Webster, 9 March 1953 (Covent Garden archives).

33   *Times* reviews, 9 June and 13 July 1953.

34   *Daily Herald*, 16 July 1953.

35   Letter dated 19 November 1953.

36   Leonard Hancock, interview with the author, 1991.

37   *Opera*, April 1954. Ludwig Hofmann was indisposed and the part of Wotan was sung at this performance by Karl Kamann, who had sung the role at Covent Garden before the war.

38   Sir Edward Downes, interview with the author, 1991.

39   Lord Harewood, interview with the author, 1991.

40   Cutting, dated 10 May 1954, from an unidentified Wiesbaden newspaper.

41   Jeremy Cullum, interview with the author, 1991.

42   "Lord of the Ring" by Michael White; *Observer Magazine*, 28 March 1982.

43   From an unpublished interview, 1985.

Chapter 12: Galley Years

1   *William Walton: Behind the Façade* by Susana Walton (Oxford University Press, 1988).
2   Interview with the author, 1991.
3   *Opera*, December 1954.
4   *The Observer*, 18 March 1956. The performance described took place on 13 March.
5   Interview with the author, 1991.
6   John Gardner, interview with the author, 1987.
7   Undated letter in Covent Garden archives.
8   *Times Educational Supplement*, 11 July 1958.
9   *The Spectator*, 6 February 1959.
10 George Hallam, interview with the author, 1991.
11 *Evening Standard* and *The Times*, 7 October 1959.
12 Minutes of meetings of the board of directors, 27 October and 24 November 1959.
13 *Financial Times*, 22 February 1960. The revival opened on 19 February.
14 David Lloyd-Jones, interview with the author, 1991.
15 Drogheda's letter is dated 18 November 1960; Webster's 21 November (Covent Garden archives).
16 Interview with the author, 1990.
17 Interview with the author, 1990.
18 Richard Nunn, interview with the author, 1991.
19 Goodall's invitation to conduct the Prom came in a letter from the BBC's concerts manager, G. J. Willoughby, dated 24 January 1961 (BBC Written Archives). The Mass ended the concert. In the first half of the programme, Sir Malcolm Sargent conducted works by Haydn, Mozart and Beethoven.
20 *The Times*, 23 August 1961.
21 Alexander Goehr, letter to the author, 3 January 1992. Goehr expanded on the letter in a subsequent conversation.
22 *The Observer*, 11 June 1961. The British Library Sound Archive has a BBC recording of the performance on 10 June.
23 At this point Solti had never conducted a complete cycle of *The Ring*.
24 James Gibson, interview with the author, 1988.
25 Joan Ingpen, interview with the author, 1992. Information about the rehearsal fee is contained in a letter from Webster to Goodall dated 26 February 1963 (Covent Garden archives).
26 Porter's letter is undated, but Drogheda noted the date he received it, 20 February 1963 (Covent Garden archives).
27 Interview, *Opera*, April 1971.
28 Suvi Raj Grubb and Brian McMaster, interviews with the author, 1992.
29 Lotte Klemperer, conversation with the author, 1989.
30 Transcript of a conversation between Klemperer and Heyworth recorded by the Canadian Broadcasting Corporation, 4 September 1969.
31 New Philharmonia Orchestra council meeting minutes, 2 August 1973.
32 Accounts of the incident from Goodall himself, etc.
33 Quotation from a BBC radio interview with John Amis, 20 August 1969.
34 George Hallam, interview with the author, 1991.
35 Sir Donald McIntyre, interview with the author, 1991.
36 *Notes from a Low Singer* by Michael Langdon (Julia MacRae, 1982).
37 John Copley, conversation with the author, 1991. Other memories from Jean Korn, and Patrick and Hilda Connell.

Chapter 13: Triumph

1   Foss's letter is dated 19 May 1966; Arlen replied on 23 May (English National Opera archives).
2   Proposal reported in the minutes of a meeting of the Sadler's Wells Trust opera sub-committee, 10 August 1966 (ENO archives).
3   Minutes of a meeting of the Covent Garden-Sadler's Wells co-ordinating committee, 25 October 1966 (ENO archives).
4   Minutes of a meeting held on 12 January 1967.
5   Goodall's reaction is recalled in a letter Victor Godfrey wrote to him on 12 August 1974.
6   *Financial Times*, 18 January 1960; *The Times*, 7 October 1960.
7   Terms stated in a letter to Goodall from Arlen's personal assistant, Patricia Bancroft, 15 April 1967. Goodall signed his contract on 7 August.
8   Norman Bailey, interview with the author, 1991.
9   Richard Fisher, interview with the author, 1991.
10   Letter from Hancock to Goodall, 20 October 1967.
11   From Tracey's obituary of Arlen, *Opera*, March 1972
12   Alberto Remedios, interview with the author, 1989.
13   Derek Hammond-Stroud, interview with the author, 1991.
14   Wilfred Stiff interviewed on the television programme, *The Quest for Reginald Goodall*, shown on BBC1, 16 September 1984. Other details about the first night provided by Nicholas Payne, Brian McMaster, etc.
15   Edmund Tracey, interview with the author, 1991.
16   *The Times*, 1 February; *Sunday Telegraph*, 4 February 1968.
17   *The Times*, 15 February 1968. The interviewer was Alan Blyth
18   Letter from Arlen to Solti, 1 March 1968 (ENO archives).
19   Letter from Eleanor Goodall to Maisie Aldridge, 7 March 1968.
20   Minutes of a meeting of the Sadler's Wells Trust's opera sub-committee, 5 March 1968 (ENO archives).
21   Minutes of a meeting of representatives of Sadler's Wells and Covent Garden to discuss the implications of the move to St Martin's Lane, 28 March 1968. Those present were Lord Drogheda, Sir David Webster, John Tooley, Lord Donaldson, Stephen Arlen and David McKenna, chairman of the Sadler's Wells Trust (ENO archives).
22   Minutes of the meeting, 22 May 1968 (ENO archives).
23   Letter from Arlen to Lord Donaldson, 24 May 1968 (ENO archives).
24   Minutes of a meeting of the Sadler's Wells Trust's opera sub-committee, 1 May 1968 (ENO archives).
25   *The Observer, Sunday Times*, 1 September 1968; *Financial Times*, 26 August 1968.
26   Stage management reports (ENO archives).
27   BBC radio interview, 20 August 1969.
28   Minutes of a meeting of the Sadler's Wells Trust's opera sub-committee, 3 October 1968 (ENO archives).
29   Minutes of the meeting (ENO archives) and an interview with Edmund Tracey, 1991.
30   Letter from Edmund Tracey to Porter, 17 April 1968.
31   Letter dated 7 May 1968.
32   Goodall talking to the author in 1986.
33   *Wait till the Sun Shines, Nellie* by Rita Hunter (Hamish Hamilton, 1986).
34   Minutes of a meeting of the Sadler's Wells Trust's opera sub-committee, 9 January 1969 (ENO archives).
35   *Evening Standard*, 25 January 1969; *Sunday Times*, 26 January.
36   *The Times*, 27 January 1969.

37 Ande Anderson, interview with the author, 1991.
38 *The Observer*, 23 February 1969.
39 Gwynne Howell, interview with the author, 1992.
40 Letter from Hammond to Goodall, 7 October 1969.
41 *New Statesman and Nation*, 13 February 1970.
42 *The Quiet Showman* by Montague Haltrecht, op. cit.
43 Letter quoted in *The Quiet Showman*, op. cit.
44 Minutes of a Covent Garden board meeting, 16 October 1968. Originally the revival had been scheduled for the 1969–70 season (Covent Garden archives).
45 Interview with the author, 1986. The meeting took place on 11 June 1969 (Goodall's diary).

Chapter 14: Resounding Ring

1   An account of the dispute is given in *Charles Mackerras: A Musician's Musician* by Nancy Phelan (Gollancz, 1987).
2   John Blatchley, interview with the author, 1991.
3   Conversation with the author, 1986.
4   Sir John Tooley, interview with the author, 1991.
5   *The Observer, Sunday Times*, 25 April 1971; *Daily Telegraph*, 22 April.
6   Minutes of a meeting of the Covent Garden board's opera sub-committee, 19 May 1971 (Covent Garden archives).
7   Interview with the author, 1991.
8   *Daily Express*, 4 November 1971. The concert was on 3 November.
9   *Music and Musicians*, May 1972.
10 Draft of letter to Hazel Vivienne and John Denman, first clarinet in the Sadler's Wells Orchestra. They had written to Goodall on 10 April to ask how he was.
11 Letter to Goodall from John C. Goldsmith, director of Unicorn Records, 9 May 1972.
12 Lord Harewood quoted in "The hidden genius of opera" by Geoffrey Wheatcroft, *Sunday Telegraph*, 27 February 1983.
13 From "Master and an institution" by Lord Harewood, *The Times*, 5 June 1986.
14 Incident recounted to Sir Donald McIntyre by an architect who was working on the site.
15 Goodall received the news in a letter from Richard Fisher that was waiting for him when he arrived at the rehearsal.
16 *Wait till the Sun Shines, Nellie*, op. cit.
17 Interview with the author, 1986.
18 Lord Harewood's letter was published on 23 March 1973, Frau Furtwängler's on 29 March.
19 Edmund Tracey, interview with the author, 1991.
20 Interview with the author, 1991.
21 *New York Times*, 29 August 1973.
22 Letter from Lord Harewood to Goodall, 9 October 1973.
23 Letter from Lord Harewood to Goodall, 19 December 1973.
24 Draft of letter to Lord Harewood, 16 February 1974.
25 The article had appeared in *The Times* on 30 December 1974.
26 Peter Moores, interview with the author, 1988.
27 Letters from Lord Harwood to Goodall, 12 May and 5 August 1975. All three of the 1976 cycles were conducted by Charles Mackerras, who had taken the complete *Ring* on tour in 1974 and 1975.
28 *Evening Standard*, 18 January 1974.
29 Letter from Peter Moores to Goodall, 9 September 1976; letter from Moores to Jeremy Caulton of the ENO, 19 July 1976; *Daily Telegraph*, 4 January 1977.
30 *The Times*, 26 August 1978; *The Gramophone*, August 1978.

31   The performance, given before an invited audience, was recorded on 4 May 1974, and broad-
     cast on 22 August. Beethoven's second *Leonora* overture, which preceded the symphony, was
     not broadcast.
32   *The Spectator*, 12 October 1974.
33   *Sunday Times*, 19 October 1975. The performances were on 8 and 9 October.
34   *The Observer*, 4 April 1976.
35   Letter from John Tooley to Goodall, 31 January 1974 (Covent Garden archives).
36   Robert Slotover, interview with the author, 1992.
37   Richard Armstrong, interview with the author, 1992.

Chapter 15: Tristan

1   From "Goodall on 'Tristan'", a conversation with Andrew Cornall and John Kehoe, *Opera*,
     October 1981.
2   "Talking of 'Tristan' with Reginald Goodall" by Angela Arratoon, *Wagner*, July 1981. A short-
     ened version of this interview appeared in the July 1981 issue of *Friends of English National
     Opera*.
3   Jeremy Caulton, interview with the author, 1992.
4   *Wait till the Sun Shines, Nellie*, op. cit.
5   Memo from Rosemarie Cave to Lord Harewood and Jeremy Caulton, 27 September 1978.
6   Notes on a planning meeting at the Coliseum attended by Goodall, Harewood, Tracey and
     Caulton, 16 January 1979.
7   Brian McMaster and Richard Armstrong, interviews with the author, 1992.
8   Letter from Margherita Stafford to Brian McMaster, 1 May 1979.
9   Richard Armstrong, interview with the author, 1992.
10   Linda Esther Gray, interview with the author, 1992.
11   Letter from Sir Peter Hall to Goodall, 4 January 1978.
12   *Financial Times*, 12 September 1979.
13   *The Spectator*, 15 September 1979.
14   *Opera*, November 1979.
15   The account of Goodall's gift to the Britten-Pears Library is based on a memorandum to the
     author (dated 1 August 1991) from Rosamund Strode, who drew both on her own memories
     and on notes made by Isador Caplan on the day following his lunch with Goodall.
16   The restored score bears the inscription, "This manuscript was presented to the Britten-Pears
     Library in January 1979 by Reginald Goodall. The expense of its repair & binding by Her
     Majesty's Stationery Office Bindery at the British Museum was borne by the British Library
     Board as a gift to the Britten-Pears Library in June 1981."
17   Donald Mitchell, letter to *The Observer*, 20 April 1980.
18   "Talking of 'Tristan' with Reginald Goodall," op. cit.
19   Edmund Tracey, interview with the author, 1991.
20   Letter from Lord Harewood to Goodall, 15 September 1981.
21   *Daily Telegraph*, 24 August 1981.
22   Brian McMaster, interview with the author, 1992.
23   *New York Times*, 24 January 1982.
24   Letter from Sir Peter Pears to Goodall, 25 September 1980.
25   "English maestro's fascist folly", by Nicholas Farrell, *Sunday Telegraph*, 13 May 1990.
26   *Financial Times*, 20 February 1984.
27   *The Guardian*, 20 February 1984 (*Valkyrie*); 28 January 1985 (*Tristan*).
28   *The Observer*, 3 February 1985.
29   Letter from Harewood to Herz, 22 November 1983.
30   Interview in *Wagner News*, journal of the Wagner Society of America, February 1982.

31   Letter from Goodall to Byam Shaw, 5 April 1970.
32   Letter from Jeremy Caulton to Andrew Porter, 8 March 1985.
33   Tom Sutcliffe, *The Guardian*, 17 March 1986.
34   Letter from Tracey to Andrew Porter, 24 August 1983.
35   *The Times*, 17 March 1986.
36   *Daily Telegraph*, 31 March 1986.
37   *Sunday Times*, 17 August 1987.

Chapter 16: The Final Years

1   Patrick Connell, interview with the author, 1990.

Discography
The recordings of Reginald Goodall

1 **TCHAIKOVSKY**. Overture, *1812*.
National Symphony Orchestra. Recorded at Kingsway Hall, London, 28 November 1945.
Decca, K1349-50 (78 r.p.m).

2 **BEETHOVEN**. Overture, *Coriolan*.
National Symphony Orchestra. Kingsway Hall, London, 29 November 1945.
Decca, matrix nos AR 9875-1-2; AR9876-1 (78 rpm.). *The World's Encyclopedia of Recorded Music* by Francis F. Clough and G. J. Cummings attributes a catalogue number, K1355, to this recording, but it seems it was never issued. Goodall's own test pressings have survived.

3 **BEETHOVEN**. Overture, *Leonora No. 1*
National Symphony Orchestra. Kingsway Hall, London, 9 January 1946.
Decca, matrix nos AR9970-1-2; AR 9971 (78 rpm). As with *Coriolan* (above), *WERM* attributes a catalogue number, K1471, but again it seems to have remained unissued. Test pressings of side 1 only have survived.

4 **BRITTEN**. *The Rape of Lucretia*, abridged.
Nancy Evans, Peter Pears, Joan Cross, Norman Lumsden, Denis Dowling, Frederick Sharp, Flora Nielsen, Margaret Ritchie, English Opera Group Chamber Orchestra. A photograph taken at the sessions suggests that Goodall himself played the piano for the recitatives.
Recorded at No. 1 Studio, Abbey Road, London; 16-19 July, 19 October 1947 and released in 1948 on eight 78 rpm. discs, HMV C 3699-706. The CD version (1993), in a box of historic Britten recordings, EMI 7 64727 2, has an extra number, 'Here the thirsty evening' from Act 1, that was not included in the original release

5 **BRITTEN**. *Peter Grimes*, excerpts.
Peter Pears, Joan Cross, Tom Culbert (the rector); BBC Theatre Chorus and Orchestra of the Royal Opera House, Covent Garden. No 1 Studio, Abbey Road, London; 12, 14, 16, 17 July 1948. Eleven 78 r.p.m. sides were recorded by Columbia, but none was released until 1972, when eight of them were included in a three-disc LP set, *Stars of the Old Vic and Sadler's Wells* (HMV, RLS 707). Finally, in 1993, all eleven appeared on CD in an EMI Britten box that also includes Goodall's *Rape of Lucretia* recording (No. 4, above). For more about these discs see pp 112 and 117-118.

6 **MEYERBEER**. *L'Africaine:* 'O Paradiso!'
Walter Midgley, Royal Opera House Orchestra. Kingsway Hall, London, 8 June 1951.
HMV matrix nos 2EA 15690-1-2 (78 rpm). Unpublished; matrices destroyed in 1953.

7   **FLOTOW**. *Martha*: 'M'appari'.
Walter Midgley, Royal Opera House Orchestra. Kingsway Hall, London, 8 June 1951.
HMV matrix nos 2EA 15691-1-2 (78 rpm). Unpublished, but a matrix survives in the EMI archives.
Midgley (1912-1980) frequently sang Calaf, Manrico and Des Grieux for the Covent Garden company, with Goodall conducting. The tenor refused to allow the two arias listed above to be released because he believed they favoured the orchestra too much. The notes for EMI's *Record of Singing, Volume 4, The Anglo-American School* (LP: EX 7 69741 1; CD: CHS 7 69741 2) wrongly lists Goodall and the Royal Opera House Orchestra as accompanists for Midgley's version of 'Dalla sua pace' from *Don Giovanni*, recorded on 16 August 1951. The orchestra used for the session was the Philharmonia under Walter Susskind.

8   **WAGNER**. *The Mastersingers*, in English.
Norman Bailey, Alberto Remedios, Margaret Curphey, Noel Mangin, Derek Hammond-Stroud, Gregory Dempsey, Ann Robson, Stafford Dean, etc, Sadler's. Wells Opera Chorus and Orchestra. Live recording, Sadler's Wells Theatre, London, 10 February 1968.
Chandos CD, CHAN 3148.

9   **WAGNER**. *Das Rheingold*: 'Abendlich strahlt der Sonne Auge'.
David Ward, Royal Opera House Orchestra. Recorded at Kingsway Hall, 23 February 1968, and released as part of a two-LP set, the *Royal Opera House, Covent Garden, Anniversary Album*.
Decca MET/SET 392-3.

10 **BRUCKNER**. Symphony No. 8 in C minor.
BBC Symphony Orchestra. Recorded live at the Royal Albert Hall, London, 3 September 1969.
BBC Legends CD, BBCL 4086-2.

11 **WAGNER**. *Parsifal*.
Norman Bailey, Louis Hendrikx, Jon Vickers, Donald McIntyre, Michael Langdon, Amy Shuard, etc, Chorus and Orchestra of the Royal Opera House, Covent Garden. Live recording, Royal Opera House, 8 May 1971.
Royal Opera Heritage Series, CD ROHS 012.

12 (a) **WAGNER**. *Tristan und Isolde*, Prelude
    (b) **WAGNER**. *Wesendonck-Lieder*
    (c) **BRUCKNER**. Symphony No. 7 in E major.
Janet Baker (*Wesendonck-Lieder*), BBC Symphony Orchestra. Concert recorded live at the Royal Festival Hall, London, 3 November 1971.
BBC Legends CDs, BBCL 4086-2 (Wagner items); BBCL 4147-2 (Bruckner).

13 **WAGNER**. *Twilight of the Gods*, Act 3, scenes 2 and 3, in English.
Rita Hunter, Alberto Remedios, Norman Bailey, Margaret Curphey, Clifford Grant, Sadler's Wells Opera and Chorus. St Giles's Church, Cripplegate, London, 30-31 December 1972.
Unicorn LP UNS 245-6; Chandos CD CHAN 6593.

14 **WAGNER**. *Siegfried*, in English.
Alberto Remedios, Gregory Dempsey, Norman Bailey, Rita Hunter, etc, Sadler's Wells Opera Orchestra. Recorded live at the London Coliseum by EMI in association with the Peter Moores Foundation, 2 (dress rehearsal), 8, 21 August 1973.
LP: SLS 875; CD: CMS 7 63595. Re-released on CD by Chandos: CHAN. 3045.

15   **BRUCKNER**. Symphony No. 9 in D minor.
BBC Symphony Orchestra. BBC Studios, Maida Vale, London, 4 May 1974.
BBC Legends CD, BBCL 4174-2.

16   **WAGNER**. *Die Meistersinger*, Prelude.
English National Opera Orchestra. Recorded live at Snape Maltings, Suffolk, 27 October 1974.
BBC Legends CD, BBCL 4147-2

17   **WAGNER**, *The Rheingold*, in English.
Norman Bailey, Katherine Pring, Emile Belcourt, Derek Hammond-Stroud, Gregory Dempsey, Robert Lloyd, Clifford Grant, etc, English National Opera Chorus and Orchestra. Recorded live by EMI at the London Coliseum in association with the Peter Moores Foundation, 10 (dress rehearsal), 19, 25, 29 March 1975.

18   **WAGNER**. *The Valkyrie*, in English..
Alberto Remedios, Margaret Curphey, Norman Bailey, Rita Hunter, etc, English National Opera Orchestra. Recorded live by EMI at the London Coliseum in association with the Peter Moores Foundation, 18 (dress rehearsal), 20, 23 December 1975.
LP: SLS 5063. CD: CMS 7 63918 2. Re-released on CD by Chandos: CHAN. 3038.

19   **WAGNER**. *Twilight of the Gods*, in English.
Rita Hunter, Alberto Remedios, Aage Haugland, Margaret Curphey, Katherine Pring, etc, English National Opera Chorus and Orchestra. Recorded live by EMI at the London Coliseum in association with the Peter Moores Foundation, 6 (dress rehearsal), 13, 27 August 1977.
LP: SLS 5118. CD: CMS 7 64244 2. Re-released on CD by Chandos: CHAN. 3060. Complete *Ring* issued as a box set: CHAN 3065

20   **WAGNER**. *Tristan und Isolde*.
John Mitchinson, Linda Esther Gray, Anne Wilkens, Phillip Joll, Gwynne Howell, etc, Welsh National Chorus and Orchestra. Brangwyn Hall, Swansea, 17–21 November 1980, 19-24 January 1981.
Decca LP: D250D 5. CD: 443 682-2.

21   **WAGNER**: *Parsifal*.
Warren Ellsworth, Waltraud Meier, Donald McIntyre, Phillip Joll, etc, Welsh National Opera Chorus and Opera. Brangwyn Hall, Swansea, 17–25 June 1984.
EMI LP: EX 27 0178 3. CD: CDS 7 49182 8.

Choir repertory of St Alban the Martyr, Holborn, 1929–1936

The choir records were lost in the fire that destroyed the church on the night of 16 April 1941 and the list that follows of music performed during Goodall's time as organist and choirmaster at St Alban's has been compiled from advance notices of services found in the *Daily Telegraph*, the *St Alban's Monthly Paper* and the *Church Times*. Since the notices often appeared sporadically and the information they contained was sometimes sketchy, the list may not be complete, particularly in the case of the motets, but it does show the range of music that Goodall gave at St Alban's. Works known to have been introduced into the repertory by Goodall are marked *. Works given with instrumental accompaniment are marked #.

1   *Works performed in the context of church services*

ANERIO, Felice	*Christus factus est*
	O Jesu, mi dulcissime
ARCADELT	*Ave Maria*
BEETHOVEN	Mass in C major#
BRUCKNER	Mass in C major*
	Mass in E minor*
	Mass in F minor*#
	Ave Maria
BYRD	3-part Mass*
	5-part Mass
	Ave Maria
	Ego sum panis vivus
	O sacrum convivium
DVOŘÁK	Mass in D major#
ELGAR	*Ave Maria*
	Ave verum corpus
FARJEON, Harry	St Dominic Mass*
FAURÉ	*In Paradisum*
GARDINER, Balfour	Evening Hymn
GIBBONS	*O Lord, increase my faith*
GOUNOD	*Messe du Sacré-Coeur de Jésus**
	Messe solennelle de Ste Cécile#
GUILMANT	Mass in E flat major
HARWOOD	Mass in A major
HAYDN	*Theresienmesse*#
HOWELLS	*A Spotless Rose**
HUMMEL	Mass in B flat major
	Mass in D major

INDY, D'	*Ave Regina coelorum*
LISZT	*Ave verum corpus*
MOZART	*Missa brevis* in B flat major K272b
	Ave verum corpus K618
MUL	*Missa: Causa nostra laetitiae*[*]
	Missa quarta[*]
PALESTRINA	*Missa: Aeterna Christi munera*
	Missa brevis[*]
RACHMANINOV	*Glory to God in the highest*[*]
	To thee, O Lord[*]
RUBBRA	*Eternitie*[*]
SCHUBERT	Mass in A flat major[*]
	Mass in B flat major
	Mass in C major
	Mass in E flat major[*] #
	Mass in F major
	Mass in G major
SÉVERAC	*Tantum ergo*
SIBELIUS	*Die Glockenmelodie*[*]
	Natus in curas[*]
STRAVINSKY	*Pater Noster*[*]
SURIANO	*Salve Regina*
TCHAIKOVSKY	*O praise the Lord*[*]
TOMBELLE, DE LA	*Ave Maria*
VAUGHAN WILLIAMS	Mass in G minor[*]
VICTORIA	*Missa: O quam gloriosum*[*]
	Ave verum corpus
	Jesu dulcis memoria
WEBER	Mass in E flat major
WILLAN	*Hail gladdening light*[*]
	O sacred feast
	Rise up my fair one*

2 *Additional works performed at concerts only*

Those marked + were given at the Mercury Theatre, Notting Hill, the remainder at St Alban's, Holborn. Those marked # were given with orchestra. Goodall was the conductor unless stated otherwise.

BAX	*Mater ora Filium*+ (with the Carlyle Singers; conductor Iris Lemare)
BRITTEN	*A Boy was Born*+ (boys only, with the Carlyle Singers conducted by Iris Lemare; also a performance with the BBC Singers conducted by Leslie Woodgate)
	Te Deum in C major+#
BRUCKNER	Psalm 150
	Te Deum#
MOZART	Requiem Mass
SZYMANOWSKI	*Stabat Mater*#

Works conducted by Goodall with the Wessex Philharmonic Orchestra, December 1939 – February 1943

ADDINSELL	*Warsaw Concerto*
BACH	Brandenburg Concerto No. 4
BARTÓK	Divertimento for strings
BATE, Stanley	Piano Concerto No. 1
	Ballet suite, *Perseus*
BEETHOVEN	Symphonies Nos 1–8
	Piano Concertos Nos 1–5
	Violin Concerto in D major
	Overtures, *Coriolan, Egmont, Prometheus, Leonora No. 3*
	Romances in F and G
	Ruins of Athens: March
BERKELEY	Serenade for strings
BERLIOZ	*La Damnation de Faust*: Dance of the Sylphs
	Overture, *Le Carnaval romain*
BIZET	Symphony in C major
	Carmen: Flower Song
BLOCKX, Jan	*Danses flamandes*
BORODIN	Symphony No. 2 in B minor
	Prince Igor: Polovtsian Dances
BRAHMS	Symphonies Nos 1 and 4
	Double Concerto in A minor
	Piano Concerto No. 2 in B flat major
	Violin Concerto in D major
	Serenade in D major – three movements only
BRAITHWAITE, S.H.	*Prelude to a Drama*
	Fanfare for trumpets
	Suite of eighteenth-century dances
BRITTEN	Violin Concerto
	Les Illuminations
	Soirées musicales
BRUCH	Violin Concerto in G minor
BRUCKNER	Overture in G minor
BRYAN, Gordon	Piano Concertos Nos 1 and 3
BURKHARD, Willy	Toccata for strings
COATES, Eric	*Knightsbridge Suite*

COPLAND	*An Outdoor Overture*
	Quiet City
DEBUSSY	*Danse sacrée et danse profane*
DELIUS	*On Hearing the First Cuckoo in Spring*
	Hassan: Serenade and Intermezzo
	Koanga: La Calinda
	A Village Romeo and Juliet: Walk to the Paradise Garden
DRAGONETTI	Double Bass Concerto in A minor
DVOŘÁK	Symphonies Nos 5, 8 and 9
	Cello Concerto in B minor
	Piano Concerto in G minor
	Overture, *Carnival*
	Three Slavonic Dances
ELGAR	Cello Concerto in E minor
	Violin Concerto in B minor
	Enigma Variations
	Pomp and Circumstance March No. 1
	Serenade for Strings
FAURÉ	*Pavane*
FINZI	Orchestration of four French songs
FRANCK	Symphonic Variations
GLAZUNOV	Violin Concerto in A minor
GLINKA	Overture, *Ruslan and Ludmila*
GRAINGER	*Mock Morris*
GRIEG	Piano Concerto in A minor
	Peer Gynt, Suite No. 1
HANDEL	Concerto for oboe and strings
	Organ Concerto No. 3
	Semele: "Where'er you walk"
HANDEL-HARTY	Suite, *Royal Fireworks Music*
	Suite, *Water Music*
HARTY	John Field Suite
HAYDN	Symphonies Nos 88, 94, 95, 101
	Cello Concerto in D major
	Piano Concerto in D major
	Overture, *Armide*
	Il mondo della luna: Entr'acte and ballet music
	The Creation: "The heavens are telling"
HOLST	St Paul's Suite
	Two Psalms
HUMPERDINCK	Overture, *Hansel and Gretel*
IRELAND	Piano Concerto
JACOB, Gordon	Concerto for piano and strings
	Suite No. 1
JÄRNEFELT	Berceuse
LIADOV	Eight Russian Folksongs, Op. 58
	Piano Concerto No. 1 in E flat major
	Hungarian Fantasy
	Hungarian Rhapsody No. 2
MAHLER	Symphony No. 5 – adagietto only

MALIPIERO	Finale
MASCAGNI	*Cavalleria rusticana*: "Voi lo sapete"; Intermezzo
MENDELSSOHN	Violin Concerto in E minor
	Overture, *The Hebrides*
MOZART	Symphonies Nos 25, 28, 29, 36, 39, 40, 41
	Clarinet Concerto in A major
	Horn Concerto No. 4 in E flat major
	Piano Concertos Nos 9, 14, 20, 23–27
	Violin Concertos Nos 4, 5, 6 (doubtful authenticity)
	Adagio for violin and orchestra K.261
	Sinfonia Concertante for violin, viola and orchestra
	Musical Joke
	Serenade, *Eine kleine Nachtmusik*
	Serenata notturna
	Six Dances K. 509
	Motet, *Exsultate, jubilate*
	Requiem Mass
	Overtures, *Le nozze di Figaro, Don Giovanni, Die Zauberflöte*
	Le nozze di Figaro: "Dove sono"
MUSSORGSKY	*Fair at Sorochintsy*: Khyvria's aria
OFFENBACH	*Les contes d'Hoffmann*: excerpts.
PALMGREN	Piano Concert No. 4
PERGOLESI-BARBIROLLI	Suite for oboe and strings
POULENC	*Mouvements perpétuels*
PROKOFIEV	Classical Symphony
PURCELL	Chaconne
RACHMANINOV	Piano Concertos Nos 2 and 3
	Rhapsody on a Theme of Paganini
RAMEAU	Suite, *Dardanus*
RAVEL	Introduction and Allegro
	Pavane pour une infante défunte
RAWSTHORNE	Three French Nursery Songs
RIMSKY-KORSAKOV	*Scheherazade*
ROSSINI	Overtures, *Il barbiere di Siviglia, L'italiana in Algeri, Guillaume Tell*
	Il barbiere di Siviglia: "Largo al factotum"
SAINT-SAËNS	Cello Concerto in A minor
	Suite, Op. 65
SCHUBERT	Symphonies Nos 4, 5 and 8
	Rosamunde: Overture, ballet music and entr'actes in B flat and G
SCHUMANN	Symphonies Nos 1, 2 and 4
	Piano Concerto in A minor
SHOSTAKOVICH	Concerto for piano, trumpet and strings
SIBELIUS	Symphonies Nos 1 and 3
	Violin Concerto in D minor
	Romance in C for strings
	Finlandia
	Suite, *Belshazzar's Feast*
	Suite, *King Christian*
	Suite, *Pelleas and Melisande*
	Valse triste

STOESSEL	Concerto Grosso for strings and piano
STRAUSS, Johann	Overture, *Die Fledermaus*
	Waltz, *The Blue Danube*
STRAVINSKY	Suite, *The Firebird* (1919)
SWINSTEAD, Felix	Suite on themes of Scarlatti
TCHAIKOVSKY	Symphonies Nos 4, 5 and 6
	Piano Concerto No.1 in B flat minor
	Violin Concerto in D major
	Chansons sans paroles
	Fantasy-overture, *Romeo and Juliet*
	Suite for Strings, elegy and finale only
	Suite, *Swan Lake*
	Marche slave
TRAPP, Max	Divertimento
	Serenade and Finale
VAUGHAN WILLIAMS	Fantasia on a theme of Thomas Tallis
	Household Music: *Three Preludes on Welsh Hymn Tunes* (first performance)
	Fantasia on Greensleeves
VIVALDI	Concerto grosso Op. 3 No. 11
WAGNER	*Siegfried Idyll*
	Lohengrin: Prelude to Act 3
	Die Meistersinger: Prize Song
WALTON	Violin Concerto
	Suite, *The Wise Virgins*
	Suite, *Façade*
WEBER	Overtures, *Oberon, Der Freischütz*
	Der Freischütz: Aria, "Leise, Leise"

Selected Bibliography

AIKIN, W. A.: *The Voice: an introduction to practical phonology* (Longmans, 1910)

ARUNDELL, Dennis: *The Story of Sadler's Wells* (Hamish Hamilton, 1965)

BAILEY, Cyril: *Hugh Percy Allen* (Oxford University Press, 1948)

BING, Rudolf: *5,000 Nights at the Opera* (Hamish Hamilton, 1972)

BLUNT, Wilfrid: *John Christie of Glyndebourne* (Geoffrey Bles, 1968)

BLYTH, Alan: *Opera on Record* (Hutchinson, 1979)

    Remembering Britten (Hutchinson, 1981)

BRETT, Philip (ed.): *Benjamin Britten: Peter Grimes* (Cambridge University Press, 1983)

BRITTEN, Benjamin, etc.: *The Rape of Lucretia: A symposium*, with contributions by Ronald
    Duncan, Eric Crozier, John Piper, Henry Boys and Britten himself (Bodley Head, 1948)

BRITTEN, Beth: *My Brother Benjamin* (Kensal Press, Bourne End, 1986)

BROOK, Donald: *Conductors' Gallery* (Rockcliff, 1945)

CAMPION, Paul: *Ferrier, A Career Recorded* (Julia MacRae, 1992)

CLARKE, F. R. C.: *Healey Willan: Life and Music* (Toronto University Press, 1983)

DEAN, Basil: *The Theatre at War* (Harrap, 1956)

DENT, Edward J.: *Opera* (Penguin Books, revised edition, 1949)

    A Theatre for Everybody: The story of the Old Vic and Sadler's Wells (T. V. Boardman, 1945)

DONALDSON, Frances: *The Royal Opera House in the Twentieth Century* (Weidenfeld and
    Nicholson, 1988)

DUNCAN, Ronald: *Working with Britten: A Personal Memoir* (Rebel Press, Bideford, 1981)

ELVIN, Laurence: *Family Enterprise: The story of some North Country organ builders* (Elvin,
    Lincoln, 1986)

EVANS, John/REED, Philip/WILSON, Paul: *A Britten Source Book* (Britten-Pears Library,
    Aldeburgh, 1987)

FAWKES, Richard: *Welsh National Opera* (Julia MacRae, 1986)

FINDLATER, Richard: *Lilian Baylis: The Lady of the Old Vic* (Allen Lane, 1975)

FISHER, Hugh: *The Sadler's Wells Theatre Ballet* (A & C Black, 1956)

FORSYTH, James: *Tyrone Guthrie* (Hamish Hamilton, 1976)

GREENE, Harry Plunket: *Interpretation in Song* (Macmillan, 1912)

GREIG, David: *In the Fullness of Time: A History of the Church of St Mary Magdalene, Toronto*
    (St Mary Magdalene, 1990)

GUTHRIE, Tyrone: *A Life in the Theatre* (Hamish Hamilton, 1960)

HALTRECHT, Montague: *The Quiet Showman: Sir David Webster and the Royal Opera House*
    (Collins, 1975)

HAWKINS, Frank V.: *A Hundred Years of Chamber Music* (South Place Ethical Society, 1987)

HEADINGTON, Christopher: *Britten* (Eyre Methuen, 1981)

HEWISON, Robert: *Under Siege: Literary Life in London 1939–45* (Weidenfeld and Nicolson, 1977)

HEYWORTH, Peter (ed.): *Conversations with Klemperer* (Gollancz, 1973)

HUNT, John: *Furtwängler and Great Britain* (Wilhelm Furtwangler Society, London, 1985)

HUNTER, Rita: *Wait till the Sun Shines, Nellie* (Hamish Hamilton, 1986)

JARMAN, Richard: *A History of Sadler's Wells Opera* (English National Opera, 1974)

KENNEDY, Michael: *Adrian Boult* (Hamish Hamilton, 1987)
     The Hallé 1858–1983 (Manchester University Press, 1982)

KENYON, Nicholas: *The BBC Symphony Orchestra, 1930–1980* (BBC, 1981)

LANGDON, Michael: *Notes from a Low Singer* (Julia MacRae, 1982)

MCCREADY, Louise G.: *Canadian Portraits: Famous Musicians* (Clarke, Irwin; Toronto, 1957)

MILLER, Geoffrey: *The Bournemouth Symphony Orchestra* (Dorset Publishing, Sherborne, 1970)

MILLINGTON, Barry, and SPENCER, Stewart (editors): *Wagner in Performance* (Yale University Press, 1992)

MITCHELL, Donald: *Britten and Auden in the Thirties* (Faber, 1981)

MITCHELL, Donald/REED, Philip (editors): *Letters from a Life: Selected Letters and Diaries of Benjamin Britten, Vols 1 and 2* (Faber, 1991)

MOORE, Gerald: *Am I Too Loud?* (Hamish Hamilton, 1962)

MORGAN, Maude A.: *Father Eves of St Alban's, Holborn*, with an introduction by Frank de Jonge (SPCK, 1956)

NORMAN, E. R.: *Church and Society in England, 1770–1970* (Clarendon Press, Oxford, 1976)

PEARTON, Maurice: *The LSO at 70* (Gollancz, 1974)

PETTITT, Stephen J.: *Philharmonia Orchestra* (Robert Hale, 1985)

PHELAN, Nancy: *Charles Mackerras: a musician's musician* (Gollancz, 1987)

PHILLIPS, Raymond (ed.): *Trial of Josef Kramer and Forty-four Others* (William Hodge, 1949)

REID, Charles: *Malcolm Sargent* (Hamish Hamilton, 1968)

REYNOLDS, Michael: *Martyr of Ritualism: Father Mackonochie of St Alban's, Holborn* (Faber, 1965)

ROBINSON, Charles W.: *Twentieth Century Druggist* (Galen Press, Beverley, 1983)

ROSENTHAL, Harold: *Two Centuries of Opera at Covent Garden* (Putnam, 1958)

RUSSELL, George: *St Alban the Martyr, Holborn* (George Allen, 1913)

RUSSELL, John: *Erich Kleiber: A memoir* (Andre Deutsch, 1957)

RUSSELL, Thomas: *Philharmonic* (Hutchinson, 1942)
     Philharmonic Decade (Hutchinson, 1945)

SHARF, Andrew: *The British Press and Jews under Nazi Rule* (Oxford University Press, 1964)

SUMMERSON, John: *Heavenly Mansions* (Cresset Press, 1949)

TEMPLE SAVAGE, Richard: *A Voice from the Pit* (David & Charles, Devon, 1988)

THOMPSON, Paul: *William Butterfield* (Routledge & Kegan Paul, 1971)

THURLOW, Richard: *Fascism in Britain: A history, 1918–1985* (Basil Blackwell, 1987)

TREHERNE, John: *Dangerous Precincts* (Jonathan Cape, 1987)

TUCKER, Brian (ed.): *And Choirs Singing* (Leith Hill Festival, 1985)

TURING, Penelope: *New Bayreuth* (Jersey Artists, St Martin, 1969)

WALTON, Susana: *William Walton: Behind the Façade* (Oxford University Press, 1988)

WHITE, Eric Walter: *Benjamin Britten: A Sketch of his Life and Works*; revised edition (Boosey and Hawkes, 1954)

WILLIAMS, Harcourt (ed.): *Vic-Wells* (Cobden Sanderson, 1938)

WOODWARD, Reg: *Boy on a Hill* (Woodward, Gainsborough, 1984)

Articles, etc

BRYANT, Giles: Entry on Healey Willan in the *Encyclopedia of Music in Canada* (Toronto University Press, 1981)

CHAPMAN, Ernest: The Macnaghten Concerts (*Composer*, Spring 1976)

COOKE, William G.: The Diocese of Toronto and its two Cathedrals (*Journal of the Canadian Church Historical Society*, October 1985)

GODDARD, Scott: Handel's English Public Today (*Monthly Musical Record*, February 1935)

HILLSMAN, Walter: Orchestras in Anglican Services, 1870–1901 *(Musical Times*, January 1988)

KERSLEY, Leo: In Memoriam, Sadler's Wells Royal Ballet (*Dance and Dancers*, November 1990)

LLOYD, Harry Powell: Unpublished journals, deposited in the Cambridge University Library music department.

MACNAGHTEN, Anne: The Story of the Macnaghten Concerts (*Musical Times*, September 1959)

MILLINGTON, Barry: Transcript of radio interview with Reginald Goodall, Radio Three, 1976

Index